Solid Rock

Stress Testing the Gospels

Solid Rock

Stress Testing the Gospels

Peter Murfitt

SOLID ROCK–Stress Testing the Gospels by Peter Murfitt
Copyright © 2022 by Peter Murfitt
All Rights Reserved.
ISBN: 978-1-59755-637-8

Published by: ADVANTAGE BOOKS™, Longwood, FL, www.advbookstore.com

All Rights Reserved. This book and parts thereof may not be reproduced in any form, stored in a retrieval system or transmitted in any form by any means (electronic, mechanical, photocopy, recording or otherwise) without prior written permission of the author, except as provided by United States of America copyright law. Unless otherwise indicated, Scriptures marked NIV are taken from the NEW INTERNATIONAL VERSION (NIV): Scripture taken from THE HOLY BIBLE, NEW INTERNATIONAL VERSION ®. Copyright© 1973, 1978, 1984, 2011 by Biblica, Inc.TM. Used by permission of Zondervan

Short quotations are used with permission within this book from:

Simply Christian by Nicholas Thomas Wright © 2006 SPCK publishing

Mark for Everyone by Nicholas Thomas Wright © 2004 SPCK publishing

Early Christian Letters for Everyone by Nicholas Thomas Wright © 2011 SPCK publishing

Virtue Reborn by Nicholas Thomas Wright © 2010 SPCK publishing

The table and extracts from *Jesus and the Eyewitnesses* by Richard J Bauckham © 2006 are used by permission of the publisher, William B Eerdmans.

The short quotations from *What are the Gospels?* by Richard A Burridge © 2004 are used by permission of the publisher, William B Eerdmans.

Library of Congress Catalog Number: 2022930629

First Printing: May 2022
22 23 24 25 26 27   10 9 8 7 6 5 4 3 2 1

ACKNOWLEDGEMENTS

I would like to convey my thanks to all those who have helped me and encouraged me during the preparation of this book.

First of all, to my friend James Roberts, pastor of Connect Church in Chorleywood, UK for times of prayer which resulted in encouragement and new directions.

Secondly, to Steve and Helen Pollard and my niece, Fiona Parker (B.A., History), who read an early draft, for their enthusiasm for, and corrections to, the project, just when I was beginning to wonder whether it was worth all the effort.

Thirdly, to Dr Peter Williams of the University of Cambridge Faculty of Divinity and Principal of Tyndale House, Cambridge. His advice led me to completely rewrite what are now chapters 3 and 4 and to bolster up chapter 7.

Then to John Withers (B.D.), Gilbert Janthial, Geneviève Jérôme and my old friend Dan England (M.Div., M.A. (Cantab), M.Th. (Princeton T.S.) for reading later drafts and for all their helpful comments. Dan, in particular, led me to look at several points once again.

To my friend and neighbour, Maté Dobrossy, and to Tim Bennek, who helped me transform some of the material for my YouTube channel as video interviews and to Mike Hollow who helped me with other points.

I would also like to thank all those at Advantage Books, especially Mike Janiczek and Debra Grady, for their help and encouragement.

Finally, I have to thank my long-suffering family for their unflinching love and support, especially my wife, Martine, who has read and reread so many drafts, in English and in French, and yet remained loyal and generous.

Table of Contents

PREFACE	9
ABBREVIATIONS	11
ATLASES AND MAPS	14
CHAPTER 1: PREAMBLE	15
CHAPTER 2: THE COMING OF JESUS	25
CHAPTER 3: THE NEW TESTAMENT DOCUMENTS	29
CHAPTER 4: MORE ON MANUSCRIPTS, ARCHIVES AND THE NEW TESTAMENT CANON	39
CHAPTER 5: WHAT ARE THE GOSPELS?	47
CHAPTER 6: WHO WROTE LUKE/ACTS? WHEN AND WHERE?	53
CHAPTER 7: THE ORIGINS OF THE GOSPELS OF MATTHEW AND MARK	61
CHAPTER 8: THE ORIGINS OF JOHN'S GOSPEL	73
CHAPTER 9: THE BIRTH NARRATIVES	83
CHAPTER 10: SOME IMPORTANT PERSONALITIES IN THE GOSPELS	97
CHAPTER 11: JESUS' EARLY AND GALILEAN MINISTRIES	103
CHAPTER 12: JESUS' LATER VISITS TO JERUSALEM	115
CHAPTER 13: THE CHRONOLOGY AND THE GEOGRAPHY OF THE GOSPELS	133
CHAPTER 14: THE PERSON OF JESUS	149
CHAPTER 15: THE MIRACLES OF JESUS	159
EPILOGUE	167
APPENDIX 1: THE INTER-TESTAMENTAL PERIOD	169
APPENDIX 2: THE GEOGRAPHICAL AND ECONOMIC BACKGROUND	173
APPENDIX 3: OTHER ANCIENT WORKS	179
APPENDIX 4: WAS MARK THE FIRST GOSPEL TO BE WRITTEN?	183
APPENDIX 5: MAPS	185

Preface

Most people are interested in the Gospels, not as background material for our knowledge of first-century Palestine, but because they are the main source of information on Jesus of Nazareth. He is the one great figure of history to whom the other major figures, people such as Napoleon, Gandhi, Churchill, Mother Theresa or Mandela, bend the knee. He is the one who has always fascinated mankind, whether we are staunch believers or fledgling inquirers about spirituality. Therefore, it is important to know whether the Gospels can be trusted.

This book is evidence-based and addressed to a wide audience. First and foremost, to those who would not call themselves Christians, but who want to find out more about Jesus. Secondly, to ordinary Christians, Bible study, prayer and cell group leaders, who seek to open up the Gospels to new believers and, finally, to the professionals: pastors, priests and theologians. To make the book easier to read, a substantial amount of background material has been placed in Appendices.

It saddens me that the proverbial man in the street regards Jesus as a legendary figure and not as a real historical person. How can this be? It seems that every kind of intellectual mud has been flung at the Gospels, from Da Vinci codes to hallucinatory mushrooms. The aim of this book is to attempt to redress the balance: to demonstrate that, whenever we seriously investigate what the Gospels say, they turn out to be entirely reliable: they are coherent and recount events and facts that can be confirmed from other sources.

There are good reasons for a new look at the reliability of the Gospels. Since the 1990's, there has been a sea change in the academic side of Gospel Studies, led by Richard Burridge (*What?*), Richard Bauckham (*Jesus, Eye, Test*) and N T (Tom) Wright. Richard Bauckham's thesis that the Gospels are based on eye-witness testimony has, in the words of Graham Stanton, Professor of Divinity at the University of Cambridge, *"shaken the foundations of a century of scholarly study of the Gospels."* Secondly, since the end of World War II, there have been some important archeological finds in Israel, which shed new light on the Gospels.

Travelling with friends in Israel in 2014, I saw some of these archeological finds at first hand. That stimulated me to reread Josephus' Jewish War, on the high-speed train journey between Colmar and Paris. Nevertheless, I had the impression that not even Richard Bauckham had dared to ask all the questions. It seemed to me that the whole question of the origins of the Gospels, in particular their places and dates of writing, needed to be looked at again, in the light of Bauckham's work. Then, when I thought I had found a systematic method of doing just that, I shot out of the starting blocks.

I have to admit that my formal academic and research training is in science and engineering. However, this is no barrier to being an amateur historian, because we use many of the same tools: logic, maps, sketches, diagrams, time charts, flow sheets and all sorts of plans.

Nevertheless, I think it necessary to explain my training in theology and biblical research. Studying Chemical Engineering in my fourth year at Cambridge University, I could not find anywhere else to stay except in an Institute of Biblical Research. There I lived, studied, ate and drank coffee under the same roof as many to whose work I refer in this book. I spent most time with Dan England (who was studying theology and who is now pastoring in the USA), Max Turner (who was working on his Ph.D. on the Holy Spirit in Luke/Acts and is now Emeritus Professor of New Testament at the London School of Theology; most of the coffee was his) and Don Carson (who was working on his Ph.D. on John's Gospel and is now Emeritus Professor of New Testament at Trinity Evangelical Divinity School, Illinois, USA, co-founder of the highly influential Gospel Coalition and author of countless books, among them *CJohn*).

The late Dick France (*FMatt, FMatt2, FMark*) had already established his academic credentials and was the librarian; he later became the warden and then Honorary Research Fellow at Bangor University. The late Colin Hemer (archaeologist and *HSC*), a benign owl-like boffin with round spectacles and an eternal beige V-neck lambswool pullover, lived in the older part of the complex. Richard Bauckham (*Eye, Test, Jesus*), working on his history Ph.D., and Bruce Metzger (world-renowned expert on the original biblical manuscripts and member of many Bible translation committees) dropped in for afternoon tea and Michael Green (*GActs*) came to lecture.

They were all extremely kind and accessible, and I asked them (and the numerous Ph.D students who came to lunch) many, many questions, often quite aggressively. They responded very graciously. So, there I was: signed up unbeknown to me for a dense course in biblical theology and the methods of biblical research. I doubt if many Ph.D. students in theology have a list of tutors as prestigious as me.

When I left, for a post as a research scientist in a Civil Service laboratory, which led to my own Ph.D. in Chemical Engineering, Max gave me a meaty theological commentary on Paul's Epistle to the Colossians, together with a list of similar works on other New Testament books. Thus, I started out on a shadowy parallel life as a clandestine theologian and biblical researcher, trying to keep abreast with developments in New Testament studies.

Finally, anyone working in this field must acknowledge his debt to the late FF Bruce (*FFBR, FFBA, FFBJ*), Rylands Professor of Biblical Exegesis at the University of Manchester, whose 1959 book *"The New Testament Documents: are they reliable?"* deservedly remains the bench mark.

I have enjoyed the research which has gone into the writing of this book enormously. I have also become a fan of Irenaeus. I try to imagine what he must have felt like when he was in Rome and learnt of the martyrdom of his bishop Pothinus. What went through his head when he was told to go back to Lyons and take over Pothinus' job? Did the authorities in Rome say *Au revoir* or *Auf wiedersehen*, or were they honest and said "Sorry, we probably shall not see each other again this side of heaven"? I am filled with admiration for Justin Martyr, Irenaeus, Blandina and the church fathers, partly for their intellect, but mainly for their courage. So my dream is that the Church in the West wakes up, becomes more combative, and lives up to the example of men and women such as these.

My research has convinced me that the Gospels are absolutely trustworthy, and that the power of the love and compassion of their central character, Jesus of Nazareth, the Messiah and Son of God, can transform us all. I trust this book will convince readers of that.

ABBREVIATIONS

Annals: Tacitus, "The Annals of Imperial Rome." Translated by Michael Grant, Penguin Classics, 1971. Includes a useful timeline.

AH: St Irenaeus of Lyons, *"Adversus Haereses"* or "Against Heresies." (c. 180) Translation published by Beloved Publishing, USA, 2015.

Ant: Flavius Josephus, "Jewish Antiquities." Translated by William Whiston, Wordsworth Classics, 2006.

Apol: Justin Martyr, "The Apologies."

BAH: Werner Keller, "The Bible as History." Translated by William Neil, Twelfth Impression, Hodder and Stoughton, London, 1966.

Baker: Simon Baker, "Ancient Rome," BBC Books, London, 2006.

BAV: E-M Stirnemann, "Brigandages Au Vatican," Publications de l'Association Képhas-Colombes, 2008.

BJ: Flavius Josephus, "The Jewish War." Translated by G A Williamson, Penguin Classics, 1970.

Caesars: Suetonius, "The Twelve Caesars." Translated by Robert Graves, Penguin Classics, 1969.

CJohn: D A Carson, "The Gospel According to John," IVP, 1991.

Crudens: Alexander Cruden, "Cruden's Complete Concordance to the Old and New Testaments," Revised Edition, Lutterworth Press, 1969.

DBLuke: Darrell L Bock, "Exegetical Commentary on the New Testament: Luke," Baker Academic, 1994.

Dissert: James Smith FRS, "Dissertation on the Life and Writings of St Luke," incorporated in "The Voyage and Shipwreck of St Paul," Fourth Edition, Longmans, London, 1880. Now available Wipf and Stock Publishers, Eugene, Oregon, 2001.

DVC: Eusebius of Caesarea, "De Vita Constantini."

Eye: Richard J Bauckham, "Jesus and the Eyewitnesses," Eerdmans, 2006.

Echoes: Richard B Hays, "Echoes of Scripture in the Gospels," Baylor University Press, Waco, Texas, 2016.

Ep: Pliny the Younger, "Letters," Translated by Betty Radice, Penguin Classics, 1969.

FFBR: F F Bruce, "The New Testament Documents: Are They Reliable?" Bottom of the Hill Publishing, 2013.

FFBA: F F Bruce, "The New London Commentary on the Book of Acts," Marshall, Morgan and Scott, 1977 edition, London.

FFBJ: F F Bruce, "The Gospel of John," Eerdmans, 1983.

FMatt: R T France, "Tyndale New Testament Commentaries: Matthew," IVP, 1992.

FMatt2: R T France, "The New International Commentary: Matthew," Eerdmans, 2007.

FMark: R T France, "The New International Greek Testament Commentary: Mark," Eerdmans, 2002.

GActs: Michael Green, "Acts for Today," Hodder and Stoughton, London, 1993.

H&G: edited by Elijah Hixson and Peter J Gurry, "Myths and Mistakes in New Testament Textual Criticism," IVP Academic, 2019.

HE: Eusebius of Caesarea, "Ecclesiastical History." (c. 300) Translated by CF Cruse, Hendrickson, 2014.

Hist: Tacitus, "The Histories." Translated by Kenneth Wellesley, Penguin Classics, 1968.

HRNT: Craig L Blomberg, "The Historical Reliability of the New Testament," B&H Academic Press, Nashville, Tennessee, 2016.

HSC: Colin J Hemer, "The Letters to the Seven Churches of Asia in their Local Setting," Eerdmans, Cambridge UK, 2001.

IHML: I Howard Marshall, "New International Greek Text Commentary: Gospel of Luke," Paternoster Press, Exeter, 1978.

Jesus: Richard J Bauckham, "Jesus: A Very Short Introduction," Oxford University Press, 2011.

Life: Flavius Josephus, "The Life of Flavius Josephus," Translated by William Whiston.

MTAC: Josh and Sean Mc Dowell, "More than a Carpenter," Authentic Media, 2014.

LMark: William L Lane, "The New London Commentary on the New Testament: Mark." Marshall, Morgan and Scott, London, 1974.

ME: Kenneth E Bailey, "Jesus Through Middle Eastern Eyes," SPCK, London, 2008.

New: Peter J Williams, "New Evidences the Gospels were Based on Eyewitness Accounts," lecture (video 2019) available on https://www.divinity.cam.ac.uk/directory/peter-williams.

NBD: "New Bible Dictionary," Third Edition, IVP Press, Leicester, 1996.

Paul: Sir William Mitchell Ramsay, "St Paul the Traveller and the Roman Citizen," Aberdeen University Press, 1896, reprinted by Forgotten Books.

SC: Sir William Mitchell Ramsay, "The Letters to the Seven Churches of Asia," London, 1904.

Star: David Hughes, "The Star of Bethlehem Mystery," J M Dent & Sons Ltd., London, 1979.

Test: Richard J Bauckham, "The Testimony of the Beloved Disciple," Baker Academic, 2007.

Trust?: Peter J Williams, "Can We Trust the Gospels?" Crossway, Wheaton, Illinois, 2018.

TTQ: Amy Orr-Ewing, "Why Trust the Bible? Answers to Ten Tough Questions," IVP, UK, 2005.

TWActs: Tom Wright, "Acts for Everyone," SPCK, London, 2008.

TWJohn: Tom Wright, "John for Everyone," SPCK, London, 2004

TWLuke: Tom Wright, "Luke for Everyone," SPCK, London, 2004

TWMatt: Tom Wright, "Matthew for Everyone," SPCK, London, 2002

TWMark: Tom Wright, "Mark for Everyone," SPCK, London, 2004.

TWNT: Tom Wright, "The New Testament for Everyone," SPCK, London, 2011.

TWRomans: Tom Wright, "Paul for Everyone: Romans," SPCK, London, 2004.

TWPrison: Tom Wright, "Paul for Everyone: the Prison Letters," SPCK, London, 2004.

TWSC: Tom Wright, "Simply Christian," SPCK, London, 2006.

VQJ: Miriam Feinberg-Vamosh, "La Vie Quotodienne au Temps de Jésus," Editions LLB, Valence.

Voyage: James Smith FRS, "The Voyage and Shipwreck of St Paul," Fourth Edition, Longmans, London, 1880. Now available Wipf and Stock Publishers, Eugene, Oregon, 2001.

What?: Richard A Burridge, "What are the Gospels?" Second Edition, Eerdmans, Cambridge UK, 2004.

ATLASES AND MAPS

Corazin: L'Israël que Jésus a Parcourue, Editions Corazin, Israël, 1991.

NIVA: Maps from NIV Bible, Hodder and Stoughton.

PAB: Picture Archive of the Bible, Lion Publishing, UK, 1987.

RDBA: Reader's Digest Atlas of the Bible, edited by J L Gardner, Reader's Digest Ass Inc, 1981.

SBA: Student's Bible Atlas, edited by H H Rowley, Lutterworth Press, London, 1965.

PART I: INTRODUCTION

Chapter 1

PREAMBLE

DOES IT MATTER?

Does it matter whether the Gospels are reliable or not? The short answer is YES - because if we want to know about Jesus of Nazareth, the figure who towers over human history, we have to study the Gospels.

The French Emperor Napoleon Bonaparte was in many ways the founder of the modern French state. He had a complex relation with Christianity. However, he was profoundly attracted to the person of Jesus Christ. On many occasions he compared himself and other great men. Here are some of the things he is reported as saying about Jesus:

"The nature of Christ's existence is mysterious, I admit; but this mystery meets the wants of man. Reject it and the world is an inexplicable riddle; believe it, and the history of our race is satisfactorily explained."

"I know men; and I tell you that Jesus Christ is no mere man. Between Him and every person in the world there is no possible term of comparison. Alexander, Caesar, Charlemagne, and I have founded empires. But on what did we rest the creation of our genius? Upon force. Jesus Christ founded His empire upon love; and at this hour millions of men would die for Him."

"His Gospel, His apparition, His empire, His march across the ages and the realms, is for me a prodigy, a mystery insoluble, which plunges me into a reverence which I cannot escape, a mystery which is there before my eyes, mystery which I cannot deny or explain. Here I see nothing human. The nearer I approach, the more carefully I examine, everything is above me, everything remains grand – and of a grandeur which overpowers."

"He asks for the human heart; He will have it entirely for himself. He demands it unconditionally; and forthwith His demand is granted. Wonderful! ...All who sincerely believe in Him, experience that remarkable, supernatural love toward Him...This is it, which strikes me most; I have often thought of it. This is it which proves to me quite convincingly the Divinity of Jesus Christ."[1]

It is clear that, for Napoleon, Jesus was both human and divine and the only one who could explain the mystery of human existence. John's Gospel (14:9) goes further: Jesus shows us the real face of God.

---

[1] http://justjesus.typepad.com/blog/2009/11/napoleon-bonaparte-and-jesus-christ.html

Secondly, Leo Tolstoy, inspired by the Gospels, wrote a thesis called *"The Kingdom of God is Within You,"* in which he portrayed the kingdom in terms of non-violent resistance to evil, a notion which impressed itself on the young Gandhi and would prove particularly effective in his political life and work[2]. Coming down to the present day, Nelson Mandela based his policies as the first black President of South Africa on the Christian doctrine of reconciliation, brought about by Jesus Christ, and a major theme of the Epistles of Paul[3]. Thus, people inspired by the teaching of Jesus Christ have changed the world, peacefully and without violence.

However (and this is the third point), no transformation of the world can last, unless the heart of man is also transformed. The Gospels recount, and Christian people believe, precisely this: that Jesus, on the cross forgave us our sins, liberated us and thus renewed our hearts.

Therefore, there are at least these three good reasons why the historical reliability of the Gospels is crucial. We come to the Gospels to get to know Jesus, the real face of God and the only hope for the world. On the other hand, if the Gospels are not trustworthy, then Christianity, the worship of Jesus the Son of God, is just an empty box, of no interest whatsoever.

Opposition

It is therefore not surprising that over the last two centuries, the Gospels have been subjected to an unprecedented intellectual artillery barrage. These attacks have not been precise and they have frequently been based on very poor scholarship[4], but they have been unceasing and have constituted an extremely successful propaganda screen. The opposing voice, that the Gospels are historical, has been drowned out by the deafening onslaught, so much so that the man in the street now believes Jesus to be a mythical character.

The aim of this book is, along with the efforts of others, to redress the balance: to demonstrate that, whenever we seriously investigate what the Gospels say, they turn out to be entirely trustworthy. They are coherent and recount facts and events that can be confirmed from other sources.

CORRESPONDENCE AND COHERENCE

The thrust of this book is to examine the reliability of the Gospels with respect to the notions of truth of correspondence and coherence. Both of these conceptions of truth have deep historical roots.

Correspondence can be traced back to Plato and Aristotle in the third and fourth centuries BC. In essence, it means that a true statement or proposition reflects reality itself. Correspondence is commonly viewed as the traditional and common sense understanding of truth. Our theories or beliefs, be they scientific, historical or religious, need to square up with reality.

---

[2] Simon Ponsonby, "And the Lamb Wins," David C Cooke, Eastbourne, UK, 2008, p51.

[3] This is the thesis of John Carlin's book "Playing the Enemy," Atlantic Books, London, 2008, on which Clint Eastwood's superb film "Invictus" is based.

[4] This is the thesis, for example, of Etienne Stirnemann, "Brigandage au Vatican" Editions Kephas-Colombes, 2008.

They must also not be self-contradictory, from which we obtain the concept of coherence. Immanuel Kant popularised the notion of coherence from the late 1700's, but its roots go way back[5]. For there to be coherence, a body of propositions must be consistent within itself.

Clearly, it is not sufficient to have only one point of correspondence with reality. For a theory or body of propositions to be true, it should ideally be shown to square up with reality, whenever and wherever it can be tested, and to be consistent within itself – to correspond and to be coherent. In practice, of course, the ideal of total correspondence and complete coherence is rarely found, in science or in other fields. This is because our theories and the information on which they are based, are not engraved on marble tablets, but rather evolve over time. This is clearly true of science, but it is also true of history[6], because new discoveries in archaeology may give us new insights and transform our views of how people lived at the time.

An example from the physical sciences may be helpful here. Towards the end of the nineteenth century, the first, second and third laws of thermodynamics seemed among the most solid in science. They explained and predicted the behaviour of gases, the conservation of energy, the cycles of heat engines and much else besides. However, they could not describe in fine detail the type of light emitted from black bodies ("Black body radiation"). On this one point correspondence with reality was lacking. Max Planck proposed a theoretical solution which explained the experimental data, but to do so he had to break and remake the ground rules. He proposed that energy was not available as an infinite continuum; it was only available in whole numbers of small finite packets which he called *quanta*. Thus, the quantum theory was born, which would revolutionise modern science, and correspondence was re-established. However, the new theory confronted Einstein with a problem of coherence, because it did not fit into his theory of General Relativity.

CORRESPONDENCE AND COHERENCE AND THE RELIABILITY OF THE GOSPELS

As we transfer these ideas of correspondence and coherence to the study of the reliability of the Gospels, several points need to be made.

We will be able to test the correspondence of the Gospels with reality, because they are historical books. We can therefore compare what these books relate with other historical documents and archaeological finds from the same periods[7].

There are, of course, four Gospels in the New Testament: Matthew, Mark, Luke and John. It is important to demonstrate that these four documents are coherent, meaning that they cover the same main events in the same places at the same time, and paint similar portraits of the person of Jesus. Nevertheless, if indeed, as John's Gospel itself maintains, these accounts originated in eye-witness testimony, then it would be suspicious if they coincided in every detail. A detective or defence lawyer, faced with four witness statements which were identical, would conclude that the four had colluded in order to present a common front, which was probably a pack of lies. The

---

[5] Neal V Dawson, "Correspondence and Coherence in Science: a brief historical perspective," Judgement and Decision Making, vol 4 No 2, March 2009, pp 126-133.

[6] One might almost say that it is especially true of history, because the relatively recent application of high technology in archaeology is likely to reap huge dividends in the future.

[7] Much of the background information in the Appendices confirms the correspondence of the Gospels with reality.

four Gospels, on the other hand, do vary in some of their details, which is a gauge of their authenticity. Therefore, when we examine the coherence of the four Gospels, we must avoid splitting hairs and allow for some differences in detail.

Scope

A few words on the scope of this book: we do not have the space to deal with the cultural references in the parables of Jesus, or the multiple echoes of the Old Testament in the Gospels. The former is covered extremely well in *"Jesus Through Middle Eastern Eyes" (ME)* by Kenneth E Bailey, the latter equally well in *"Echoes of Scripture in the Gospels" (Echoes)* by Richard B Hays. Nor, at the other end of the scale, is it a work covering the question of the relationship between science and religion[8].

THE EVIDENCE OF THE EARLY GENTILE WRITERS

The earliest Gentile historian who mentions the person of Jesus is Thallus. In about AD 52, he wrote a work tracing the history of Greece and its relations with Asia, from the Trojan War to his own day. He has been identified with a Samaritan of that name, who is mentioned by Josephus (*Ant* 18.6) as being a freedman of the Emperor Tiberius. Unfortunately, the works of Thallus have not survived apart from fragments quoted by later writers. Julius Africanus, a Christian author on chronology in about AD 221, knew the writings of Thallus and says, when discussing the darkness which fell on the land during the crucifixion of Christ:

"Thallus, in the third book of his histories, explains away this darkness as an eclipse of the Sun-unreasonably, as it seems to me (unreasonably, of course, because a solar eclipse could not take place at the time of the full moon, and it was at the season of the Paschal full moon that Christ died)."

From this it can be deduced that Jesus' death was already known about in non-Christian circles in Rome towards the middle of the first century AD (*FFBR* p91; *TTQ* p58).

The British Museum possesses a manuscript preserving the text of a letter written sometime after AD 73. This letter was sent by a Syrian named Mara Bar-Serapion to his son Serapion. Mara Bar-Serapion was in prison at the time, but he wrote to encourage his son in the pursuit of wisdom. He pointed out that those who persecuted wise men were overtaken by misfortune, taking the deaths of Socrates, Pythagoras and Christ as examples:

"What advantage did the Athenians gain from putting Socrates to death? Famine and plague came upon them as a judgment for their crime. What advantage did the men of Samos gain from burning Pythagoras? In a moment their land was covered with sand. What advantage did the Jews gain from executing their wise King? It was just after that that their kingdom was abolished. God justly avenged these three wise men: the Athenians died of hunger; the Samians were overwhelmed by the sea; the Jews, ruined and driven from their land, live in complete dispersion. But Socrates did not die for good; he lived on in the teaching of Plato. Pythagoras did not die for good; he lived on in the statue of Hera. Nor did the wise King die for good; He lived on in the teaching He had given."

---

[8] Those interested in this area should consult the works of Professors John Polkinghorne, Alister McGrath and John Lennox.

The writer cannot have been a Christian, or he would have stated that Jesus lived on by being raised from the dead. But all this shows that, although Christianity in the first hundred years of its existence, was regarded by the Romans as an obscure, disreputable, oriental superstition, nevertheless the person of Christ was already well known by Gentile philosophers and historians (*FFBR* p92).

ON THE HISTORIANS AND CHURCH FATHERS

Here we consider the major secular historians of the New Testament period and then the most important early church historians, whose work we will be using in the rest of this book. We begin with the most important Roman historians.

THE ROMAN HISTORIANS

Suetonius

Gaius Suetonius Tranquillus (Suetonius) was probably born in AD 69. He practised briefly at the bar and became chief secretary to the Emperor Hadrian (AD 117-138). He lived to a good old age. He had access to the Imperial and Senate archives, checked his facts as much as possible, and much of his information about Tiberius, Caligula and Nero came from eye-witnesses. *"The Twelve Caesars"* is the only complete book which has come down to us. He was a close friend of Pliny the Younger.

Tacitus

Publius (or Gaius) Cornelius Tacitus was born somewhere between AD 56-7, and probably survived the Emperor Trajan, who died in AD 117. He was an orator and a senator in the bleak days of Domitian (AD 81-96), but he later rose to Consul (AD 97) and, fifteen years later, to Governor of Anatolia (Asia). His short monographs *"Agricola"* and *"Germania"* appeared in about AD 98. His *"Histories"* told the story of the Roman Emperors from Nero's death in AD 68 to AD 96, though only AD 68-69 is preserved. *"The Annals"* was supposed to cover AD 14 to 68, but Book V is partly missing, Books VII-X are missing and Book XVI breaks off in AD 66. Tacitus was a friend of Pliny the Younger and married the daughter of Agricola – Governor in Britain between AD 78 and AD 84.

Pliny the Younger

Pliny the Younger, nephew and adopted son of Pliny the Elder, lived from AD 61-113. His letters contain his account of the destruction of Pompei and his celebrated correspondence with the Emperor Trajan about the early Christians. He was a lawyer and was appointed consul at the very early age of 39. He rose through the ranks of the Empire, even during the reign of the hated Domitian. He was a friend of Tacitus and Suetonius. His final appointment was as imperial magistrate of Bithynia and Pontus under Trajan.

Flavius Josephus

Joseph ben Matthias, who was later to call himself Flavius Josephus, was born in AD 37, the year of Caligula's accession and died in Rome in AD 100. By birth right a Jewish priest and, on his mother's side, the descendant of kings, he was precocious and became a politician, soldier, orator and, finally, historian. During the early stages of the Jewish Revolt, when the Jerusalem priestly classes were still trying to canalise the rebellion, he rose to become the youthful Governor of Galilee in AD 66. He was taken prisoner by Vespasian and, in a final effort to save his skin, "prophesied" that Vespasian would become Emperor. This did indeed happen and Josephus thereafter served the Romans, notably as Titus' interpreter during the AD 70 siege of Jerusalem. The works which have come down to us are, in probable order of publication: *"The Jewish War," "Antiquities of the Jews," "Life," "Against Apion."* Most commentators accept that Josephus often writes to justify his own change of allegiance but, apart from this qualification, *"The Jewish War"* is by far the most accurate record we have of these events and the vast *"Antiquities of the Jews"* gives great insight into the history and customs of the Jewish nation.

EARLY CHURCH HISTORIANS

Papias

Papias was bishop of Hierapolis and we will introduce him in more detail later. In the words of Richard Bauckham (*Eye* pp 12-15): Papias belonged…to a generation that had been in touch…with the apostles. Although Papias wrote between AD 100 and 107, his recollections date from around AD 80.

Justin Martyr

Justin Martyr was born in Flavia Neapolis (modern-day Nablus), a Greek-speaking town in Samaria. In his *"Dialogue with Trypho"* he explains how he became a Christian, having passed by most of the different schools of Greek philosophy.

The *"First Apology"* (*Apol* 1) was an early work of Christian apologetics, addressed to the Emperor Antoninus Pius between AD 155 and 157. It may have been provoked by the martyrdom of Polycarp. Its aim was to stop the persecution of individuals solely because they were Christians. The much shorter *"Second Apology"* (*Apol* 2) was addressed to the Roman Senate.

Justin Martyr invented a new *genre* of Christian apologetics which was later refined by authors such as Tertullian.

Clement of Alexandria

Clement of Alexandria lived between about AD 150 and 215. He had pagan parents. In around AD 180, he reached Alexandria, leaving in 202-203.

Tertullian

Tertullian who lived between about AD 155 and 240 was from Carthage. He was the first Christian author to produce an extensive corpus of Latin Christian literature and theology. He wrote against the heresies of Gnosticism and Marcion.

Origen

Origen lived between AD 184/5 and 253/4 and was a prolific scholar and early Christian theologian who spent the first half of his career in Alexandria. He moved to Caesarea in 231/2.

Eusebius

Eusebius was probably born between AD 260 and 265 in Caesarea Maritima, where he lived for most of his adult life. Through the activities of Origen and Pamphilius, Caesarea became a centre of Christian learning. Eusebius wrote *"Demonstrations of the Gospel," "Preparations for the Gospel,"* and *"On discrepancies between the Gospels."* But he is most remembered as the "Father of Church History" with the books *"Ecclesiastical History"* (written between AD 290 and 300), *"On the Life of Pamphilius," "The Chronicle,"* and *"On the Martyrs."*

In his *"Ecclesiastical History"*, his vital concern was to record facts before they disappeared and before eyewitnesses were killed and libraries were burned and destroyed in persecutions by Rome. He had access to the impressive biblical and theological library at Caesarea, which included Origen's *"Hexapla"* and *"Tetrapla"* and a copy of the original Aramaic version of the Gospel of Matthew[9]. He faithfully transcribed the most important existing documents of his day, so that future generations would have a collection of factual data to interpret. He thus richly deserves the title of "Father of Church History."

He became bishop of Caesarea soon after AD 313. Eusebius enjoyed the favour of the Emperor Constantine and, as such, presented the creed of his own church to the Council of Nicaea in AD 325. He died in AD 339/40.

UNBROKEN CHAINS OF WITNESSES

Irenaeus

Irenaeus was one of the most important early church historians.

He was a Greek, born in Polycarp's home town of Smyrna in Asia Minor, now Izmir in Turkey. He lived between roughly AD 130 and 202 and his major work *"Adversus Haereses"* (against the Gnostic heresy) was written c 180, when he was in Lyons. He died as a martyr in Lugdunum in Gaul (present-day Lyons in France).

Irenaeus was brought up in a Christian family and was therefore not an adult convert. As a young man in Smyrna, the aged bishop Polycarp was his mentor, who in turn was a hearer of the apostle John and later died as a martyr. They both went to Rome, where Irenaeus met Justin Martyr. Then Irenaeus was sent as a missionary to Lyons, where many Christians were martyred during the persecution of the Roman Emperor Marcus Aurelius. However, in AD 177, Irenaeus was sent to Rome as a delegate of the churches in Gaul, with a letter for Pope Eleuturus concerning Montanism and, while he was there, another violent wave of persecution hit Lyons. Returning to Gaul, Irenaeus succeeded the martyr Pothinus and became the second bishop of Lyons.

However, Irenaeus is best known for his work *Adversus Haereses (AH)* or "Against Heresies" (c. 180), which was a detailed attack on Gnosticism, especially that of Valentinus. Irenaeus found that the Gnosticism of Valentinus was extremely sophisticated, dangerous and prevalent in Gaul. Indeed, Valentinus had nearly made it to bishop of Rome in AD 130. Irenaeus' aim with *Adversus Haereses (AH)* was to protect his flock and to convert Gnostics to knowledge of the saviour Jesus Christ. He is an extremely solid historical witness for several reasons.

---

[9] Timothy Barnes, "Constantine and Eusebius," Harvard University Press, 1981, p94.

Firstly, Irenaeus was one of the greatest ever systematic theologians. According to Emil Brunner, the eminent Swiss theologian[10]: *"that, though Irenaeus has more title than any other to be regarded as the founder of ecclesiastical* (dogmatic or systematic) *theology, nevertheless in him the New Testament witness, Johannine and Pauline, the specifically New Testament and the whole-Biblical, are united in hardly any other until Luther."*

Secondly, because there was little historical evidence on Gnosticism, over the years Irenaeus' attacks on it were deemed to be exaggerated. However, the discovery in 1945 in Egypt, at Nag Hammadi, of 13 leather-bound codices, containing 52 gnostic treatises (the most famous being the *Gospel of Thomas*), recording gnostic teaching of the second century AD, has shown Irenaeus' treatment of the subject to be largely fair.

Thirdly, and this is crucial, Irenaeus in his youth in Asia Minor, had access to important historical witnesses. Indeed, Irenaeus valued his memories of Polycarp *because they put him in touch with Jesus by way of only two intermediaries: Polycarp and the Apostle John.* This was only possible because both were very long-lived: John survived, according to Irenaeus, into the reign of Trajan, which began in AD 98 (*AH* 3.3.4), while Polycarp was 86 when he was martyred in Smyrna somewhere between AD 156 and 167 (*Eye* p457).

The other oral source of Irenaeus' information about John was doubtless the church of Ephesus (*AH* 3.3.4), which he would have known when he lived in Smyrna. Finally, Irenaeus had a written source: the works of Papias which he cites once (*AH 5.33.4*).

Irenaeus also refers generally to the elders, the circle of revered teachers in the province of Asia, contemporaries of Polycarp and Papias, who had been disciples of John and the other apostles or disciples of Jesus who had settled in the area (*AH 5.33.3*). All this is resumed in Table 1.1 and demonstrates that Irenaeus is a very sure historical witness.

Unfortunately, *Adversus Haereses (AH)* and *"The Demonstration of the Apostolic Preaching"* are the only works of Irenaeus which survive today. However, and this is the fourth point, even though no complete version of *Adversus Haereses (AH)* in its original Greek exists, we do possess the full ancient Latin version, probably from the third century, as well as 33 fragments of a Syrian version and a complete Armenian version of Books 4 and 5.

Hence, for all these reasons, Irenaeus is an extremely valuable and solid historical witness. Above all, there is an unbroken chain of witnesses between him and the apostles and Jesus (see Table 1.1). He also substantiates what we know from Papias, in the extracts recorded by Eusebius (*HE*).

Quadratus (*Eye* pp54-5), who wrote in AD 130 evokes another similar chain of witnesses:

"The deeds of our Saviour," said Quadratus, *"were always before you, for they were true miracles; those that were healed, those that were raised from the dead, who were seen, not only when healed and when raised, but were always present. They remained a long time, not only while our Lord was on earth, but likewise when he had left the earth. So that some of them have also lived to our own times."* (*BAV* p139 and *HE* 4.3.1-2)

There was thus no gap separating Jesus and the writers of the Gospels from the early church, but rather several continuous chains of witnesses.

In the next chapter we look at the coming of Jesus.

---

[10] Quoted in Paul R Hinlicky, "Divine Complexity: the Rise of Creedal Christianity," p138.

Table1.1: IRENAEUS' CHAIN OF WITNESSES

(Based on *Eye* Table 17 p471, with some modifications; references are to *AH*)

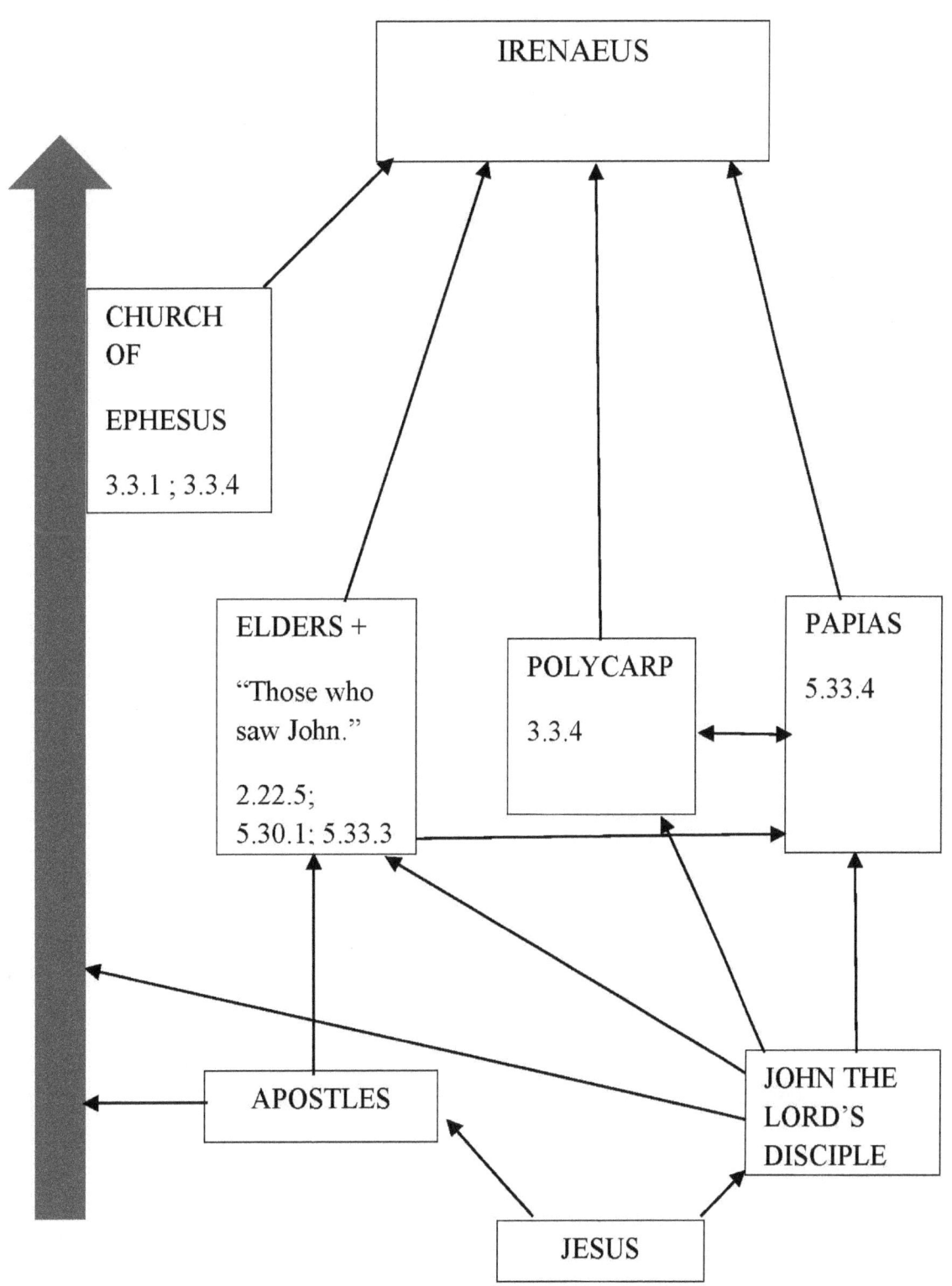

Chapter 2

THE COMING OF JESUS

We shall discover in Chapter 9 that Jesus was born in 6-7 BC. Caesar Augustus was in power in Rome; Herod the Great ruled over Palestine, appointed by Mark Anthony, and then by Augustus, as "King of the Jews." He massacred all the baby boys under two years of age, in and around Bethlehem, before dying in 5 BC.

Herod the Great

Herod the Great was a blood-thirsty, paranoid megalomaniac. No visitor to modern Israel can fail to be impressed by the legacy of land-marks left by Herod's megalomaniac passion for building. There are the twin palaces of Masada, the palace, theatre, stadium and port at Caesarea (Maritime), his palace and mausoleum at Herodium, his palaces at Jericho and Machaerus, the immense shrine for the patriarchs at Hebron and, of course, the enormous platform left after the destruction of Herod's Temple at Jerusalem.

Herod was not an ethnic Jew, which may have been the source of some of his insecurity and paranoia. On his father's side, he was Idumean; his ancestors had converted to Judaism. His mother was Arab, a Nabatean (*BJ* 1.181). He sought legitimacy by marrying into the Hasmonean aristocracy, but they opposed him which, paradoxically, made the Essenes his allies. He gained influence by distributing land to selected nobles, who supported him, and became known as the "Herodians."

So, he was no descendant of David. He nevertheless appointed the High Priests, Hasmoneans to begin with, but when their opposition grew, he chose an obscure priest from Babylon, called Ananias. Herod gained power and maintained order brutally, using Roman troops, based in the Fortress Antonia in Jerusalem.

His paranoia led him to execute, early in his reign, his predecessors Antigonus II (*Ant* 15.8-10) and Hyrcanus II (*Ant* 15.173-178) together with large numbers of their supporters (*Ant* 15.6) and, eventually, all the remaining members of the Hasmonean family (*Ant* 15.260-66). Even those Hasmoneans directly related to him by marriage: his brother-in-law (*Ant* 15.53-55), mother-in-law (*Ant* 15.247-51) and even his favourite wife Mariamme (1) (*Ant* 15.222-36) were killed. In his final years, he killed his three eldest sons (Alexander, Aristobolus and Antipater) on suspicion of plotting to seize the throne (*Ant* 16.392-94; 17.182-87) (see Table 2.1 The Chief Members of Herod's Family). He ruled with spies (*Ant* 15.366-69) and by the ruthless suppression of political opposition (*Ant* 15.280-90). This accelerated between 7 and 5 BC.

"I would prefer to be Herod's pig than his son," said Augustus Caesar (*VQJ* p13). To cap it all, in 5 BC, Herod, who was extremely ill, ordered that the Judean nobility should be arrested, imprisoned and killed on his death, the idea being that the Jews would then mourn his passing. His daughter Salome (1) began by carrying out his orders, but finally freed the nobles (*Ant*

17.174-78). His massacre of all the baby boys under two years of age in the region of Bethlehem (Matthew 2:16-18) was, unfortunately, entirely in character.

The End of the Exile?

Jesus was born in 6-7 BC (*HRNT* p104). What were the hopes and aspirations of ordinary Jews in 7 BC? They were not free. God had not spoken to them through prophets for 420 years. The so-called King of the Jews was not even an ethnic Jew, let alone a descendant of David. He had been appointed by a pagan Emperor and maintained power using foreign troops. Even if the High Priest came from the line of Aaron, he was appointed by a "king" who was appointed by Rome; the office had become a political appointment and had nothing to do with worshipping God. (In fact, Herod the Great never took an important decision without consulting Augustus, which is tantamount to saying that Caesar appointed the High Priests). All this was a far cry from the three-fold hierarchy[11], with each branch being anointed by the Holy Spirit: the Davidic kings, the prophets to keep the kings in line with the will of God, and the priests to gather up the worship of the people.

The chief priests, based in Jerusalem, were almost certainly all tarred with the same corrupt brush. Perhaps the ordinary priests, living outside Jerusalem, like Zechariah (Luke 1:5-6), were still righteous, but what influence could they have? Everywhere there was spiritual drought (which the beginning of Luke's Gospel captures very well), oppression, violence and corruption. The "exile" of the Jews was not yet over.

So, our ordinary Jews in 7 BC, in the synagogues, where they read the Hebrew Scriptures together, were waiting for the Messiah. He would:

- Be a king from the line of David (2 Samuel 7:14-16)
- Decisively defeat Israel's pagan enemies, notably the Romans
- Rebuild and/or cleanse the Temple
- Bring justice and righteousness (*TWMark* p235).

And the teachers in the synagogues, those who could read the Hebrew Scriptures for themselves, would be reading the prophet Daniel, because he had got everything right so far. According to Josephus, they were reading Daniel Chapter 9[12].

Daniel 9 is mostly a prayer. Daniel prayed about the prophecy of Jeremiah, that the exile would only last for seventy years, and this did indeed happen. His prayer was answered by a heavenly visit from the angel Gabriel who informed him that the prophecy was not for seventy years but for "seventy weeks of years": *"Seventy weeks of years are decreed for your people and your holy city to finish the transgression, to put an end to sin, to atone for wickedness, to bring in everlasting righteousness, to seal up the vision and prophecy and to anoint the most holy One."* (Daniel 9:24).

---

[11] For more on this, see Appendix 1: The Inter-Testamental Period.
[12] This whole argument is based on Tom Wright, "Justification," pp 37-45, SPCK, London 2009.

The prophecy continues with descriptions of the rebuilding of Jerusalem, the cutting off of the "anointed one," the setting up of "an abomination that causes desolation" and an ultimate destruction.

So, the question was, since Daniel was popular reading in the synagogues in the first century AD, when would the 70 x 7 = 490 years be up? When would this greatest of all prophecies be fulfilled? When would the redemption finally happen? When would this extended term of "exile" finally be over?

Well, it all depended on when you counted from; when did the countdown of the 490 years begin? The Jews of the first century would have begun counting from anywhere between 522 and 445 BC. Thus, they would have reckoned that the events of Daniel 9 were due somewhere between 32 BC and 45 AD, or perhaps even later.

So, the coming of Jesus coincided exactly with the Jews expecting the end of the period of extended exile and the coming of the Messiah. For them, it was not some vague future promise; it was imminent; it dominated their thinking. They were confidently expecting the coming of the Messiah, the defeat of the Romans and the rebuilding/cleansing of the Temple within their lifetime.

After Herod the Great

Octavius Caesar was a cunning, ruthless and courageous young man (*Caesars*: Augustus) but, on gaining supreme power as Augustus, proved to be a wise and diligent ruler. He was a womanizer; however, he only really loved one woman, his wife Livia. Morally, he was an example for the Romans. Suetonius (*Caesars*: Augustus) says the only mistake he made was in the choice of his heir: Tiberius.

On Herod the Great's death, Augustus thought long and hard over the succession to Herod's sons (see the Table 2.1: Chief Members of Herod's Family). Augustus finally distributed the land to Herod the Great's sons, giving Trachonitis, Gaulantis and Batanea to Philip with the title of Tetrarch; Galilee and Perea to Herod Antipas, also as Tetrarch and the superior title of Ethnarch to Archelaus, along with Judea, Samaria and Idumea (*Ant* 17.318). Two minor regions were attributed to Salome (1). There was no longer a "King of the Jews."

However, even before arriving in Rome for the decision, Archelaus had already provoked the massacre of 3,000 people by his troops in Jerusalem (*BJ* 2.7-26). (No wonder Joseph (Matthew 2: 22-23) did not want to live in his territory and decided to settle in Nazareth in Galilee). This was followed by spontaneous uprisings throughout the country. As the terror and anarchy spread, Varus, the Governor of Syria, went into action. He retook and burnt cities throughout Palestine and crucified 2,000 rebels. Jerusalem was in flames.

The Roman Province of Judea

Archelaus treated the Jews and Samaritans so cruelly that both peoples sent embassies to Rome, to accuse him before Caesar. As a result, Archelaus was banished to Gaul in 6 AD. Augustus instituted direct rule by uniting Judea, Samaria and Idumea as the Roman Province of Judea, under a Roman Prefect, Coponius (*Ant* 17.200-344)[13].

---

[13] For more on this see Appendix 2: The Geographical and Economic Background.

Table 2.1 CHIEF MEMBERS OF HEROD'S FAMILY

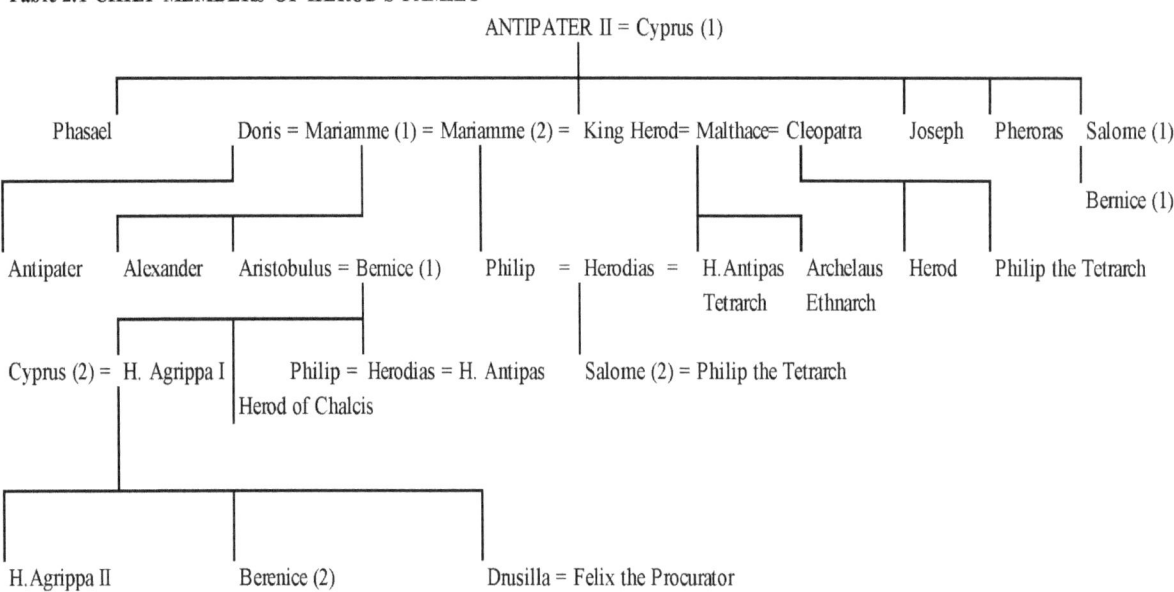

NOTES

This chart is based on *BJ* p405

Only a few members of this vast family with its numerous internal and at times incestuous alliances are shown above.

King Herod is known to have had ten wives and fifteen children.

Cleopatra is not the Egyptian Cleopatra, mistress of Julius Caesar and Mark Anthony

Cyprus (2) was in fact the grand-daughter of Phasael

Bernice (2) had two husbands and was mistress to Vespasian, Titus and probably her own brother Herod Agrippa II, the last monarch of Herod's line, who retired like Josephus to Rome, where in AD 100, both died.

Meanwhile Philip the Tetrarch ruled wisely and without major incident until his death in AD 34. He was happily married to Salome (2), the daughter of Herodias by his half-brother Philip (not the Tetrarch, see the Table 2.1 Chief Members of Herod's Family). Herod Antipas is the Herod we hear of during the ministry of Jesus, because he ruled over Galilee and Perea (Perea was on the east bank of the Jordan). He built his new capital Tiberias, named after Augustus' successor, on the shores of the Sea of Galilee. Thus, the Jewish nation at the time of Jesus was comprised essentially of the Roman Province of Judea (including Samaria and Idumea) and Herod Antipas' territories of Galilee and Perea.

Finally, Augustus died and Tiberius became emperor. He began his reign with a reputation for military courage, caution and persuasion. However, from 31 AD onwards, perhaps as a result of illness, his pedophile tendencies and violence began to dominate. A reign of terror ensued which continued under Caligula (*Annals* 5.2-6.50).

Tiberius nominated Gratus as Prefect over the Province of Judea, who deposed the High Priest Ananus (*Ant* 18.29-35) and designated successors. However, no one suited him, until he chose Joseph Caiaphas, who held office from AD 18-36.

In Part II we begin to look at the New Testament documents and, in particular, at the ancient manuscripts that record them.

PART II: THE DOCUMENTS

Chapter 3

THE NEW TESTAMENT DOCUMENTS

Authors, Bookshops and Publishing in the First and Early Second Centuries AD

Obviously modern methods of printing and publication did not exist in the Graeco-Roman world. However, in order to understand how the New Testament writings were transmitted in the earliest stages, we must examine the techniques of book production and circulation at the time. Timothy N Mitchell does this in *H&G*.

At the time, books took the form of scrolls and codices. The scroll, made of parchment (prepared animal skin) or papyrus, was written by hand in continuous columns and then rolled up with the text on the inside. The codex, on the other hand, was made from sheets of parchment or papyrus stacked together, folded down the centre and then stitched along the folded spine. The writing (also by hand) was on both sides of the pages (*H&G* p28).

Although booksellers existed (*H&G* p30), the circulation of literature occurred mainly through acquaintances and making personal copies of these borrowed books. The works of Pliny the Younger (c 61-115) give us an insight into both the commercial and private circulation of books. Writing to his friend, the famous Roman historian Suetonius, he wants to hear *"that my friend's books are being copied, read and sold"* (*Ep* 5.10).

Pliny also describes his own process of writing:

"First of all, I go through the work myself; next I read it to two or three friends and send it to others for comment. If I have any doubts about their criticisms, I go over them again with one or two people, and finally read the work to a larger audience; and this is the moment, believe me, where I make my severest corrections." (*Ep* 7.17)

During these stages, Pliny worked with a scribe (*Ep* 9.16). Once satisfied with the piece, he "released" the work to be circulated by his associates and acquaintances, by giving or lending a copy to a friend, sending a copy to a bookseller or deposing the book in a library. At this point of relinquishing control of the piece, Pliny signalled that the work was ready to be copied and circulated (*H&G* p32).

Martial (*Epig* 1.66 cited in *H&G* p32) declared that once a work had been circulated in a community, the writing could not be significantly transformed without these actions becoming widely known. Once a document was completed and released for circulation there was a possibility that further copies could be made under the control of the authors (*H&G* p39).

Also, in the same way as Pliny the Younger kept copies of his letters in view of future publication, the apostle Paul could well have kept copies of his epistles and circulated them as a collection (*H&G* p41). Tom Wright suggests that the first trace of the codex is to be found in 2 Timothy 4:13, written in AD 64, where Paul, who is once again in prison in Rome, asks Timothy to bring him *"the scrolls* (biblia) *and especially the books* (membranas)*."* Here, the *membranas* would be sheets of papyrus or parchment stitched together to form a flat volume or *codex*[14].

Whether this is true or not, the early Christians certainly went for the codex, because it was so much easier to put short documents together in a collection, such as the four Gospels.

Hence, when we turn to the New Testament documents, we may conclude that they also would only have been circulated once their text was finalised by the author and authorized for copying. Once circulated, they could not have been significantly transformed. Copies may have been made after release under the control of the authors. An author, such as Paul, may have kept copies of his epistles and circulated them as a collection (*H&G* pp46, 47).

Peter J Williams (*Trust?* p23) points out that the rapid spread of Christianity means it would have been hard to shape its message and beliefs and bring about changes to the New Testament documents.

SOME BASIC IDEAS

It is generally accepted that the closer the date of writing is to the events that the document describes, the more reliable the document. This tenet concerns the veracity of the contents of the document. If, for example, the document depends on eyewitness testimony, then a short time difference between the events and writing will mean that the witnesses will not have suffered memory loss, that a large number of witnesses will still be alive, and that there will have been insufficient time for more "legendary" aspects to develop and be included in the document.

In future chapters we will demonstrate that Jesus of Nazareth was born in 7 BC and pursued his public ministry between 27 and 30 AD. Future chapters will also determine the origin of the Gospels. It turns out that a major proportion of the New Testament documents was written before the martyrdoms of Peter and Paul at the height of Nero's persecution in AD 64/65. The earliest document is doubtless Paul's Epistle to the Galatians, penned in AD 49, closely followed by 1 and 2 Thessalonians in AD 51 and 52 respectively and by 1 Corinthians in AD 55. Matthew probably wrote the Semitic version of his Gospel in Palestine or Syria between AD 55 and 57; Mark produced his in Rome in AD 59 or 60; Luke produced his Gospel and Acts in Rome between February AD 60 and February AD 62. The Epistle of James must date from before his death in AD 62; similarly, 1 Peter and 2 Peter were written before the apostle's death, probably in AD 59 and 60 respectively. The latest major documents of the New Testament, Revelation and John's Gospel, were written respectively in AD 95-96 and 97-98. However, even these were authored by John, one of the last living eyewitnesses of Jesus' public ministry, who had been a young lad in AD 27-30.

Hence, a huge proportion of the New Testament (the Gospels of Matthew, Mark and Luke, Acts, Paul's Epistles, 1 and 2 Peter, James), was already written by AD 64/65 and the totality was finished by AD 100. *Thus, the totality of the New Testament was completed within the*

---

[14] Tom Wright, "Paul for Everyone: The Pastoral Letters," SPCK, London, 2003, pp131-2. Incidentally, for some reason, the NIV translation inverses scrolls and books.

lifetime of the eyewitnesses of the events. This is already a huge gauge of reliability for the New Testament documents.

We note, in passing, that the works of Suetonius, Tacitus and *The Jewish War* of Josephus were also written not long after the events which they describe, so that, according to this criterion, these works may also be considered to be reliable.

After this first basic concept, there are two others which appear, at first sight, to be intuitively correct:

- The closer the date of the first good copies is to the date of writing, the more reliable the document, because textual variations in the document are likely to accumulate over time.
- The more copies we have in our possession, the more certain we can be of the original text.

There is a certain amount of truth in these two ideas, but the real picture is more complicated and will lead us into the *science of textual criticism*. Among the questions we shall ask are the following:

- How many manuscripts exist of the New Testament?
- What are the different types of New Testament manuscripts?
- How do we catalogue the New Testament manuscripts?
- What determines the value of a New Testament manuscript?
- How do we determine the age of a New Testament manuscript?
- When can a later manuscript be better?
- Were the copyists well trained?
- How many textual variants are there in the New Testament manuscripts and are they significant?
- Was there any deliberate corruption of the New Testament manuscripts? Can it be detected?

How many manuscripts exist of the New Testament?

Jacob W Peterson (*H&G* p48) explains that, when it comes to the number of manuscripts, the New Testament documents are in rarefied company among the wider field of classical authors. As a general rule there are more of them, many are earlier, and they tend to be more complete. But the bulk, while more complete, are not early. The early ones are fragmentary and few in number. So, are the numbers useful?

Categories of manuscripts

Greek New Testament manuscripts are classified according to the Gregory-Aland (GA) system into four categories: papyri, majuscules (or onciales), minuscules and lectionaries. Papyri are designated by a capital P followed by a number (e.g. P100), majuscules by a number prefixed by a zero (e.g. 042), minuscules by a plain number (e.g. 1739) and lectionaries by a lowercase l (e.g. l249) (*H&G* p50).

The system is a little peculiar because papyri is a material-based category, but the others are not. Majuscules and minuscules are script-based, while lectionaries can be either majuscules or minuscules. Kurt Aland founded the Institute for New Testament Textual Research (INTF) in 1959, which is now responsible for the official registry of Greek New Testament manuscripts, commonly known as *die Liste*.

Counting the manuscripts

Counting the number of Greek New Testament manuscripts is difficult. On the one hand, new ones appear all the time. There again, some are found to be complements to, or part of, existing classified manuscripts, which enhances the value of the initial manuscript. On the other hand, some are lost or destroyed by fire, flood or insects (*H&G* p55).

The best estimate (*H&G* p61) is of 5,100-5,300 Greek New Testament manuscripts.

Determining the age of a manuscript

Elijah Hixson (*H&G* p91) explains that the earliest manuscript for 1-2 Peter and Jude is P72 (Bodmer VII-VIII), but it seems to have been written by a sloppy scribe. So, an early manuscript is not necessarily the best.

Some manuscripts can be dated with precision, through notes on the copy or by when and where it was found. Unfortunately, techniques such as radiocarbon dating cannot usually be used, because this means destroying at least a part of the manuscript (*H&G* p101). Therefore, most are dated according to the styles of handwriting (*palaeography*), which results in a range of 50 years (*H&G* p95). For the earliest New Testament manuscript, the famous P52 Rylands manuscript, containing five verses from John 18, the most recent dating suggests AD 100-200 (*H&G* p109).

Weighing manuscripts

Taking two extreme examples: Codex Sinaiticus contains the whole New Testament, whereas P12 has parts of a single verse from the Epistle to the Hebrews (*H&G* p64). Clearly, they do not have the same value. Many factors need to be taken into account when we consider the value of a manuscript: its date, size, contents, quality and whether it comes from a reliable textual stream. More of this later.

Dates of manuscripts

Of the 5,300 New Testament Greek manuscripts, 83% come from after AD 1000 and the remaining 17% from before.

Contents of manuscripts

The standard divisions of the New Testament in Greek manuscripts are: the Gospels (represented by *e*), Acts and the General (or Catholic) Epistles (*a*), the Pauline Epistles (*p*) and Revelation (*r*). It is very common to find the Gospels transmitted alone and Acts and the Catholic Epistles together with the Pauline Epistles, but these are not rules and almost any combination can be found (*H&G* p63). The Gospels are the best represented books of the New

Testament over the first millennium, with 356 manuscripts (*H&G* Figure 3.2 p64). They are also well-represented in the early manuscripts, with 6 from the second century and a further 30 from the third century (*H&G* Figure 3.3 p65).

Different sizes of manuscripts

As we have already seen, a manuscript may range from part of one verse to the contents of the entire New Testament. So how complete is the earliest manuscript evidence for some books?

Of the Gospels, Mark is the least well attested over the second and third centuries. The only manuscripts of Mark from this period are P45 (absent for 78% of the Gospel) and the recently-found P137, which contains only parts of six verses from Mark 1[15]. This means that, overall, 22% of Mark's Gospel is preserved in manuscripts prior to the fourth century.

John, on the other hand, is very well represented over this early period. John is found in several early manuscripts (P45, P66 and P75) that cover the majority of the Gospel, and then in several smaller ones that fill in the gaps. Only fourteen verses do not find a witness over the second and third centuries. This means that, overall, 98% of John's Gospel is preserved in manuscripts prior to the fourth century (*H&G* p66).

However, we shall see further on that later manuscripts are also valid. The fact is that the bulk of the papyri found at the beginning of the twentieth century, and more recent manuscript discoveries, have not significantly changed the text of the New Testament. The text is remarkably stable and can be reconstructed without them (*H&G* p67).

Can a later manuscript be better?

Gregory R Lanier has tackled this question. Logically, a later manuscript can be better if, for example (*H&G* p112):

1. It is shown to come from a stable text stream

2. It can be shown that a later manuscript in fact contains an earlier reading of the text

3. If the later scribe proves to be an expert in textual criticism

The extremely talented and vigilant scribe Ephraim worked in Constantinople (Byzantium) and produced manuscripts in the mid 950's. He was probably involved in Family 1 for the Gospels. Family 1 includes at least the minuscules 1, 22, 118, 131, 205, 209, 872, 1192, 1210, 1278, 1582, 2193, 2542. Of these, 1 (c 1100's) and 1582 (c 900's) are the most prominent. They are independent copies of a much older manuscript, denoted by A-1 from about 700, which no longer exists. In turn, A-1 probably comes from an earlier manuscript dating from 500. In this way, a later manuscript can be a faithful copy of a much earlier one (*H&G* p120). Gregory R Lanier gives other similar fascinating examples.

Later scribes could also correct copies using earlier readings from Irenaeus, Clement, Origen, Eusebius and Basil (*H&G* p124). It also seems that Irenaeus himself was an expert textual critic, amongst all his other talents.

---

[15] This manuscript news made it into the world press because scholars were hoping for a first century Mark manuscript. Therefore, there was disappointment when it turned out to be from the late second or early third century. It is nevertheless the oldest manuscript of Mark 1 (*H&G* p14).

In conclusion, then, later manuscripts can have better readings than some earlier manuscripts. The core textual tradition of the New Testament remains remarkably stable over time. Later scribes show they were conscientious, seen in their choice of early manuscripts and in their choice to correct their manuscripts.

Were the early copyists well-trained?

In the preceding section we have seen that scribes, like Ephraim, who were incorporated into scriptoriums were extremely well-trained. Was this also the case for the scribes of the earliest period, who were copying the New Testament manuscripts, before Constantine became Emperor (he reigned from 306-337)? Were they, in the words of Zachary J Cole (*H&G* p133), energetic but inexperienced or – on the contrary - professional, careful, scrupulous and well-trained, like their Jewish counterparts?

Zachary J Cole has investigated this and cites (*H&G* p137) Kim-Haines-Eitzen in her monograph *"Guardians of Letters"* to answer the question:

"What is striking about our earliest Christian papyri is that they all exhibit the influences of literary and documentary styles, and they all seem to be located in the middle of the spectrum of experience and level of skill. The scribes who produced these copies fit well into the portrait of multifunctional scribes – both professional and nonprofessional – whose education entailed learning how to write a semi cursive style."

Zachary J Cole underlines the *"all"* in the above quotation. Far from being the work of amateurs, the early Christian copyists seemed to have been trained in both literary and documentary domains. It is worth considering some of the most significant early examples.

- P45 is a copy of the four Gospels and Acts that dates from the third century. Thirty folios (or sixty pages, counting front and back) remain of an original 220 folios (440 pages). It is the work of a consistent and practised scribe (*H&G* p140).

- P46 is a collection of Paul's Letters that dates to the third century. Eighty-six folios (172 pages) remain of the manuscript. By all accounts, it is also the work of a skilled transcriber (*H&G* p142).

- P75 is a substantial copy of Luke and John that dates to the third century. It appears to be a "Rolls Royce" production. Scholars widely recognize the high-quality work found in P75 (*H&G* p141).

The exceptions to this rule of high-quality transcription by early Christian copyists are P72, a third-century copy of 1-2 Peter and Jude[16] and P47, a third century papyrus of Revelation. In the first case the manuscript is noticeably rough and unclear. Scholars believe it was intended for private use rather than congregational worship. In the second case, the letter size is not consistent. Nevertheless, the significant majority appear to be competent transcribers (*H&G* p142). This is shown in the fact that legibility does not fall off as the texts of the manuscripts progress, as might be expected with untrained copyists. Trained copyists, on the other hand, would take account of their tiredness and take a break so that legibility did not suffer.

---

[16] Further on, we will see there is another reason for treating this papyrus with precaution.

We must avoid the typical error of modern man in considering the ancient peoples, writers and copyists as ignorant and uneducated. By the year AD 290, the Library of Alexandria, founded by Ptolemy, boasted more than 30,000 works. Later, in the fourth century AD, Eusebius had access to the considerable library at Caesarea Maritime.

We may add two further points. For the Jews, one had to master several languages, including Greek, to be a member of the ruling Sanhedrin. Greek was taught in the rabbinical schools. So, when in Acts 6:7, we learn that many priests come into the Christian faith, that means an influx into the early church of educated and cultivated people (*BAV* p133). The early church had no shortage of competent people to draw on. Secondly, there is evidence from Acts that John Mark may have been trained as a clerk or scribe.

Were the early copyists faithful transcribers?

It is generally accepted that 01, 03 and P75 are accurately copied texts. Early papyri, such as P1, P4, P64 + 67, and P77+103 show strong textual affinities with Codex Sinaiticus (01) and Vaticanus (03). This demonstrates a faithful copying over time:

- Second century: P4, P64+ 67   Luke and Matthew
- Third century: P1, P66, P75   Luke and Matthew and John
- Fourth century: 01, 03 Complete New Testament

They all agree closely in their wording (*H&G* pp147-8), which means we can have a high degree of confidence in the text, even during the early years of transmission. This, in turn, leads most scholars to agree that we have a very good idea of what the apostles originally wrote (*H&G* p150).

In conclusion, the earliest copyists of the New Testament manuscripts were, in their large majority, competent transcribers. New Testament manuscripts show the same degree of care, experience and accuracy as one could reasonably expect with any ancient text. The structure of the New Testament is remarkably stable, especially in comparison with other ancient works.

On textual variants

Nobody tries to hide the fact that there are some significant variants in the New Testament text. However, there are a large number of variants simply because there are a large number of New Testament manuscripts. This, in turn, means that we can have a clearer view of what the original text was. Such variants occur in:

- John 7:53-8:11   The story of the adulteress
- Mark 16:9-20   The end of Mark's Gospel
- John 5:4   Omitted in modern translations

In most modern translations, the first two passages are accompanied by the mention that they are absent from the earliest and most reliable manuscripts. The third is present "in some less important manuscripts." In this case, it seems that some later scribe wanted to add some detail that John appeared to have left out (*H&G* p146). In the case of the ending of Mark's Gospel,

Tom Wright suggests that Mark's original *"ending is missing...and that later copyists were determined to fill in the gap"* (*TWMark* pp221-2).

Gurry (*H&G* p200-3) notes two significant New Testament variants, in addition to those cited above. They concern Mark 1:1 and Luke 23:34. Williams (*Trust?* p117) adds Matthew 16:2b-3 and Luke 22:43-44. None of these affect Christian doctrine, because it is clearly upheld in other passages.

Williams (*Trust?* pp118-120) illustrates the question of variants by considering the first fourteen verses of John's Gospel. Five completely different editions have exactly the same number of words and even letters:

- Erasmus's edition from 1516, made on the basis of two twelfth-century manuscripts
- The 1979, 1993 and 2012 editions of the German Bible Society, used by most scholars
- The 2005 edition by Maurice Robinson who prefers Byzantine manuscripts
- The 2010 edition by Michael Holmes, made under the auspices of the Society of Biblical Literature
- The 2017 edition made at Tyndale House, Cambridge.

The editions of the German Bible Society, the Society of Biblical Literature and Tyndale House follow different editorial philosophies in consulting the vast range of manuscripts of John's Gospel – including the two earliest papyri (P66 and P75), which are regularly dated to the third century.

But when these opening verses of John's Gospel, a sequence of 188 words or 812 letters, are examined, there are *no differences* found in these editions. Erasmus was, on the basis of his two manuscripts, able to do just as well as twenty-first century scholars, who have all the discovered manuscripts at their disposal.

Therefore, it is absolutely rational to suppose that the text of the Gospels has been passed down through the centuries with integrity.

Was there any deliberate scribal corruption of the New Testament? Can it be detected?

According to Robert D Marcello, there is some evidence of scribes introducing deliberate corruptions into the New Testament text. This is known as *orthodox corruption* and can be detected by comparison with the (majority) reading of other manuscripts (*H&G* p211)[17].

There seem to be two cases of real corruption (*H&G* pp220-222). One concerns the Western-D text of Acts within Codex Bezae, which probably contains an anti-Jewish bias. The other concerns P72 (containing Jude and 1-2 Peter), where the divinity of Jesus is overstressed, so that, for example, *"God"* replaces *"Jesus"* in 1 Peter 5:1.

---

[17] The big corruption case, that the apostles made it all up, will be dealt with in Chapter 15.

SUMMARY

1. The totality of the New Testament was completed within the lifetimes of the eyewitnesses of the events, on whose testimony the Gospels were based. This is a huge gauge of reliability for the New Testament documents.

2. The New Testament documents would only have been circulated once their text was finalised by the author and authorized for copying. Once in circulation, they could not have been significantly transformed.

3. An author, such as Paul, may have kept copies of his Epistles and then circulated them as a collection.

4. Both early and later Christian copyists were well-trained and were faithful transcribers.

5. As a general rule, there are more New Testament manuscripts compared with other ancient works and they are earlier, but the numbers are difficult to count and may not be that useful. There are about 5,300 Greek New Testament manuscripts, and a few thousand in other ancient languages.

6. Most manuscripts are dated by palaeography, according to styles of handwriting. This results in a dating range of 50 years.

7. The value of a manuscript depends on many factors: its date, size, contents, quality and whether it comes from a reliable textual stream.

8. The Gospels are the best represented New Testament documents in the early manuscripts, followed by the Pauline Epistles and then by Acts and the General or Catholic Epistles. Of the Gospels, Mark is the least well represented, while John is superbly represented, over the second and third centuries.

9. A later manuscript may sometimes be better if:

    - It comes from a stable textual stream
    - It can be shown that a later manuscript in fact contains an earlier reading of the text
    - The later scribe was an expert in textual criticism

10. There are variants in the text of the New Testament but few are truly significant and none affect Christian doctrine.

11. Scribal bias has occurred in at least two non-Gospel manuscripts, but it can be easily detected and eliminated by textual criticism.

CONCLUSION

As Tom Wright puts it (*TWSC* p153):

"Yes, scribes may have introduced alterations here and there. But the massive evidence available means that we are on extremely secure grounds for getting at what the biblical authors actually wrote."

And, as we have already pointed out: *the Gospels were based on the testimony of eyewitnesses. They wrote about what they had seen with their own eyes.*

Chapter 4

MORE ON MANUSCRIPTS, ARCHIVES AND THE NEW TESTAMENT CANON

In the previous chapter we showed that textual criticism was a useful tool for analysing manuscripts and to get as close as possible to the original text of the New Testament.

NEW TESTAMENT MANUSCRIPTS IN OTHER ANCIENT LANGUAGES

A few thousand New Testament manuscripts exist in other ancient languages, such as Latin, Syriac, Coptic, Armenian, Slav etc (*H&G* p303). From the second century onwards, we also have records of numerous people (such as Irenaeus) quoting the Gospels (*Trust?* p114).

The Greek New Testament was first translated into Latin. It is the closest ancient language structurally to the original Koine Greek of the New Testament (*H&G* p280). However, even here there are important linguistic differences: there are no articles in Latin, whereas Greek has the definite article (*"the"* in English). We then have to decide whether the translator into Latin tried to show the Greek article or to hide it. Therefore, it is too difficult to use Latin versions of the New Testament in the textual criticism of the Greek text (*H&G* p303).

Following Latin, the New Testament was translated into other ancient languages such as Coptic and Syriac not later than the third century (*Trust?* p114). By the late fourth century, the New Testament had also been translated into Gothic, Ethiopian and Armenian. These are all even more distant structurally from New Testament Greek. So, the best use of the New Testament versions in these ancient languages is as a control of the transmission of the Greek text. Indeed, these translations confirm the remarkable integrity with which the New Testament text was transmitted across time and geography (*H&G* p284).

Coming back to the Latin versions, the Gospels and Pauline Epistles were translated into Latin by the end of the second century and the rest of the New Testament by the end of the third. The early Latin translations are simply known as Old Latin.

While the (Latin) Vulgate is traditionally associated with St Jerome (347-420), he was only responsible for the translation of the Gospels. He revisited the Old Latin texts and revised them towards a Greek text with strong similarities to Codex Sinaiticus (01). Others followed with the rest of the New Testament in the fourth and fifth centuries, in greater conformity with Greek vocabulary and grammar. This means that the Vulgate is more suited to studying the Greek source than the Old Latin texts (*H&G* pp286-288).

The exact number of New Testament manuscripts in Latin cannot be obtained (*H&G* p279). The Syriac manuscript tradition is rich, beginning in the second century and with 120 copies in the seventh century alone (*H&G* p290). There are also 350-370 copies of the New Testament in the Coptic Saladic dialect (*H&G* p299). Thus, Jeremiah Coogan gives the very conservative estimate of a few thousand non-Greek New Testament manuscripts (*H&G* p303).

Archives and Neutral Documents

The early Christians boasted that what they said was confirmed by "neutral documents," that could not be supposed to be influenced by the Church.

For example, writings of the Gnostic school of Valentinus (in Gaul) show that, before the middle of the second century, most of the New Testament books were as well known and venerated in that heretical circle as they were in the early church (*FFBR* p19).

Justin Martyr, the philosopher, could write to the Emperor Antoninus Pius in about AD 150 suggesting that he should check the official archives (*Apol* 1.34), because there he would find confirmation *"of the birth of Jesus Christ at Bethlehem, of the passion of Christ and of his miracles."* He also appealed to the Roman archives dealing with Jesus' death under Pontius Pilate (*Apol* 1.35, 48). Since Justin's objective was to obtain an interruption in the persecution of Christians, he could not have taken the risk of referring to documents which did not exist – he would have ruined his case (*BAV* p139).

THE COMPARISON OF THE MANUSCRIPT ATTESTATION OF THE NEW TESTAMENT WITH THAT OF OTHER ANCIENT WORKS

There are difficulties in comparing the number of New Testament manuscripts and those of other ancient works. For the New Testament textual critic, every manuscript is of interest, even though some may be more valuable than others. On the other hand, classicists do not count those manuscripts which are derived from others. This means that the count of New Testament copies is inclusive whereas that of ancient classical works is functional and exclusive (*H&G* pp78-79). Nevertheless, few classical works (such as Herodotus, Sophocles, Suetonius, Plato, Caesar's Gallic Wars, Tacitus' Annals, Thucydides, Josephus, Livy etc) are attested by more than a couple of hundred manuscripts, and many have far less[18]. Clearly, the New Testament is in a different ball park with its 5,100-5,300 Greek manuscripts, not forgetting the few thousand in other ancient languages (see section above).

The New Testament has more early texts than other ancient works, including probably half a dozen from the second century, that is within a hundred years of the final document being written. Here only Thucydides gets even close: we possess some papyrus fragments from the third century BC, that is 200 years after the writing of the original. For many ancient classical works, our first copies date from 750-1350 years after the writing of the original text[19]. Furthermore, there are basically no chronological gaps in the manuscript record of the New Testament.

Thus, in general, the New Testament is much better attested in the manuscript record than other classical works from antiquity. In other words, if we cannot trust the New Testament, then we cannot trust any ancient text (*H&G* p84).

---

[18] See Clay Jones, "The Bibliographical Test Updated," CRJ 35, no.3 (2012):32-37 and *H&G* pp 86-87.
[19] Ibid.

We will continue to consider all these ancient writings as genuine. Nevertheless, we must always keep in mind the fact that their textual authority is much less than that of the New Testament documents.

THE NEW TESTAMENT CANON

Contrary to popular theories played out in recent thriller novels, the New Testament Canon was not an attempt to present a socially or politically acceptable theology[20]. As Tom Wright remarks, these debates were going on during periods of fierce, if intermittent, persecution. Rather, the impetus came from opposing heretical teachers, such as the Roman Marcion, who preached that only the Gospel of Luke and ten of the Epistles of Paul were authentic and authoritative (*Dict* p172; *AH* 3.12.12; *TWSC* p153).

It appears that, very shortly after the writing of John's Gospel, the four Gospels were united in one collection known as "The Gospel." We know this from the works of Ignatius, bishop of Antioch, writing in about AD 115. By about AD 170, an Assyrian Christian named Tatian attempted to harmonise the four Gospels in one volume, known as the *Diatessaron*.

Irenaeus

By the time of Irenaeus who, although originally from Asia Minor, was bishop of Lyons in about AD 180, the idea of a fourfold Gospel had become so axiomatic in the Church at large that he can refer to it as an established and recognized fact, as obvious as the four points of the compass or the four winds:

"For, since there are four zones of the world in which we live, and four principal winds, while the Church is scattered throughout all the world, and "the pillar and ground" of the Church is the Gospel and the spirit of life; so it is fitting that she should have four pillars, breathing out immortality on every side and vivifying men afresh. From which fact, it is evident that the Word, the Artificer of all, He that sitteth upon the Cherubim and contains all things, He who was manifested to men, has given us the Gospel under four aspects, but bound together by one Spirit." (*AH* 3.11.8)

A closer examination of *AH* reveals that Irenaeus quoted from 20 of our New Testament books, appealing to their authority in his combat against the Gnostics (see the Table 4.1[21] on the next page):

Some say Irenaeus quotes Paul's Epistle to Titus, but I could not confirm this. There is also a probable echo of Hebrews in *AH* 2.30.9; echoes of James and 2 Peter are less convincing and there is no mention of Philemon, Jude or 3 John. It is clear that Irenaeus considered the four Gospels, Acts, all the letters of Paul and Hebrews, 1 and 2 John, 1 Peter and Revelation to be authoritative Scripture that he could use in his doctrinal drive against the Gnostics in Gaul. The fact that Irenaeus probably did not use Paul's letter to Philemon, or the Epistles of James, 2 Peter, 3 John or Jude does not necessarily mean he did not regard them as authoritative – they were probably merely less useful in the development of his arguments.

---

[20] See also Appendix 3: Other Ancient Works.
[21] This Table is not exhaustive; there are certainly more quotes from the Gospels and Paul's Letters.

Table 4.1: Irenaeus' Quotations from the New Testament

New Testament Book	Paragraphs from Irenaeus' *AH*
Matthew	3.16.2; 3.8.1; 3.9.2
Mark	3.10.1-5
Luke	3.14.3; 3.10.1, 2, 3
John	3.11.1; 3.8.3; 3.11.2; 3.13.2
Acts of the Apostles	3.14.1; 3.12.1-14
Romans	3.16.3; 3.13.1; 3.16.9
1 Corinthians	3.3.5; 3.13.1
2 Corinthians	3.7.1
Galatians	3.22.1; 3.13.3; 3.16.3
Ephesians	5.2.3
Philippians	4.18.4
Colossians	1.3.4; 3.14.1
1 Thessalonians	5.6.1
2 Thessalonians	5.25.1; 3.7.2
1 Timothy	1.16.3
2 Timothy	3.14.1
Titus	3.3.4?
1 Peter	4.9.2
1 John	3.16.5, 8
2 John	1.16.3
Revelation	5.28.2

Now what of the other church fathers? Which New Testament books did they regard, or report as, authoritative?

The Debate

Justin Martyr (AD 100-165) wrote:

"On the day called Sunday there is a gathering together to one place of all those who live in cities or in the country and the memoirs of the apostles or the writings of the prophets are read as long as time permits."[22]

Reading through the work of Eusebius (*HE*), we get a good impression of the process of the internal debate in the church concerning the value of the respective documents. He mentions the work of Clement of Alexandria, who wrote somewhere around AD 200, and Origen, who wrote a little later, around AD 210-240. They talk about two categories: firstly, those books universally regarded as scriptural (*homolegoumena*); secondly, those books whose scriptural status is disputed by some but recognized by the majority (*antilegoumena*). In Table 4.2, we list the four earliest lists from the early church concerning the New Testament books which they regarded as authoritative.

---

[22] Justin Martyr, "The First Apology of Justin Martyr, Addressed to the Emperor Antoninus Pius," 1.67, Griffith, Farren, Okeden and Welsh, London, 1891.

Table 4.2: THE DEBATE ABOUT THE BOOKS

Author	Date AD	Reference	Undisputed NT Books	Disputed NT Books
Irenaeus	180	*AH*	Four Gospels plus Acts, 13 Pauline letters plus Hebrews, 1 Peter, 1 and 2 John, Revelation	
Clement of Alexandria	200	*HE* 6.14.1-7 *HE* 3.24.17	Four Gospels plus Acts, 13 Pauline letters plus Hebrews, 1 John	James, 1 and 2 Peter, 2 and 3 John, Jude, Revelation
Origen	210-240	*HE* 6.25.3-13	Four Gospels plus Acts, 13 Pauline letters plus Hebrews, 1 Peter, 1 John, Revelation	James, 2 Peter, 2 and 3 John, Jude
Eusebius	c 325	*HE* 3.25	Four Gospels plus Acts, 13 Pauline letters plus Hebrews, 1 Peter, 1 John	James, 2 Peter, 2 and 3 John, Jude, Revelation

All this evidence shows that, from an early date, the Christians in the early church, began to collect together the writings of the apostles and the evangelists and to treat them as authoritative and scriptural (*TTQ* pp64-65). It is also clear that, as early as the time of Irenaeus (about AD 180), the four Gospels of Matthew, Mark, Luke and John, Paul's letters, Hebrews and at least 1 Peter and 1 John, and probably Revelation, were already considered to be authoritative scripture. The rest of what we regard today as the New Testament was accepted by most (James, Jude, 2 Peter, 2 and 3 John), but there was a continuing open debate on the subject, as we can see from the slightly different positions of Clement of Alexandria, Origen and Eusebius. Origen suggested that whether 2 and 3 John were scripture or not was no big deal – after all they added up to less than 100 lines when they were put together (*HE* 6.25.10)!

Reading between the lines, we can see that two essential criteria were emerging for discriminating between scripture and the rest: apostolicity (links to an apostle) and usage (whether the book was widely read or used in worship).

There are two or three interesting cases. Firstly, the authority of the Epistle to the Hebrews was undisputed, although its author was unknown (Eusebius describes much speculation on this matter), even if the thirteenth chapter of the book suggests it originated in Paul's circle. However, it was widely read, presumably especially as the Jewish Revolt of AD 66-74 began to loom on the horizon. Eusebius himself seemed to argue against the Apostle John's authorship of Revelation but, as with the General Epistles, it finally made it into the Canon. On the other hand, even the epistles of Clement, one of Paul's later co-workers and the third bishop of Rome, did not make it into the Canon.

We must conclude that, although the debate in the early church on what was scriptural and what was not, was wide and open, the final consensus was extremely solid and based on demanding criteria. With hindsight, we can only applaud their wisdom, because their choices have stood the test of time.

Thus, the Canon of the New Testament was established by consensus over time in the early church and not by the decisions of an ecclesiastical committee of powerful men. By the time of Irenaeus in AD 180, the major contents of the Canon were already agreed upon; only relatively peripheral choices were still to be made. And by AD 367, Athanasius already gave a list which was identical to our Canon:

"Again, it is not tedious to speak of the books of the New Testament. These are the four Gospels, according to Matthew, Mark, Luke and John. Afterwards the Acts of the Apostles and Epistles (called Catholic), seven viz. of James, one; of Peter, two; of John, three; after these one of Jude. In addition, there are fourteen Epistles of Paul, written in this order. The first, to the Romans; then two to the Corinthians; after these, to the Galatians; next to the Ephesians, then to the Philippians; then to the Colossians; after these, two to the Thessalonians, and that to the Hebrews; and again, two to Timothy; one to Titus; and lastly one to Philemon. And besides the Revelation of John."[23]

This list was then rubber-stamped by the Synod of Hippo in AD 393 and confirmed by the Council of Carthage in AD 397.

As FF Bruce remarks:

"When at last a Church Council – the Synod of Hippo in AD 393 – listed the 27 books of the New Testament, it did not confer on them any authority which they did not already possess, but simply recorded their previously established canonicity."[24]

MODERN TRANSLATIONS

There are essentially two approaches to modern translations of the New Testament (at least in the fortunate western world): *form-based* and *meaning-based* (Edgar Battad Ebojo in *H&G* p306). Form-based translation attempts to follow the form of the source language and is known as literal translation. Meaning-based translation makes every effort to communicate the meaning of the source language text in the natural forms of the receptor language. Such translation is known as idiomatic. In practice, the cursor for any given translation will be placed somewhere between these two extremes.

Since 2014, the Greek source text most widely used for translating the New Testament is the standard shared text of the United Bible Societies (UBS) and Nestlé-Aland, now in their 5th and 28th editions respectively (*H&G* p309). This is the product of an inter-confessional editorial committee. The 2014 edition included the use of the P117-P127 papyri. Nevertheless, apart from

---

[23] Athanasius L 552, quoted in Josh McDowell, "The New Evidence that Demands a Verdict," p24 Thomas Nelson, Nashville, 1999.

[24] FF Bruce, "The Books and Parchments: How we got our English Bible," p117, Pickering and Inglis, Basingstoke, 1984.

the spelling, the text in the UBS 3rd (1979) to 5th editions (NA 26th-28th) is identical (*Trust?* p118 note 6).

AN OVERVIEW OF THE HISTORIC TRANSLATIONS

In his age, Desiderius Erasmus (1466-1536) was reputedly the world's most learned man. In 1516, he produced the first printed edition of the New Testament in Greek. For the Gospels he had only two manuscripts to work with: the minuscules 1 and 2, both dating from the twelfth century (*Trust?* p112). His *Textus Receptus* was used for the original German Luther Bible, the translation of the New Testament into English by William Tyndale, the Authorized or King James Version (KJV) as well as other translations into Spanish and Czech. It remained largely unchallenged until 150 years ago.

Since Erasmus's time a couple of thousand Greek manuscripts of the Gospels have been discovered or identified. Most are medieval, but some are much earlier. We now have two important manuscripts of all four Gospels (Codex Vaticanus (03) and Codex Sinaiticus (01)) from approximately 350 AD, both of which became available during the nineteenth century (*Trust?* p113). In the twentieth century, partial manuscripts of all four Gospels from the third century were discovered. Some of the early fragments of Matthew and John may even date from the second century. Hence, the gap, between the earliest available manuscripts and the writing of the Gospels themselves, has narrowed massively since the time of Erasmus, from about 1100 years down to 100 years!

It may seem amazing, but this has made only a slight difference to our modern translations of the Gospels (*Trust?* p113). Readers, such as myself, who are familiar with both our modern translations and the KJV, find it surprising that there are so few real differences.

The most noticeable differences between a sixteenth century copy of the Gospels (in the original Greek or as a translation into a modern language) concern the ending of Mark's Gospel (after Mark 16:8) and the twelve verses in John 7:53-8:11. Most scholars now believe that these were later additions to the Gospels (*Trust?* p114). But Erasmus already knew about this. Minuscule 1 told him of the uncertainty at the end of Mark and also omitted the passage in John.

Therefore, even though we have nearly a thousand times more manuscripts than were used by Erasmus in his first edition, and the gap between the earliest discovered manuscripts has narrowed by nearly a thousand years, not much has changed (*Trust?* p116). This is a further witness to the remarkable stability of the New Testament Greek text over time and over geographical boundaries.

SUMMARY

1. There are a few thousand non-Greek New Testament manuscripts.

2. They cannot be used in textual criticism of the Greek text, but they confirm the remarkable integrity with which the New Testament was transmitted across time and geography.

3. In general, the New Testament is much better attested in the manuscript record than other classical works from antiquity. In other words, if we cannot trust the New Testament, then we cannot trust any ancient text.

4. Modern translations of the New Testament are based on the standard shared Greek text of the United Bible Societies (UBS) and Nestlé-Aland, now in their 5th and 28th editions respectively. This is the product of an inter-confessional editorial committee.

5. Even though we have nearly a thousand times more manuscripts than were used by Erasmus in his first edition in 1516, and the gap between the earliest discovered manuscripts has narrowed by nearly a thousand years, not much has changed. This is a further witness to the remarkable stability of the New Testament Greek text over time and over geographical boundaries.

CONCLUSION

It is simply not true to suggest that the New Testament Canon was adopted in order to support a view of Jesus which was convenient for the ruling authorities, in the fourth century AD, when Christianity was becoming the official religion of the Roman Empire.

We have demonstrated that the synods of Hippo and Carthage, in AD 393 and 397 respectively, merely confirmed the list of New Testament books which the early church already considered as authoritative and scriptural. This "rubber-stamping" came after a wide and open debate over about two centuries had led to a consensus across the Church, based on the books' links with the apostles and their universal use, notably in worship. However, most of the contents of the Canon (the four Gospels, Acts, Paul's Letters, the Epistle to the Hebrews, 1 Peter, 1 John and probably Revelation) were already clearly identified by the time of Irenaeus (c 180) - only relatively peripheral choices were left to be made in the debate over the following two hundred years.

In the next chapter we will consider the nature of the four canonical Gospels.

Chapter 5

WHAT ARE THE GOSPELS?

As we indicated in the Preface and Preamble, one of the reasons for the writing of this book is the sea change which is occurring in Gospel Studies. The tide began to turn in the early 1990's but, in order to understand why this is important, and how it came about, we first of all need a brief historical overview. We begin with the Enlightenment.

A BRIEF HISTORICAL OVERVIEW OF GOSPEL STUDIES

The Enlightenment

The philosophers of the European and American Enlightenment (David Hume, René Descartes, Voltaire, Jean-Jacques Rousseau, Adam Smith and Immanuel Kant) came to the fore in the eighteenth century. They kicked God upstairs. Science, they said, showed that miracles did not happen and that God did not intervene in the world he had created. They signalled the end of belief in a personal, loving God (*theism*) who had revealed himself in the person of Jesus of Nazareth. For them, Jesus had most certainly not risen from the dead.

The Enlightenment substituted *deism* for *theism.* God was like a master watch-maker: he made the mechanism of the universe and set it working, but then he went away and left it. He did not intervene in his creation; he was far away and had lost interest. We, humans, were the captains of our own fate. We no longer needed God; he was not useful to us.

Now there were consequences, many and varied, to this change in worldview. Firstly, we the enlightened humans largely inhabited Western Europe and the newly independent United States of America. Therefore, according to this worldview, we had a responsibility to enlighten the indigenous savages in foreign parts. Sometimes Christian missionaries were sent, but the main impulsion was Empire: economic and military power. There were political, social, industrial, moral and religious consequences too, but we do not have the space to deal with these.

Form Criticism

There were repercussions in studies of the Gospels. For Karl Ludwig Schmidt[25] and Rudolf Bultmann[26], the Gospels were extended cultic legends. They had arisen from independent oral traditions within the post-Easter church and had little to do with the life of the historical Jesus of Nazareth. The seams between the units of oral tradition could be seen in the Synoptic Gospels of Matthew, Mark and Luke. They had been strung together, like pearls on a piece of string, by the Gospel writers. They were not real literature (*Hochliteratur*) because there was no room for the author's intentions or literary pretensions. They were *Kleinliteratur,* folk books, not biography

---

[25] K.L. Schmidt, "Der Rahmen der Geschichte Jesu," Trowitzsch und Sohn, Berlin, 1919
[26] R. Bultmann, "The History of the Synoptic Tradition," Second Edition, 1931

but cult legend, because the Gospel writers did not come from the educated classes and so could never have written real literature. In addition, the Gospels could not be placed in any literary category, convention or *genre*. This view dominated for more than half a century (*What?* p11).

Form Criticism focussed attention on the oral transmission of units of Gospel tradition. It was not interested in the Jewish or Semitic background to the Gospels. Nor did it treat the secular historians of the Gospel period, such as Josephus, Tacitus and Suetonius, as worthy of trust. In this way, the Form Critics could ignore the historical evidence that was contrary to their affirmations. Form Criticism bore down like a tidal wave and engulfed the majority of Protestant theological colleges, seminaries and university theological faculties in Germany, Britain and America. Few resisted. Some of those resisting in Germany, Britain and America called themselves Evangelical: they still believed the New Testament to be historical, while using some of the tools of biblical criticism, such as textual criticism.

For the man in the street, however, the damage was done. He no longer considered the Gospels to be reliable and, in his mind, Jesus became the subject of legend; he was no longer a real figure of history.

Redaction Criticism

However, after World War II, the intellectual opposition to Form Criticism began to be organised. The 1960's and 1970's brought the rise of Redaction Criticism in New Testament studies for several reasons. Firstly, the development of folklore studies showed that oral tradition did not grow in steady stages as Form Criticism had postulated. Secondly, Form Criticism had concentrated so much on the individual parts of the Gospels that the significance of the whole had been missed. Redaction Criticism was interested in the theological purposes of the Gospel writers. The Christian community was no longer the sole actor in the formation of the Gospel material; the author also had a role. This meant that questions about their literary intentions, including *genre* could not be far behind (*What?* p15).

Redaction Criticism was a healthy development because it placed the emphasis once again on the author and his text. However, New Testament studies continued to talk of oral tradition and the communities in which it had developed. Some of the real questions were not yet being asked.

Roman Catholic Biblical Studies

Until the 1970's, biblical studies in the Roman Catholic Church seemed relatively immune from the disease of Form Criticism. However, Stirnemann's perceptive analysis (*BAV* pp15-23) shows that, in reality, the enlightenment views of Kant were already widely accepted, along with their philosophical consequences:

- The Gospels did not have any historical value
- Since the bodily resurrection of Jesus did not happen, Christianity could only be based on a "leap of faith," a leap into the emptiness without any evidence to back it up.

The malaise finally came to the surface in April 1970, when the most respected Catholic scholars came together in Rome at the St Dominic Institute, for a Symposium on the Resurrection of Jesus, under the direction of the Jesuit, P E Dhanis. In 1974, they published their conclusions under the title *"Resurrexit"* (He is risen) – Stirnemann comments wryly that they should have entitled it *"Non resurrexit"* (He is not risen) – with an introduction, the speech and blessing of Pope Paul VI, as if the Symposium had the full authority of the Vatican. In fact, Pope Paul had remained firm on the historicity of the Gospels and the bodily resurrection of Jesus, but the damage was done: the International Symposium on the Resurrection of Jesus, published by the Vatican, stated that the Gospels had no historical value and that Jesus had not risen physically from the dead (*BAV* p45).

The Catholic Church had to wait until 2008, when Benedict XVI courageously reiterated the historic teaching of the church and stigmatised *"the atheism of modern biblical scholars"* and *"a philosophy which denied the revelation of the divine in the world"* (*BAV* p21).

The Tide Begins to Change

The tide began to change in the 1990's. In 1992, Richard Burridge published a study comparing the Gospels with 10 Graeco-Roman biographies (*bios*), 5 predating the Gospels (including Satyrus' *Euripides* and Philo's *Moses*), and 5 post-dating the Gospels (including Tacitus' *Agricola* and Suetonius' *Lives of Julius Caesar* and *Augustus Caesar*). He showed that the four canonical Gospels (Matthew, Mark, Luke and John) shared the same generic features as these Graeco-Roman biographies (*What?* p235). So, the four canonical Gospels are biographies of Jesus. They are *Hochliteratur*, not *Kleinliteratur*. They may be other *genres* as well, but essentially, they are biographies of Jesus, written in the Greek or Roman style of the period. This might seem to be a trivial or unimportant conclusion, but it is not and we shall come back to it[27]. Furthermore, the non-canonical gnostic gospels, which were written much later, are not *bios*, because they lack the narrative, chronological and geographical settings which are characteristic of the *bios* family (*What?* p242)[28].

In the same year, N T Wright published the first volume of his blockbuster series *Christian Origins and the Question of God* which came to dominate Jesus scholarship. However, the real breakthrough came in a paper by Richard Bauckham in 1995. In it, he criticised the consensus views about the Gospels originating in Gospel communities, suggesting that such theories treated the Gospels almost as allegories of their communities. Yet the sheer diversity of the reconstruction of these communities rendered them not really credible: because communications were good during the first century AD, the Christian communities were relatively homogeneous. Moreover, drawing on Burridge's work, he suggested that these approaches were based on a *genre* mistake: they treated the Gospels like letters and not like *bios* (*FMark* p36; *What?* p295). Thus, Burridge could say that the Gospels were not written "by committees, about concepts, for communities." Instead, they were essentially biographies of Jesus written "by a person, about a person (Jesus), for other persons." Then, in 2006, Richard Bauckham published his masterpiece *Jesus and the Eyewitnesses: the Gospels as Eyewitness Testimony*, inviting his readers to make a clear break with Form Criticism, and to end the classic scholarly division between the "historical Jesus" and the "Christ of faith", proposing instead the "Jesus of testimony" as presented by the Gospels. He demonstrated that the Gospels were historical and based on eyewitness testimony.

---

[27] When Graham Stanton, the Lady Margaret Professor of Divinity at the University of Cambridge states, in his foreword to Burridge's book, that "very few books on the gospels have…influenced scholarly opinion more strongly" he means that it's a game-changer.

[28] For more information on this point please see Appendix 3.

On the Catholic side, Stirnemann also considered the question of *genre*, coming to the same conclusions as Bauckham, and declining 14 hermeneutic principles concerning the interpretation of testimony (*BAV* pp62-72).

The Present Day

Therefore, as we write, there is a sea change occurring in Gospel Studies. All the tenets and methods of Form Criticism have been shown to be erroneous and void. The raft of Form Criticism has finally disintegrated under the influence of the intellectual waves beating against it. None of its postulates stand up to scrutiny and nobody believes in its piece of string any more. The recruitment of specialists in the period between the Old and New Testaments[29] into the university theological faculties has meant that the Jewish and Semitic background to the Gospels is now taken into account. Classicists have re-examined the secular historians of the Gospel period to throw light onto their historical and political context. The pearls of oral tradition originating in the post-Easter Christian communities were largely a figment of the Form Critics' imagination, although this fact will take time to trickle down into the theological colleges and seminaries because it remained a postulate of Redaction Criticism.

The sea change has come about through the detailed, painstaking research work of philosophers, linguists, classicists, historians, archaeologists, literary and folk-lore specialists, lawyers and even the odd theologian. However, we must return to our unanswered question: why is the *genre* of the Gospels important?

WHY IS THE *GENRE* OF THE GOSPELS IMPORTANT?

Whenever we take a document into our hands to read, we immediately have, consciously or unconsciously, an idea of what we expect to find in it. We do not treat a gas bill in the same way as, say, a letter from a close friend. In the first case, we would be interested in how much we have to pay, we would check that we had indeed consumed roughly that amount of gas and, if we were concerned for the environment, we might hope that we had polluted the atmosphere less than in the past. All these things would be in our mind as we began to read the gas bill. On the other hand, for the letter from the close friend, we might be interested in where he was writing from, and how long he was staying there but, above all, we would be hoping that he and his family were prospering and in good health. We do not expect the letter from the friend to inform us about our consumption of gas; nor do we expect the gas bill to tell us how our friend's family is getting on. Why not? Because quite clearly the two documents are not of the same type, category or *genre*.

The *genre* helps us in our approach to a document and also guides us in how to interpret it. Burridge (*What?* p36) puts it this way: "*Genres* are conventions which assist the reader by providing a set of expectations to guide his or her understanding. Such expectations are corrected and further refined in the light of actual reading."

It also follows that, if Jesus is the biographical centre of the Gospels, then the Gospels are the study of Jesus Christ in narrative form. And every passage must be interpreted in the light of what the author tells us about Jesus (*What?* p289-303). It is also noteworthy that there were no

---

[29] The "Inter-Testamental" Period, see Appendix 1.

rabbinic biographies. Rabbinic anecdotes are directed more towards sayings than actions. Sage stories would have been about the Torah, not about a given rabbi. Jesus is the centre of Christianity and that is why we have the Gospels. And they were written *"that you may believe that Jesus is the Christ, the Son of God, and that by believing you may have life in his name."* (John 20:31).

WHAT ARE THE OTHER POSSIBILITIES?

Burridge has shown conclusively that the Gospels are essentially *bios*, that is biographies written in the Graeco-Roman style of the period. Without in any way questioning this fundamental finding, since the frontiers between different literary *genres* are porous and leaky, we are allowed to seek other subsidiary possibilities. Primarily the Gospels are *bios*, but are they secondarily something else as well?

The best other candidate is that the Gospels might also be histories[30].

John's Gospel

Richard Bauckham, accepting that John's Gospel is basically a *bios*, makes out a case for it being secondarily written in the style of a Graeco-Roman history (*Test* pp93-112). It is true that John places great emphasis on the place and time settings. He also exhibits the selectivity, narrative asides, eyewitness testimony, discourses and dialogues which would have been expected of the *genre* at the time.

The Synoptic Gospels

Luke's introduction to his Gospel:

"Many have undertaken to draw up an account of the things that have been fulfilled among us, just as they were handed down to us by those who from the first were eye-witnesses and servants of the word. Therefore, since I myself have carefully investigated everything from the beginning, it seemed good also to me to write an orderly account for you, most excellent Theophilus, so that you may know the certainty of the things you have been taught."

(Luke 1:1-4)

And particularly his statement that he has *carefully investigated everything from the beginning* would seem to suggest that he was writing a history. Nevertheless, the evidence for Luke's Gospel being essentially *bios* remains overwhelming. Thus, Luke's Gospel is a biography of Jesus with history overtones and it is probably best to regard Matthew and Mark in the same way.

In Part III we examine the origins of the Gospels, beginning with Luke/Acts and we introduce the method of our investigation.

---

[30] The technical term is historiography, which includes the writing of histories or historical monographs, the body of literature dealing with historical matters, the body of techniques of historical research, the narrative presentation of history based on a critical evaluation of sources and so on. Unfortunately, the word is not widely understood so we will use the term "histories."

PART III: THE ORIGINS OF THE GOSPELS

Chapter 6

WHO WROTE LUKE/ACTS? WHEN AND WHERE?

METHOD

The classic method for examining the origins of the Gospels has two parts:

1. First of all, we examine the evidence from the Gospel documents themselves – what historians and theologians call the *internal evidence*.

2. Then we link the information we glean from Acts, the New Testament Letters and the historians, notably Josephus, Suetonius, Tacitus, Papias, Irenaeus and Eusebius. This is the *external evidence*.

In this investigation we add two further steps:

3. We derive timeline charts to find when and where the appropriate people would have had the time, the means and the opportunity to research and write the Gospel concerned. This adds to the external evidence.

4. We follow Richard Bauckham in considering a literary device known as an *inclusio* (*Eye* pp 124-130). An author uses an *inclusio* to underline the importance of the testimony of a character, by citing his name first and last in the document. It is thus a form of internal evidence.

This method attempts to be systematic and to allow both the internal and external evidence to speak. It also seeks to avoid the rather sterile and inconclusive A-says-this-but-B-claims-that sort of dialogue, which fills many Bible commentaries.

We will try to avoid coming to the evidence with fixed ideas. We will not prejudge, for example, whether Mark, Luke and Matthew's Gospels are intimately linked, or were written independently or whether there was some degree of "cross fertilization" (see *FMark* pp 41-44) or, for example, whether Mark's Gospel was written first. This debate feeds many Bible commentaries. We hope to be pointed in the right direction by the evidence. In the same vein, the fact that Mark, Luke and Matthew's Gospel share approximately the same chronology is not taken to indicate that the three Gospels are intimately linked. They are perhaps simply describing the same order of real events (*BAV* p75).

Allow me to disagree firmly with the (skeptical) idea that, because Matthew, Mark and Luke all talk about the destruction of the Temple in Jerusalem, which occurred under the command of

Titus in AD 70, that these Gospels must have been written after this date. We know from experience that the charismatic gift and ministry of prophecy are much more than mere prediction. However, they do include prediction. Once the skepticism is removed, the argument falls, and is in fact turned right around. If Jesus, as a prophet, is predicting the fall of the Temple so that his followers can discern the signs and escape the coming terror, then these passages strongly suggest that all three Gospels were written before AD 70 (see also *Trust?* pp47-49). Darrell Bock (*DBLuke* p17) states Jesus could have predicted the fall of Jerusalem from his perspective of how God reacts to covenant unfaithfulness. In other words, it was foreseeable! He also concludes, as do many others, that the three Synoptic Gospels were written before AD 70.

Another trap, into which many (*LMark* p18) have fallen, is the concept that certain events were necessary (such as the Jewish War from AD 66-74, the devastation of the Temple in AD 70, and the subsequent dispersion of the Jewish church, or the martyrdoms of Peter and Paul in AD 64/65) to trigger the writing of the Gospels. This inevitably pushes their dates of writing into the 70's or 80's.

However, any intelligent observer of the situation in Jerusalem (which the early Jewish Christians surely were) would have seen many disquieting events much earlier, such as (see the Paul and Luke Timeline Chart 6.1 or the Peter and Paul Timeline Chart 7.1) the Emperor Caligula's attempt to install his own statue in the Temple in AD 41, the 30,000 crushed to death under Cumanus, the arrival of the *sicarii* assassins in AD 57, or even the fact that the eyewitnesses of Jesus' life were gradually getting old.

But all this betrays a lack of understanding of the mindset of the early disciples. The trigger event for the Gospel writers was the life, death and resurrection of Jesus. They needed no other. They saw the whole nature and future of the universe in terms of this one life; they were prepared to use any legal means of proclaiming that "Jesus is Lord," and sought to invent new ways of communicating this message. That was their motivation for writing.

That said, our investigation will show that each Gospel writer had his own specific reasons for writing when he did. Matthew wanted to leave his companions a solid basis for faith, before he relocated (*HE* 3.24.6). Mark probably started making notes of Peter's preaching at Rome and then he realized he had gold dust in his hands. He then turned these notes into a work of substance. Luke himself admits (Luke 1:1) that he set out to write down an ordered account, based on eyewitness testimony. Finally, John seems to have been urged by *"his fellow disciples and bishops"* to write down the fourth Gospel. We detect this in the Muratorian Canon, compiled in Latin in Rome, towards the end of the second century (*FFBJ* p10).

In the previous chapter we have shown that the Gospels were not written *"by committees about concepts for communities,"* but were essentially biographies of Jesus, written *"by a person, about a person (Jesus) for other persons"* (*What?* p295). Therefore, we do not try to read the Gospels between the lines, to discover that what is really going on is not about Jesus at all, but about Matthew's (or Mark's or Luke's or John's) theology and about the life of their communities, and so on[31]. Elsewhere the same author calls these circular arguments, rather like

---

[31] Tom Wright, "Virtue Reborn" p89, SPCK, London, 2010.

"someone trying to reconstruct the other end of a telephone conversation from what we could hear at this end[32]."

Hengel argues in his study "The Titles of the Gospels"[33] that, as soon as more than one written version of the Gospel was in circulation, some label would be necessary in order to distinguish between them, and the only such labels we have are the traditional *"according to Matthew," "according to Mark"* etc. He also quotes Tertullian as typical of the view that a "Gospel" not bearing the name of its author would not have been regarded as authoritative. This is certainly the impression one gets from reading Irenaeus and Eusebius. As Stirnemann says, we should not fall into the trap of accepting that Josephus wrote *"The Jewish War,"* and Strabon his *"Geography,"*, but denying that Matthew wrote the Gospel of Matthew (*BAV* p22).

Having accomplished all this ground clearing, we will proceed to apply the method, beginning with the Gospel of Luke and the Acts of the Apostles.

LUKE/ACTS

1. Internal Evidence

It is generally accepted that the Gospel of Luke and the Acts of the Apostles were written by the same author (*FFBA* p15 note 1; *DBLuke* p4; *HRNT* p234), partly because of the similarity of their introductions:

"Many have undertaken to draw up an account of the things that have been fulfilled among us, just as they were handed down to us by those who from the first were eyewitnesses and servants of the word. Therefore, since I myself have carefully investigated everything from the beginning, it seemed good also to me to write an orderly account for you, most excellent Theophilus, so that you may know the certainty of the things you have been taught." (Luke 1:1-4)

"In my former book, Theophilus, I wrote about all that Jesus began to do and to teach until the day he was taken up to heaven, after giving instructions through the Holy Spirit to the apostles he had chosen. After his suffering, he showed himself to these men and gave many convincing proofs that he was alive." (Acts 1:1-3a)

And the fact that both books are addressed to Theophilus, even if we do not know who he was – his may well be a general name or title, since it means "lover of God."

We notice that the author of Luke and Acts bases his accounts on eyewitness testimony, but does not claim to be an eyewitness himself. One of the major results of the most recent research into the origins of the Gospels is exactly this (see *Eye* pp8-9). The Gospel writers were conscious of writing in one of two *genres* of history of the first century AD: either *bios* (roughly speaking a biography of a well-known figure) or history (an account with more historical details). *Both* genres *depended on eyewitness testimony because it was considered the most reliable.* Secondly, we note that Luke does not claim to be the first to have written an account of the life of Jesus. Indeed, he says that many others have done so.

---

[32] Tom Wright, "Early Christian Letters for Everyone," p187, SPCK, London, 2011.
[33] Martin Hengel, "Studies," pp64-84 quoted by *FMark* pp39-40; see also *HRNT* p11.

The Acts of the Apostles contains passages written in the first person plural rather than the third (the "we" passages) which enable us to learn about the author[34]. The first "we" passage begins in 16:10, when Paul and his companions are in Troas, and ends in 16:16 at Philippi. The second "we" passage recommences at Philippi in 20:6 (see the Paul and Luke Timeline Chart 6.1). We deduce that Paul left the author behind in Philippi to pastor the fledgling church. The second "we" passage continues through Caesarea (21:8), to Jerusalem (21:17), where Paul is arrested. The author then accompanies Paul during his imprisonment in Caesarea (23:23 to 26:32). Paul appeals to Caesar (25:10-12) and the author of Acts then goes with him to Italy (27:1), suffering shipwreck and coming aground on Malta (28:14), and so to Rome (28:14). He would then have stayed with Paul during his two years of house arrest while awaiting trial (28:30). Irenaeus (*AH* 3.14.1) says Luke and Paul were *"inseparable."*

There is some *inclusio* evidence in Luke's Gospel. Peter is the first disciple to be mentioned (4:38) and the first to be called by Jesus (5:1-11). He is also the last to be named (24:34). The suggestion is (*Eye* p 127) that Luke is paying tribute to the fact that he used the testimony of Peter. The classic view would say that he obtained this from Mark but, as we shall see later, he also met Peter regularly, so he is another possible source.

Jesus put women into the limelight and this is apparent in Luke's Gospel. There is an *inclusio* concerning the women eyewitnesses in Luke's Gospel. It begins rather late in 8:2-3, mentioning Mary Magdalene, Joanna and Suzanna by name *"among many others."* It ends in 24:10 with the mention of Mary Magdalene, Joanna and Mary the mother of James. The implication is that Luke owed some of his recorded testimony to Mary Magdalene and Joanna, although the traditional idea that he used testimony from Mary, Jesus' mother, is also attractive, because of Luke 2:19 and 51 (*IHML* p114).

It is interesting that Luke, the Gentile, non-Palestinian, at home around the Mediterranean Sea, calls the Sea of Galilee *"the lake"*, whereas Matthew (16 times) and Mark (19 times) call it *"the Sea of Galilee"* (*Trust?* pp57-8).

2. External Evidence from the Epistles and the Historians

The timing of the imprisonment of Paul and Luke at Caesarea can be known with precision by cross-checking Acts 24:27-25:12 with Josephus (*BJ* 2.279) and coins found from the time. Felix, the Roman Procurator, kept Paul and Luke in prison for two years (Acts 24:27). But his successor, Festus, dealt with the matter swiftly. This occurred in July AD 59 (*Paul* p396) and the shipwreck after the Day of Atonement (October) AD 59 (*Voyage* p84). This means that Paul and Luke arrived in Rome in February AD 60, where Paul was imprisoned, under a form of house arrest for two years (Acts 28:30-31), until December AD 61.

Colossians and Philemon were both written during Paul's period of house arrest in Rome. From Colossians 4:10 and Philemon 24 we learn that Luke and Mark have met up and, from Colossians 4:14, that Luke was a doctor. Eusebius (*HE* 2.22) informs us that Paul was released after his first trial in Rome and resumed preaching. In 2 Timothy 4:11, Luke is with him and he wants Mark to join him. (Thus, in Colossians 4:10, Mark is in Rome (AD 60) and in 2 Timothy 4:11 (AD 64) he is on his way back from Asia Minor to Rome (see the Paul and Luke Timeline

---

[34] Irenaeus of Lyons used this reasoning (*AH* 3.14.1), but I first came across it in *GActs* pp 26-28.

Chart 6.1 where AM signifies Asia Minor)). However, the mood is not the same, because in 2 Timothy 4: 16-18 Paul is again facing trial and this time he believes he will die. This confirms what we learn from the Roman historians such as Tacitus and Suetonius: at the beginning of his reign, Nero governed well and was not so brutal, so Paul could indeed have been freed the first time around (see also *HE* 2.22). However, in the year AD 62, Nero lost his two restraining counsellors: Burrus, the honest head of the Praetorian Guard, died and Seneca, his former tutor, resigned to his country estates. So, from AD 62 onwards, Nero threw all his energy into art and vice and his governance deteriorated. Finally, in AD 64, after the burning of Rome (*Caesars*: Nero 38), he began to persecute the Christians (*Annals* 15.41-44). It is supposed that both Peter and Paul met their deaths in AD 64/65 at the height of the persecutions, Paul beheaded and Peter crucified (*HE* 2.25).

Allusions to the Gospel occur as early as the epistles of 1 Clement (c. AD 95-96) and 2 Clement (c. 100). Numerous texts comment on authorship: Justin Martyr (c. 160)[35] speaks of Luke writing a *"memoir of Jesus,"* and that the author was a follower of Paul (*DBLuke* p5). The Muratorian Canon (c. 170-180) attributes the Gospel to Luke, a doctor, who was Paul's companion.

Marcion's heresy (c. 144) stimulated the early church to search for authoritative New Testament documents. This led to the Anti-Marcionite prologues to the Gospels, probably dating from Papias or Irenaeus (*FFBA* p17 note 6). The Anti-Marcionite prologue to the third Gospel (c. 175) attributes Luke/Acts to Luke the physician from Antioch. Tertullian (early third century) in *Against Marcion* 4.2.2 and 4.5.3 calls the Gospel a digest of Paul's gospel (*DBLuke* p5).

Both Eusebius (*HE* 3.4.2) and Irenaeus (*AH* 3.1.1, 3.14.1) attribute Luke and Acts to Luke, the former adding that he was born in Antioch (Syria), the latter stating that Luke and Paul were inseparable. The fact that the *"we"* passages begin in Troas (Acts 16:10), that is neither in Philippi nor in Antioch, has led to speculation. Ramsay (*Paul* p349) maintains that there were considerable trade and sea links between Macedonia and Antioch. It is quite possible therefore that Luke spent his adult life between Philippi and Antioch and thus found himself at Troas. Smith (*Voyage* p21) adds that Luke was well versed in nautical matters, and described them in the language of seamanship, without being a professional seaman.

We can therefore draw some **preliminary conclusions on authorship**: Luke and Acts were both written by Luke, an inseparable companion of Paul, who was born in Antioch in Syria, who was a doctor and non-Jewish (*DBLuke* p7), and who for a time pastored the fledgling church in Philippi. This was the position of both Irenaeus (*AH* 3.14.1*)* and Eusebius (*HE* 2.22.6). Luke was an eyewitness for much of the Acts of the Apostles, but not in his Gospel. Here he used the testimony of other eyewitnesses (*Dissert* p60).

We also know when and where Acts was written. Since Luke and Paul were inseparable (*AH* 3.14.1), it is inconceivable that if Paul had been already dead, Luke would not have mentioned this in Acts. So, Acts must have been written before AD 64/65[36]. Similarly (*FFBA* p22), Acts would not have finished on such an optimistic note if Luke's hero had already died. This confirms Eusebius (*HE* 2.22): he suggests that Luke wrote Acts during Paul's period of

---

[35] Justin Martyr, "Dialogue with Trypho," 103.19.
[36] I am indebted to my friend Dan England for this insight.

house arrest in Rome, that is between February AD 60 and December AD 61[37]. And one of the reasons that Luke wrote Acts was as a defence document for Paul's (first) upcoming trial before Nero (*TWActs* Part 2 p248; *FFBA* pp20, 23).

3. But when and where did Luke write his Gospel?

We remember our premise that Luke had to have the motive, the means (access to information from eyewitnesses) and the opportunity (the time to research the material and to write). Motivation was no problem for any of the Gospel writers, so we only need to consider the aspects of means and opportunity.

The two two-year periods that Luke spent in prison with Paul, in Caesarea or in Rome, are therefore both possibilities.

Of these, the period in Caesarea is attractive (*TWActs* Part 2 p194, *GActs* p27 and *Dissert* pp13-14) because it would have given Luke the chance to interview his Palestinian and, especially, his women witnesses. He would also have been able, for his Gospel and Acts, to consult Philip the Evangelist who resided at Caesarea (Acts 21:8-9) and Mnason, one of the early disciples, who lived in Jerusalem (Acts 21:15-16). So, it is very likely that Luke's Gospel, at least in an embryonic form, existed by the beginning of AD 59. Whether it was in its final state, or whether Luke added some finishing touches after having met Peter in Rome is difficult to say. However, the *inclusio* evidence and Irenaeus (*AH* 3.1.1) suggest that the latter position is correct.

Paul's house arrest in Rome dates from February AD 60 to December AD 61 (*Paul* p396). Paul began preaching again after his release (*HE* 2.22.2), and we cannot imagine someone of Paul's dynamic character hanging around for more than two months before getting back on the preaching trail. Thus, Paul's first period in Rome would have been between February AD 60 and February AD 62: before he was in Malta and afterwards he was on what we will call his "Fifth Missionary Journey." Since Paul and Luke were inseparable (*AH* 3.14.1), this means that Luke must have produced Luke/Acts between February AD 60 and February AD 62. This is a very solid date.

4. Conclusion

Luke and Acts were both written by Luke, an inseparable companion of Paul, who was born in Antioch in Syria, who was a doctor and non-Jewish, and who for a time pastored the fledgling church in Philippi.

Luke wrote Acts during Paul's period of house arrest in Rome, that is between February AD 60 and February 62, although he probably gleaned information for it during his time in Palestine between AD 57 and 59. One of the reasons that he wrote Acts was as a defence document for Paul's (first) upcoming trial before Nero.

Luke began his work on his Gospel during his period of imprisonment, with Paul, in Caesarea between 57 and 59 AD and finished it in Rome, after contact with Peter and Mark in AD 60-61. Luke himself states that his was not the first Gospel to be written (1:1)

These solutions respect the internal and external evidence and are very solid.

---

[37] Or not later than AD 62 for both Luke and Acts (*HRNT* p236).

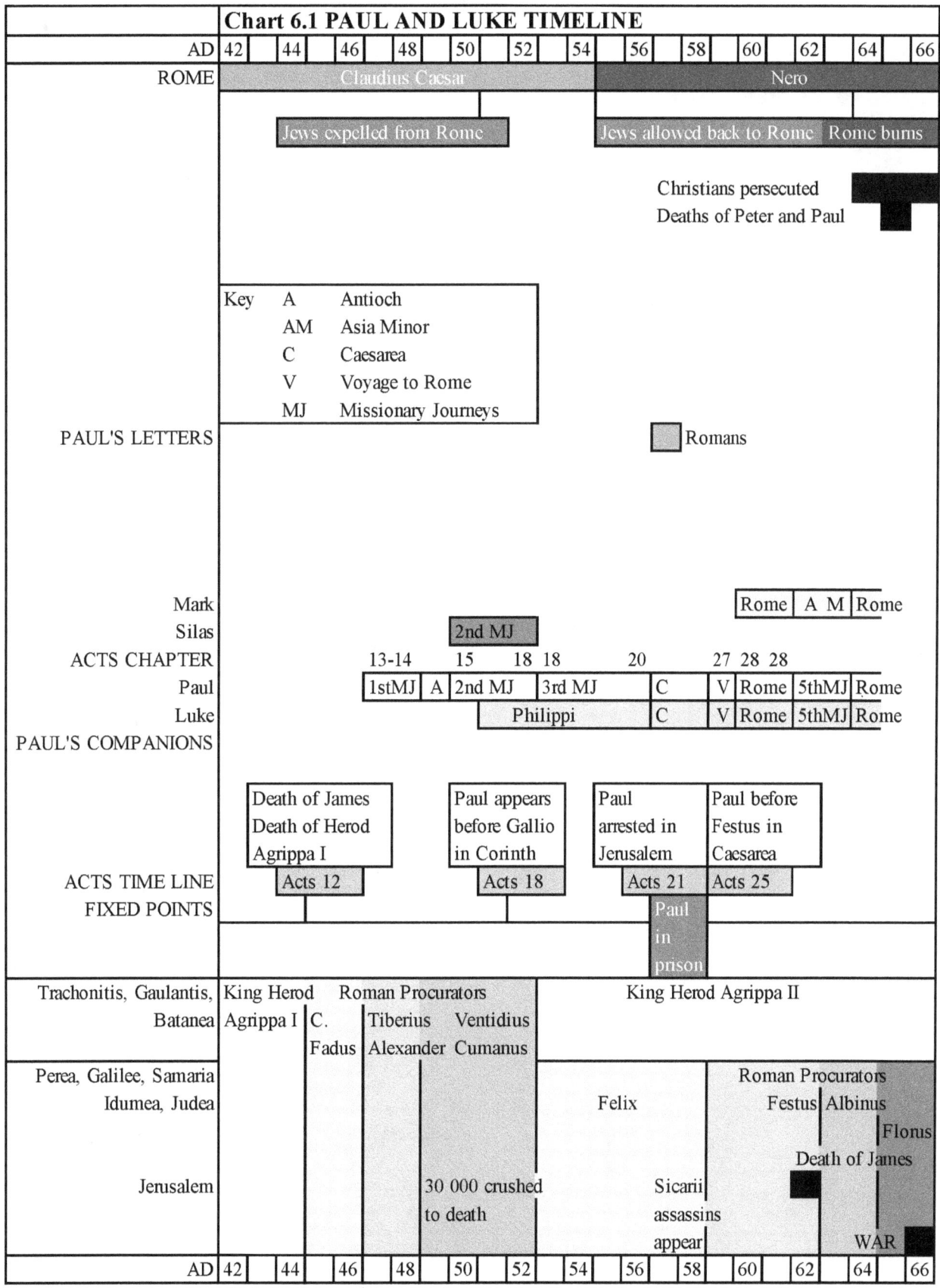

Chapter 7

THE ORIGINS OF THE GOSPELS OF MATTHEW AND MARK

MARK'S GOSPEL

Before attacking the internal evidence, a remark about first century names in Palestine is in order. Simon/Simeon and John were respectively the first and the fifth most popular male names in Palestine between 330 BC and 200 AD (*Eye* p85). Matthew/Matthias was number 9 and Levi number 17. It therefore made sense, in order to distinguish between the various Simons to call them, for example, Simon Peter. The same argument applies for John Mark. Even for Matthew, it might have been useful to have a second name, Levi.

1. Internal Evidence

Once again, we may begin with the *inclusio* evidence. The first and the last disciple to be mentioned is Simon Peter (1:16 and 16:7). Thus, Mark indicates that he depends on the eyewitness testimony of Peter.

There is also in Mark's Gospel an interesting, plural-to-singular narrative device (*Eye* pp 156-162 gives 21 instances) of which we will cite 4 examples:

"They went across the lake to the region of the Gerasenes. When Jesus got out of the boat..." (5:1-2)

"They came to Bethsaida, and some people brought a blind man and begged Jesus to touch him." (8:22)

"The next day as they were leaving Bethany, Jesus was hungry." (11:12)

"They went to a place called Gethsemane, and Jesus said to his disciples..." (14:32)

These four examples are sufficient to show the pattern: *"They"* concerns the movements of Jesus and his disciples when they come to a new place. But the transition to *"him"* or *"Jesus"* is immediate. Bauckham (*Eye* pp 156-181) draws two conclusions from this narrative device.

Firstly, Mark's Gospel is essentially the Gospel of the Twelve, because that is the *"they"* which is concerned. Secondly (see also *LMark* p11 for this), these passages read even more naturally if the *"they"* was originally *"we"*. This is potentially hugely significant, because it suggests - and we will see later that there is excellent external evidence to back this up - that behind Mark's Gospel we can hear the voice of Peter's preaching.

It is clear that Peter is the apostle who is most present in Mark's Gospel, but he is not always presented in a favourable light. He is portrayed as the *"foremost in understanding and loyalty while failing the most miserably and blatantly in both"* (*Eye* p170). Given Peter's stature in the early church, nobody else would have dared preach thus, apart from Peter himself.

In all this, the internal evidence is strong for Mark depending on the eyewitness testimony of the apostle Peter.

The internal evidence shows that Mark wrote for a Gentile (non-Jewish and non-Aramaic) audience. He provides explanations for his readers of Jewish customs (7:3-4, 19c; 14:12; 15:42) which are not present in the parallel passages in Matthew.

Mark also shows a preference for Latin or Roman technical and military terms (*LMark* p24), for example: *legion* (5:9); *praetorium* (15:16); *centurion* (15:39); *speculator* (6:27); *flagellare* (15:15); *denarius* (12:15); *quadrans* (12:42). Although such terms were used throughout the Roman Empire, it is significant that, on two occasions, common Greek expressions are explained by Latin ones:

12:42 *"two very small copper coins (lepta), which make a* quadrans.*"*

15:16 *"the palace, that is the* praetorium."

Since the *quadrans* was not in circulation in the east of the Empire, this suggests that Mark was aiming at an Italian or Roman audience.

Many readers will be wondering at this point about the evidence for the idea that Mark's Gospel was the first to be written (this is termed Markan Priority). Since this notion is based solely on a particular form of internal evidence (a comparison of the contents of Matthew's, Mark's and Luke's Gospels), it is dealt with in Appendix 4.

2. External Evidence

It is now the moment to introduce Papias. In the words of Richard Bauckham (*Eye* pp 12-15):

"Papias was bishop of Hierapolis, a city in the Lycus valley in the Roman province of Asia, not far from Laodicea and Colossae. He completed his major work, Exposition of the Logia of the Lord, *in five books, somewhere near the beginning of the second century, but sadly it has not survived…the most interesting of the fragments are those preserved by Eusebius of Caesarea."* (*HE*)

"Papias belonged…to a generation that had been in touch…with the apostles. He was personally acquainted with the daughters of Philip the Evangelist, who was one of the Seven…This Philip spent the last years of his life in Hierapolis, and two of his daughters who were well known as prophets (Acts 28:8-9), also lived out the rest of their lives there, unmarried…from Philip's daughters he learned some stories about the apostles (HE 3.39.9)."

"Hierapolis…stood at the meeting of two great roads: one running east and west, between Antioch in Syria and Ephesus, the chief city of Asia, the other south-east to Attalia in Pamphylia and north-west to Smyrna. There Papias was almost uniquely placed for collecting traditions coming direct…from Palestinian (Christian) leaders settled in Asia (a great centre of the Jewish Dispersion)."

Bauckham (*Eye* p14) states that, although Papias wrote between AD 100 and 107, his recollections date from around AD 80. Papias, in his prologue (*HE* 3.39.3-4) explains the following:

"I shall not regret to subjoin to my interpretations, also for your benefit, whatsoever I have at any time accurately ascertained and treasured up in my memory, as I have received it from the elders, and have recorded it in order to give additional confirmation to the truth by my testimony. For I have never, like many, delighted to hear those that tell many things, but those that teach the truth, neither those that regard foreign precepts, but those that are given from the Lord, to our faith, and that came from the truth itself. But if I met with anyone who had been a follower of the elders anywhere, I made it a point to inquire what were the declarations of the elders. What was said by Andrew, Peter or Philip. What by Thomas, James, John, Matthew, or any other disciples of our Lord. What was said by Aristion, and the presbyter John, disciples of the Lord; for I do not think that I derived so much benefit from books as from the living voice of those that are still surviving."

Papias talks of the Gospels of Mark and Matthew:

"And John the Presbyter also said this, Mark being the interpreter of Peter whatsoever he recorded he wrote with great accuracy but not however, in the order in which it was spoken or done by our Lord, but as before said, he was in company with Peter, who gave him such instruction (chreiai) *as was necessary, but not to give a history of our Lord's discourses: wherefore Mark has not erred in anything, by writing some things as he has recorded them; for he was carefully attentive to one thing, not to pass by anything that he had heard, or to state anything falsely in these accounts."...(HE 3.39.15)*

Of Matthew he had stated as follows: "Matthew composed his history in the Hebrew dialect, and everyone translated it as he was able." (HE 3.39.16)

Papias' statement on Mark's Gospel is the earliest explicit claim that Peter's preaching lies behind this Gospel. This links up very nicely with what we found in the internal evidence: that often the *"they"* in Mark's Gospel should more naturally be *"we", because in reality we are dealing with Peter's preaching.*

Bauckham (*Eye* pp 202-239) has examined the meaning of the Papias passage on Mark. He concludes that Papias is saying that Mark faithfully wrote down Peter's oral testimony. Peter's Greek was probably sufficiently good orally, but needed a more accomplished Greek linguist to write his preaching down (p210). *Chreiai* are brief narratives containing sayings or actions (p215) which fit what we know of Mark's Gospel rather well. The question of the ordered arrangement or not of Mark's Gospel (pp217-237) will be left until we consider Matthew's Gospel. We will now examine evidence from other primitive church historians.

Eusebius quotes Clement of Alexandria (*HE* 2.15.1-2 and 6.14.6-7) who said that the people in the church in Rome entreated Mark, as Peter's companion, to leave them a monument in writing of Peter's preaching. Peter was delighted with the result and authorised it for reading in the churches. Origen (*HE* 6.25.5) talks of Mark's as the second Gospel, *"who composed it as Peter explained it to him."*

FMark p37 adds that the Anti-Marcionite and Monarchian Prologues, Irenaeus, Tertullian, Ephraem, Epiphanus and Jerome all back up the idea that the author was John Mark (one-time companion of Barnabas, Paul and Peter), that he derived his material from the preaching of Peter, with whom he was closely associated and that the work was compiled in Rome or, more generally, in Italy.

The only remaining question in all this evidence is whether Mark wrote the Gospel before or after Peter's death. Irenaeus (*AH* 3.1.1 and *HE* 5.8.3) says that Mark wrote his Gospel after the departure of Peter and Paul. But this does not necessarily refer to their death, more likely to their relocation. Irenaeus underlines Mark as the interpreter of Peter (*AH* 3.10.5), and the view of Clement of Alexandria, that Mark wrote his Gospel before Peter's death (*HE* 6.14.6-7), seems convincing (see the argument at the beginning of the previous chapter: no event was necessary to "call forth" the writing of the Gospels, the apostles would always have been looking for new ways to communicate "Jesus is Lord.")

Moreover (*FMark* p38), Eusebius and Jerome claim to have got their information from Papias (*HE* 2.15.1-2). Therefore, the earliest and the overwhelming evidence from the early church is that Mark wrote his Gospel in Rome, as a record of Peter's preaching, before Peter was crucified in AD 64/65, and this fits the internal evidence extremely well.

3. Peter and Mark

Faced with the overwhelming historical evidence of Mark as the faithful scribe for Peter's preaching in Rome, it is interesting to try to piece together the whereabouts through time of Peter, Mark and Silas (see the Peter and Paul Timeline Chart 7.1). We begin in Acts chapter 12. Peter has just escaped miraculously from prison (12:1-11); he goes to the house of Mary, the mother of John Mark, where many people were praying for his release (12:12-19). Then Herod Agrippa I dies and we know from Josephus (*BJ* 2.223) that this was in August AD 44.

In Acts 13: 4-6 Paul, Barnabas and John Mark set off on the First Missionary Journey but, in Perga in Pamphilia, John Mark leaves them to go back to Jerusalem.

In Acts 15, all the major protagonists (Paul, Barnabas, Peter, Silas, James and possibly John Mark) are present for the Council of Jerusalem. Paul, Barnabas, Silas and John Mark then go to Antioch and spend some time there (15:30-35). Then Paul embarks on his Second Missionary Journey with Silas, while Barnabas and John Mark go off to Cyprus.

We have meanwhile no news of Peter. Clement of Alexandria, cited by Eusebius (*HE* 2.14.6) has Peter in Rome under Claudius dealing with the evil Simon Magus (this would be in AD 54 at the latest). However, this seems a little unlikely because, under Claudius, Jews were not allowed into Rome. It seems more likely that he got to Rome just as Nero was allowing the Jews back, in AD 55. Origen cited in *HE* 3.1 suggests that Peter preached his way through Pontus, Galatia, Bithynia, Cappadocia and Asia to the Jews that were scattered abroad before finally coming to Rome. This may be an interpretation of 1 Peter 1:1, but it makes sense. This would have taken him at least three years from AD 52-55. Since, in the same letter, he refers to Mark as his son (5:13), then we can suppose that John Mark accompanied him and perhaps Silas[38] too (5:12). The Epistle to the Romans, which was written from Corinth in January AD 57, was partly written because Paul hoped to go to Rome and he knew that Peter and other Jews such as his friends

---

[38] Since Silas was a rare name (*Eye* p87), Silas and the Silvanus of 1 Peter 5:12 are almost certainly the same person.

Priscilla and Aquila (Romans 16:3) were already there. Therefore, a date of AD 55 for Peter and John Mark's arrival in Rome seems eminently reasonable.

When Paul arrived in February AD 60, the two apostles worked together and there was some mixing of the teams, so that Mark is referred to in Colossians 4:10, Philemon 24 and 2 Timothy 4:11. Silas seems to have changed teams earlier, from Paul to Peter, after Paul's Second Missionary Journey. We can assume that the Gospel of Mark and 1 Peter were both written before Paul arrived to mix up the teams, that is between AD 55 and 59. Mark could not have written his Gospel later than AD 61, because by AD 62 he was probably on his way to Asia Minor (2 Timothy 4:11).

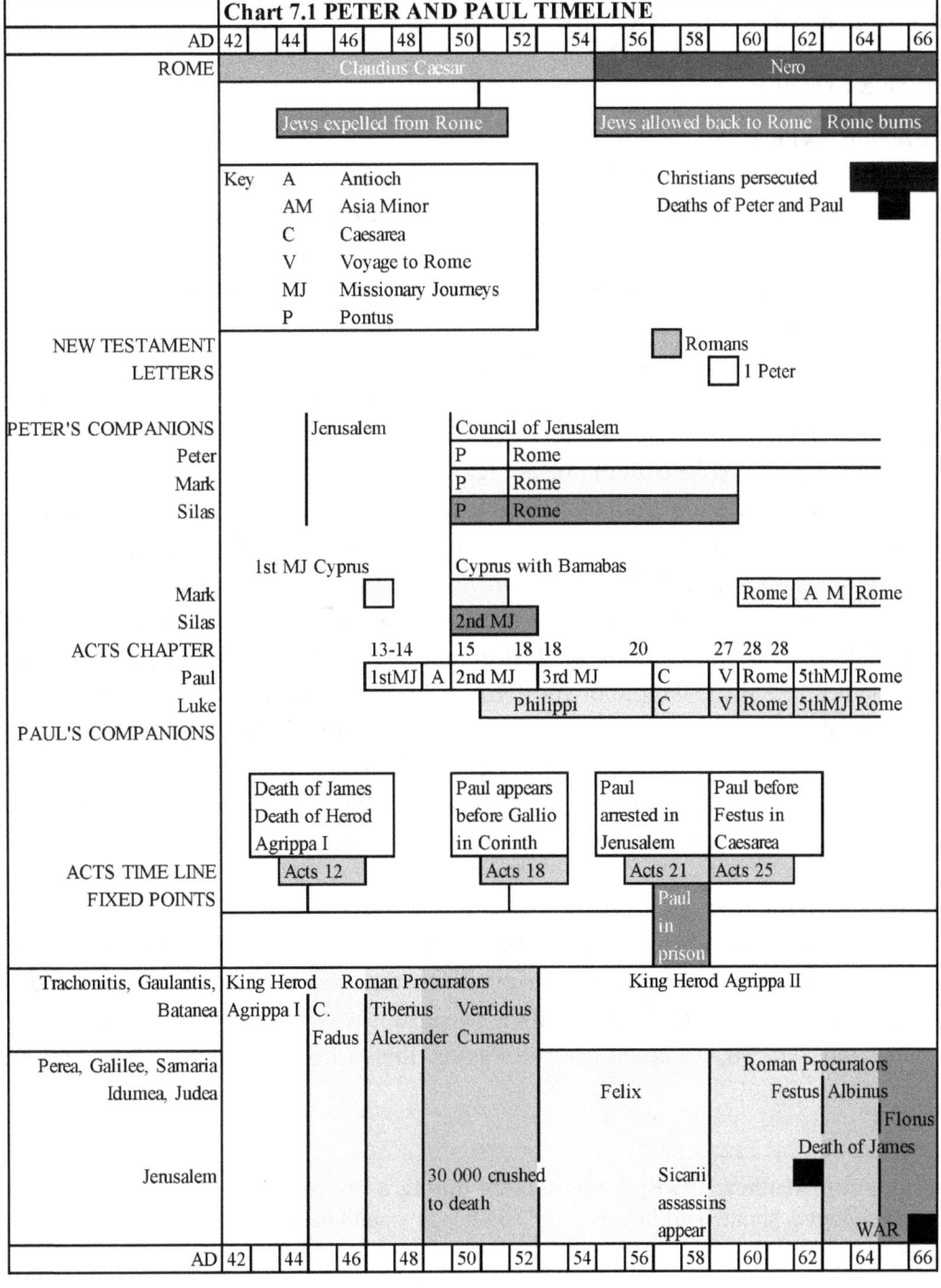

So, this gives us the Peter and Paul Timeline Chart 7.1, and a possible date of writing of the Gospel between AD 55 and 59. The same applies for the date of writing of 1 Peter, and AD 59 would seem a reasonable date.

4. Conclusion

The internal and external evidence is truly overwhelming. Mark's Gospel was written by John Mark, one-time resident of Jerusalem and companion of Paul and Barnabas on their First Missionary Journey. He later developed an almost filial relationship with the apostle Peter. Mark's Gospel is that of the Twelve, but behind it is the voice of Peter's preaching. Mark faithfully wrote down Peter's preaching, for the Gentile audience of Rome and Italy, before Peter died. This happened in Rome between AD 55 and 59.

MATTHEW'S GOSPEL

1. Internal Evidence

Unfortunately, there is no clear *inclusio* evidence to guide us.

The Gospel seems to be have written by a Jewish Christian for a largely Jewish Christian readership (*FMatt* p17). It begins with the genealogy of Jesus, which begins with Abraham, the father of the Jewish nation. There are Aramaic terms which are not translated, such as *raca* (5:22), a term of contempt or *korbanas* (27:6), referring to the Temple treasury. Unlike Mark, Matthew does not explain Jewish customs such as handwashing (15:2) or the wearing of phylacteries (23:5). He seems to assume that his readers are familiar with Jewish customs. Burridge (*What?* p204) states that Matthew was capable of Semitisms.

The "formula quotations" are an important feature of the Gospel: Matthew uses these citations of the Old Testament to demonstrate that Jesus is the fulfilment of the hopes of Israel.

We have already shown that the three Synoptic Gospels (Matthew, Mark and Luke) were written before the destruction of the Temple in Jerusalem in AD 70. After AD 70, the discussion of the Temple Tax (17:24-27) would have presented no interest whatsoever, and would indeed have been misleading because, after the destruction of the Temple, the tax was diverted by the Romans to the upkeep of the temple of Jupiter in Rome. The same argument applies to two other passages found only in Matthew which refer to the Temple (5:23-24; 23:16-22): they would have meant nothing or would have been misleading after AD 70.

Thus, the internal evidence points to the writer of Matthew's Gospel being a Jewish Christian, writing for a predominately Jewish Christian audience, before AD 70[39].

2. External Evidence

Richard Bauckham examines the Papias statements on Mark and Matthew in great detail (*Eye* pp223-233). He suggests that Papias was originally comparing Matthew and Mark and John, and that Mark did not have a typical literary order, because it was based on oral preaching. Matthew, on the other hand, did. So, we come back to Papias, the earliest external evidence on Matthew's Gospel:

---

[39] The idea that Matthew's Gospel was written during a period of hypothetical separation between church and synagogue, situated arbitrarily in AD 85 has no sound basis (see *FMatt2* p18).

Of Matthew he had stated as follows: "Matthew composed his history in the Hebrew dialect, and everyone translated it as he was able." (HE 3.39.16)

However, Papias was not alone in saying that Matthew was first written in Hebrew. Irenaeus (*AH* 3.1.1 and *HE* 5.8.1), and Origen (*HE* 6.25.4) said the same. The explanation seems to come from Eusebius himself (*HE* 3.24.6):

"Matthew also having first proclaimed the Gospel in Hebrew, when on the point of going also to other nations, committed it to writing in his native tongue and thus supplied the want of his presence to them by his writings."

Clearly, Matthew was first written in Hebrew or Aramaic, probably in Palestine or Syria (but not necessarily in Antioch (*FMatt2* p15)). Eusebius had access to the impressive biblical and theological library at Caesarea, which included Origen's *Hexapla"* and *"Tetrapla"* and a copy of the original Aramaic version of Matthew[40]. However, its translation into Greek quickly superseded it. Smith (*Dissert* p52) makes a case for Matthew himself translating his Gospel into Greek. This would explain why the Semitic version disappeared so that only the Greek version of the Gospel has come down to us. Irenaeus states (*AH* 3.1.1 and *HE* 5.8.1):

"Matthew also issued a written Gospel among the Hebrews in their own dialect, while Peter and Paul were preaching at Rome, and laying the foundations of the Church. After their departure, Mark, the disciple and interpreter of Peter, did also hand down to us in writing what had been preached by Peter. Luke also, the companion of Paul, recorded in a book the Gospel preached by him. Afterwards, John, the disciple of the Lord, who had also leaned upon His breast, did himself publish a Gospel during his residence at Ephesus in Asia."

Thus, Matthew produced his Gospel while Peter *and* Paul were preaching in Rome, which means between AD 60 and 61 (see the Peter and Paul Timeline Chart 7.1) if taken literally. If, on the other hand, as seems reasonable, we allow just Peter to have started preaching in Rome, then this would mean between AD 55 and 61.

Finally, it must be stated firmly that the Gospel of Matthew has never, in the history of the early church, been associated with anyone else but Matthew/Levi (Matthew 9:9-13; Mark 2:13-17; Luke 5:27-32), from Capernaum, who was a border tolls collector for Herod Antipas. It has also, throughout this period, been regarded as the first of the Gospels to be written (for example Origen in *HE* 6.25.4 and Irenaeus in *AH* 3.1.1).

3. Conclusion

The internal evidence points to the writer of Matthew's Gospel being a Jewish Christian, writing for a predominately Jewish Christian audience, before AD 70, probably in Palestine or Syria. The external evidence, which is not copious, tends to confirm this, raising the point that the Gospel was almost certainly written originally in a Semitic dialect, before being translated into the Greek text which has come down to us. Irenaeus adds that Matthew wrote his Gospel while Peter and Paul were preaching in Rome, which puts its date of writing at AD 60-61, or more likely between AD 55 and 61. The Gospel of Matthew has never, in the history of the early church, been associated with anyone else but Matthew/Levi from Capernaum, who was a border

---

[40] Timothy Barnes, "Constantine and Eusebius," Harvard University Press, 1981, p94.

tolls collector for Herod Antipas. It has also, throughout this period, been regarded as the first of the Gospels to be written.

SUMMARY OF THE ORIGINS OF THE SYNOPTIC GOSPELS

The internal and external evidence for the origins of the Gospels of Luke and Mark are very strong, and so our conclusions can be detailed and sound. Unfortunately, we have less evidence to work with for the Gospel of Matthew. Recalling that we have not based any of our reasoning on whether the three Gospels were written independently, or whether there was some degree of cross-fertilisation between them, we can summarise our findings in the Table 7.1: Summary of Synoptic Gospel Origins.

The first thing which strikes us in the Table 7.1 is the amazing diversity and richness in these three Gospels. As authors, we have a Gentile physician, a young Jew from Jerusalem and an older Jew from the Galilean countryside. Whereas Matthew could depend on his own eyewitness testimony as a member of the Twelve, Mark faithfully wrote down the eyewitness testimony of the apostle Peter, which he communicated in the form of short narratives known as *chreiai* in his preaching. This makes Mark's Gospel pacy and dynamic, whereas Matthew contains more blocks of teaching, notably the Sermon on the Mount. On the other hand, Luke gathered together eyewitness testimony when he was in prison in Caesarea Maritime with Paul, between June AD 57 and July AD 59. He had the time to gather in testimony from many of Jesus' contemporaries, in particular that of Philip the Evangelist, Mnason and the women close to Jesus. He then completed his Gospel after comparing notes with Peter in Rome, during the house arrest of Paul from AD 60 to 61. However, there is another possibility which is very attractive. Smith (*Dissert* p52) makes a convincing case that Luke used the Syriac version of Matthew and then completed his Gospel using Mark. On this basis, Luke could have begun his Gospel in Caesarea using the Syriac version of Matthew (in AD 57-59), the eyewitness testimony of the women close to Jesus, Mnason, and of Philip the Evangelist, and then finalised it using Peter's testimony and Mark's Gospel in Rome between Feb AD 60 and Feb AD 62.

Whereas Matthew wrote for a Jewish audience, Mark wrote for a Gentile audience in Italy. Matthew apparently wrote his Gospel in a Semitic language or dialect, even though only its Greek translations have come down to us. Luke and Mark both wrote their Gospels in Greek. So, we have great variety of scope in these three Gospels, and yet they all narrate the same wonderful life, death and resurrection of Jesus.

The remarkable result of this investigation is that all three Gospels were written at approximately the same time. In particular, we shall see that the completion dates of Luke and Mark were close together. If we regard the probable dates of completion in the Table 7.1, many of the classic sequences of the writing of the Gospels can be accommodated. The early church fathers were unanimous (for example Irenaeus and Origen (*AH* 3.1.1 and *HE* 6.25.4)) that the order of writing was Matthew, then Mark, then Luke and finally John. From the Table 7.1, this is a possibility. The view, which dominated scholarship during the nineteenth and twentieth centuries, made Mark's Gospel a primary source for Matthew and Luke. This too would be possible, if we ignored the fact that Matthew was first written in a Semitic dialect, and concentrated our attention on the Greek version which has come down to us. On the other hand, the Griesbach Hypothesis (*FMatt* p35) - that Matthew's Gospel was used by Luke and that

Mark's Gospel is a deliberate condensing of the two into a single work - is difficult to accommodate. But then it also flies against all the historical evidence. However, there is also the possibility that the three Gospels were essentially written independently, with Luke just depending on Peter's testimony in Rome to put the finishing touches to his Gospel.

This is probably as far as we need to go. However, it is possible to go further, basing our reasoning on the points we are most sure of:

1. Luke completed his Gospel in Rome between February AD 60 and February AD 62.

2. His was not the first Gospel to be written. He himself (Luke 1:1) says that others (plural) had undertaken the same task before him. He therefore probably had the Semitic version of Matthew and either Mark's Gospel in Greek, or Peter himself, by his side, as he wrote.

The testimony of Irenaeus (*AH* 3.1.1) is interesting:

"Matthew also issued a written Gospel among the Hebrews in their own dialect, while Peter and Paul were preaching at Rome, and laying the foundations of the Church. After their departure, Mark, the disciple and interpreter of Peter, did also hand down to us in writing what had been preached by Peter. Luke also, the companion of Paul, recorded in a book the Gospel preached by him. Afterwards, John, the disciple of the Lord, who had also leaned upon His breast, did himself publish a Gospel during his residence at Ephesus in Asia."

We can attempt to unpack this as follows. First of all, Matthew wrote his Gospel in Palestine or Syria, in a Semitic dialect between AD 55 and 57. At this point (AD 55), Peter has just arrived in Rome, accompanied by his "son" John Mark, having preached his way through Pontus, Galatia, Bithynia, Cappadocia and Asia. Now that they are settled in Rome, Mark, independently from Matthew, begins to write down Peter's sermons, or *chreiai*, over a period, probably between AD 55 and 59. This means that his Gospel is probably finished by the time Paul and Luke arrive in Rome in February AD 60. Then the teams of Peter and Paul are mixed up and Mark works with Paul once again (see Colossians 4:10; Philemon 24; 2 Timothy 4:11)[41].

Meanwhile, Luke has gathered together eyewitness testimony when he was in prison in Caesarea Maritime with Paul, between June AD 57 and July AD 59[42]. He has had the time to gather in testimony from many of Jesus' contemporaries, in particular that of Philip the Evangelist, Mnason and the women close to Jesus. He has also been able to use the Semitic version of Matthew's Gospel, which was available by then in Palestine. Luke, when he arrives in Rome, can use Mark's Gospel plus the eyewitness testimony of Peter, to complete his own Gospel between February AD 60 and February AD 62.

Mark leaves Rome to arrive in Asia Minor probably not later than the beginning of AD 62, which is also when (February AD 62) Paul leaves Rome to resume preaching, presumably with Luke, his inseparable companion[43]. Mark has published his finished Gospel between AD 59 and 61, before leaving Rome, and Peter authorises it for reading in the churches.

---

[41] Colossians and Philemon were almost certainly written from Rome in AD 60, before an earthquake destroyed towns in the Lycus valley in AD 60-61 (*Annals* 14.27).

[42] Craig Blomberg (*HRNT* p719) accepts the possibility that Matthew, in Hebrew or Aramaic, preceded Mark.

[43] Considering *AH* 3.1.1, we can make the same type of assumption that we made earlier: *"their departure"* (literally that of Peter and Paul) may apply essentially to Paul, in the same way that, before,

According to this scenario, based on the passage of Irenaeus, Matthew and Mark have been authored *independently* in different languages and in different countries. The fact that Mark's Gospel is a written account of Peter's (oral) preaching, leads to the notion that the dates of final publication of Mark and Luke may be quite close together, even though Luke has used Peter's testimony and both Matthew's and Mark's Gospels to construct his own.

Table 7.1: SUMMARY OF SYNOPTIC GOSPEL ORIGINS

Gospel of	LUKE	MARK	MATTHEW
Author	Luke	John Mark	Matthew
Profile of author			
Origin	Gentile	Jew	Jew
From	Antioch, Syria	Jerusalem	Capernaum, Galilee
Profession	Doctor	Clerk?	Border customs officer
Profile	Inseparable companion of St Paul Pastor of church in Philippi	One-time companion of Paul and Barnabas Then filial interpreter of apostle Peter	Member of Twelve
Basis of Gospel	Based on eye-witness testimony collected when in jail with Paul in Caesarea (AD57-59), including that of women around Jesus. Completed by Peter's testimony collected in Rome (AD60-61)	Based on Peter's eye-witness testimony expressed in his preaching (*chreiai* short narratives) Faithfully written down before Peter's death.	Based on his own eye-witness testimony as one of the Twelve.
Language	Greek	Greek	First written in Hebrew, Syriac or Aramaic, then translated into Greek.
Written for whom	Theophilus so he may be sure of the Gospel message	Gentile Christians and other Gentiles in Italy	Jewish Christians and other Jews in Palestine or Syria
Strong point	The place accorded to women	Dynamic, Gospel of the Twelve	Jesus the Messiah fulfils the hopes of Israel.
Place of writing	Caesarea, then Rome	Rome	Palestine or Syria?
Dates of Preparation	AD 57-59 (Caesarea)	AD 55-59	AD 55-57
Possible date of completion	Feb AD 60-Feb AD 62 (Rome)	AD 59-61	Semitic: AD 55-57
Probable date of completion	Feb AD 60-Feb AD 62	AD 59-60	Semitic: AD 55-57

"their preaching in Rome" applied essentially to Peter. Thus, Peter could well have stayed in Rome until his death in AD 64/65.

On the Independence of Matthew and Mark

The early church fathers and historians never mention that one Gospel writer used the material of another. Although this is admittedly an argument from silence, it is nevertheless perhaps significant (see also Appendix 4).

Are there additional good reasons for believing that Matthew and Mark were written independently? Table 7.1 shows that Matthew and Mark were probably being prepared during the same time period (AD 55-59) in different countries (Palestine or Syria for Matthew, Rome in Italy for Mark).

They were also addressing different audiences (Jewish Christians for Matthew, Gentile Christians for Mark) in different languages (Hebrew, Aramaic or Syriac for Matthew, Greek for Mark). We see this in the fact that Matthew uses Aramaic terms and talks of Jewish customs without any explanation. On the other hand, Mark tends to use Latin military terms and explains Jewish customs.

They also had slightly different objectives: Mark to faithfully record Peter's preaching, Matthew to give a solid basis for the faith to his companions before he relocated (*HE* 3.24.6).

Therefore, they both had solid reasons for writing their respective Gospels when they did, in the locality where they lived. Thus, the independence of Matthew and Mark seems a reasonable proposition. Nevertheless, whether or not this proposition is true or not, does not affect the future arguments found in Chapter 13.

We will now consider the origins of the Gospel according to John.

Chapter 8

THE ORIGINS OF JOHN'S GOSPEL

1. Internal Evidence

We will assume the unity of John's Gospel. In other words, we will take the position that chapter 21 is not just a supplement added on after the completion of the real Gospel, but rather an Epilogue or a Postface - a device which many authors ancient and modern have used - which is an integral part of the whole (*Test* pp271-284; *CJohn* pp665-668; *FFBR* pp41-42).

The Gospel according to John was written by *"the disciple whom Jesus loved"* (21:20, 24), sometimes shortened to *"the beloved disciple."* He testifies to these things and he wrote them down (21:24). *"He dwelt among us. We have seen his glory,"* he writes (1:14). It is not an exhaustive biography of Jesus, because the writer himself says there was much more (20:30; 21:25). We also know that he wrote his Gospel *"that you may believe that Jesus is the Christ, the Son of God, and that by believing you may have life in his name."* (20:31)

The *inclusio* evidence in John's Gospel is subtle and double. The first two disciples mentioned are anonymous to begin with (1:37) but, as we read on, we learn that one of them is Andrew. The other one remains nameless and it is not difficult to see *"the disciple whom Jesus loved"* behind this anonymity. Then, after Andrew, the next disciple mentioned is Simon Peter (1:40). Similarly, at the end of the Gospel, the last disciple mentioned is *"the disciple whom Jesus loved"*, just after Peter (21:19).

So, we have a double *inclusio*, with *"the disciple whom Jesus loved"* taking priority over Peter. In other words, although the former insists he wrote the Gospel, and that his witness takes priority, he nevertheless admits his indebtedness to the testimony of Peter.

There are even some quotations which are closer to Hebrew and Aramaic than to Greek (*CJohn* p71) and Burridge (*What?* pp226-7) states that the Gospel contains some Semitisms, trilingual and eastern Mediterranean features. All this points to the author being a Jew from Palestine who had also lived in Asia Minor. But who was *"the disciple whom Jesus loved"* or *"the beloved disciple"*?

After the anonymity of 1:37, we first meet him at the Last Supper (13:23), where he was reclining next to Jesus, and so may pass on Peter's question. He was at the foot of the cross (19:25-27), where Jesus commissions him to take care of his mother, Mary. He was present at the empty tomb, outrunning Peter (20:2-4). Finally, he was present in chapter 21, where we learn that he is the author of the Gospel.

There are basically two views concerning his identity[44]. The traditional view is that he was John, the son of Zebedee, but that he avoids using his name, substituting *"the disciple whom*

---

[44] Throughout the 1970's and 1990's, studies in John's Gospel were dominated by the idea that the Gospel was produced by and for the so-called Johannine Community. This school of thought began with

Jesus loved", as a literary device to emphasise Jesus' love for him and, by extension, Jesus' love for each one of us. The other (*Test* pp33-50) is that he was not a member of the Twelve, but from a priestly family in Jerusalem which would have given him access to the High Priest's courtyard (18:16). However, this latter view depends above all on the interpretation of certain strands of external evidence. Therefore, for the moment, we will pursue the internal evidence which supports the traditional view (*CJohn* p72; *FFBR* pp41-42; *HRNT* p156):

a) We know that the beloved disciple was present at the Last Supper (13:23) which, according to Mark 14:17 and the other Synoptic Gospels, makes him one of the Twelve.

b) Jesus, at least in the Synoptic Gospels, seems to have an inner circle of three (Peter and James and John, the sons of Zebedee), so it seems logical to suppose that *"the disciple whom Jesus loved"* is one of these three.

c) The beloved disciple is constantly distinguished from Peter, although their relation is close. He is one of the seven disciples who go fishing in chapter 21, but he is not Peter, nor Thomas or Nathanael, because these are named in the text. He is therefore either a son of Zebedee or one of two unnamed disciples (21:2). He cannot be James, the son of Zebedee, who was martyred in AD 44 (see Acts 12:1-2), because the beloved disciple lived long enough to lead people to suppose that he would not die (21:23).

d) So, combining b) and c), we conclude that *"the disciple whom Jesus loved"* is John, the son of Zebedee.

We may further comment that if the beloved disciple is not John, the son of Zebedee, then his anonymity in the Gospel, and that of his brother James, is most odd. If it is not a literary device, then other explanations must be produced and, in general, they are not forthcoming. Overall, it seems much more reasonable to suppose that John was just a lad when Jesus called him. Jesus then "took him under his wing", having a special fondness for this bright and utterly trustworthy young man. Later, Jesus entrusted him with his mother and John lived for many more years[45].

Another intriguing subject concerns the disclosure of some names in the Gospel according to John, who remain nameless in the Synoptic Gospels, notably Mark.

Selective or Protective Anonymity

As many readers of the Bible will have noticed certain characters, which are not named in the Gospel of Mark, are named in John's Gospel. This becomes particularly apparent when we compare the two arrest and passion narratives. This suggests that John's Gospel was written later than Mark's. Mark covered up the identity of certain people so they would not have trouble with the police! This is known as *selective or protective anonymity* (*Eye* pp194-201).

We will consider the three clearest cases to begin with.

Jean-Louis Martyn and was developed by Raymond Brown (see *Test* pp9-16). The work of Burridge (*What?*) and Bauckham (*Eye* and *Test*) has countered this hypothesis.

[45] Private communication from Dan England on what somebody said during a Bible Study he was leading.

(a) The woman anointing Jesus in Bethany. She is mentioned in Mark 14:3 and Matthew 26:7 (not in Luke). We do not know her name in either case, but in John 12:3 we learn that she is Mary, the sister of Martha and Lazarus.

(b) The man who cut off the ear of the high priest's servant. He remains anonymous in all three Synoptic Gospels (Mark 14:47; Matthew 26:51; Luke 22:50) but in John 18:10 we learn that it is Simon Peter.

(c) In the same verses in the Synoptic Gospels, the name of the high priest's servant is not revealed, but in John's Gospel we learn that his name was Malchus.

Now Malchus was not just *a* servant of the high priest but *the* servant of the high priest; in other words, a man of considerable influence. If it had been known that Peter was responsible for his injuries, Simon Peter would have faced criminal charges. Hence the anonymity, which can be waived later in John's Gospel, when either Peter is dead, or far away from Jerusalem, or Malchus has died.

For Mary, the reasoning is slightly different. The raising of Lazarus, we learn in John's Gospel, was such a remarkable event that the Jewish authorities sought to kill Lazarus (12:9-11) and it also provoked the decision to kill Jesus (11:50). Therefore, Lazarus, Mary and Martha would all have been in immediate danger, the sisters because they had been witnesses to the event. Mary's anointing of Jesus was also a prophetic act, indicating he was the Messiah, the anointed one. This explains why Mary's name as the anointer and the account of the raising of Lazarus only occur in John's Gospel, when the danger to the family had passed.

There is a final interesting case of a man we meet in John's Gospel, but not in the Synoptics: Nicodemus. Whereas in Matthew (27:57-60), Luke (23:50-56) and Mark (15:42-46), it is Joseph of Arimathea who takes Jesus' body down from the cross and places it in his own tomb, we learn from John's Gospel that he was accompanied by Nicodemus. Now Nicodemus was extremely wealthy, from one of, if not the, richest families in Jerusalem[46]. Joseph of Arimathea had made a conscious courageous decision to declare his allegiance to Jesus at this terrible time. But for Nicodemus, such a commitment at that time would have been very dangerous. Later, it could be disclosed.

Other Points

We therefore conclude that John's Gospel was written after the last of the Synoptic Gospels, that is after AD 62. Although it is an argument from silence, the fact that John does not refer to the destruction of the Temple in AD 70, suggests that the Gospel was written when the Jewish War was well and truly over, say after AD 74.

Conclusion

From the internal evidence, it is clear that the Gospel was written by *"the disciple whom Jesus loved"*. Moreover, the internal evidence strongly suggests that *"the disciple whom Jesus loved"* should be identified with John, the son of Zebedee, a member of the Twelve, a Jewish fisherman from Bethsaida (1:44) in the Tetrarchy of Philip. He was a young man during the time of Jesus'

---

[46] See *Test* pp137-172. The name Nicodemus was very rare and Richard Bauckham has managed to piece together his family tree. More on this later.

ministry and therefore represented no threat to the élites in Jerusalem, although he knew them (18:16). He could thus also live for a long time after Jesus' ascension (21:23).

He used his own eyewitness testimony and that of Peter to write his Gospel, which had an evangelistic purpose (20:31). The internal evidence places the writing of the Gospel somewhere between AD 74 and AD 130; to narrow this down we must look at the external evidence.

2. External Evidence

Gnostic writers were already quoting from John's Gospel early in the second century AD. Basilides (c.130) quoted from John 1:9 and Valentinus (c. 140) seems to allude to John 1:14 (*CJohn* pp24-5; *FFBJ* p7 notes 23 and 24).

However, early Christian apologists such as Justin Martyr, writing between AD 155 and 157, also alluded to John's Gospel (*Apol.* 1.61 seems to depend on John 3:3-5). Similarly, Justin's disciple Tatian quoted huge swathes of John's Gospel in his *Diatessaron*, a harmony of the Gospels, which was written c. 170. Carson (*CJohn* p26) states that Theophilus of Antioch (c. 181) quoted unambiguously from John's Gospel and that, even before this date, Claudius Apollinaris (bishop of Hierapolis) and Athenogoras were doing the same. So, once again, John's Gospel must have been written before AD 160.

To further narrow things down, we begin once again with the Eusebius citation of Papias:

"I shall not regret to subjoin to my interpretations, also for your benefit, whatsoever I have at any time accurately ascertained and treasured up in my memory, as I have received it from the elders, and have recorded it in order to give additional confirmation to the truth by my testimony. For I have never, like many, delighted to hear those that tell many things, but those that teach the truth, neither those that regard foreign precepts, but those that are given from the Lord, to our faith, and that came from the truth itself. But if I met with anyone who had been a follower of the elders anywhere, I made it a point to inquire what were the declarations of the elders. What was said by Andrew, Peter or Philip. What by Thomas, James, John, Matthew, or any other disciples of our Lord. What was said by Aristion, and the presbyter John, disciples of the Lord; for I do not think that I derived so much benefit from books as from the living voice of those that are still surviving." (*HE* 3.39.3-4)

From this Bauckham (*Eye* p417) deduces that Papias knew the Gospel of John (i.e. it had already been written) because the list of the disciples corresponds with that found in John (1:35-51; 21:2). Furthermore, the first six names (Nathanael is omitted by Papias) occur in the order in which these characters first appear in the Gospel (1:40, 41, 43; 11:16; 21:2).

At first sight, Papias distinguishes between disciples of the Lord and a second category of elders (Aristion and John). This leads Bauckham to follow Hengel (*Test* p34) and to suggest that John the Elder was the beloved disciple (a resident of Jerusalem and not a member of the Twelve) and the author of the Fourth Gospel and the Johannine letters. The idea that this elder was a priest comes from a letter written in the last decade of the second century by Polycrates, bishop of Ephesus (*HE* 5.24.2-7). But there are other similar Christian references (*Test* p45), the most important being that James the Lord's brother was a priest. Neither seems credible: for example Josephus, although he describes how James was killed, does not mention this aspect (*Ant* 20.200).

Prudence is necessary, because we are dealing with extracts, and so we do not know the context. In this situation, we must beware of concentrating too much on the meaning of the Greek words, and charging them with a load they cannot withstand.

However, there are good reasons to suppose (*CJohn* p70) that the Greek syntax really means *"Ariston and the aforementioned elder John"*. The distinction Papias is making in his two lists is then, not between apostles and elders of the next generation, but between first generation eyewitnesses (what they *said*) and the first-generation witnesses who are still alive (what they *say*) (*CJohn* p70 and *Eye* p419). Nor are apostle and elder mutually exclusive (see 1 Peter 1:1 and 5:1).

It is clear also that (*CJohn* p70; *Eye* p424) Eusebius had his own agenda. He wanted to make a distinction between the two Johns (see *HE* 3.39.5-8) in order to attribute the authorship of Revelation to John the Elder, whom he did not regard as a disciple of Jesus. He could thus describe Revelation as non-apostolic and non-canonical.

So, the Papias extracts show that John's Gospel existed when Papias wrote between AD 100 and 107 (*Eye* p14). The view that John's Gospel and the Johannine letters were written by a second figure, John the Elder, a priestly resident of Jerusalem and not a member of the Twelve, strains the Papias extract to its limit. On balance, it seems more likely that the extract supports the authorship of John the disciple, the son of Zebedee. This will become clearer as we examine the rest of the external evidence.

For Irenaeus, the beloved disciple is John the son of Zebedee and author of John's Gospel:

"Afterwards, John, the disciple of the Lord, who had also leaned upon his breast, did himself publish a Gospel during his residence at Ephesus in Asia." (*AH* 3.1.1 and *HE* 5.8.4)

This is clearly a reference to John 13:23, which means the writer of the Gospel was a member of the twelve (*HRNT* p153). Irenaeus knew Polycarp personally. Polycarp was intimate with the apostles and was bishop of the church at Smyrna (*HE* 3.36.1). He was martyred in AD 156 at the age of 86 (*CJohn* p26). Irenaeus reports Polycarp's *"converse with John and the others who had seen the Lord, how he remembered their words, and what were the things concerning the Lord which he heard from them, including his miracles and teaching, and how Polycarp had received from eyewitnesses the word of life, and reported all things in agreement with the Scriptures."* (*HE* 5.20.5-6)

The inference is that Polycarp is referring to John the son of Zebedee, the author of the Fourth Gospel (see again *AH* 3.1.1).

The importance of Irenaeus's witness cannot be overestimated. Table 1.1 (Bauckham's Table 17 (*Eye* p471)) shows Irenaeus's sources of information and they constitute a direct line back to Jesus (the references are to *AH*). He knew Polycarp and would have had information from the churches at Ephesus when he lived nearby in Smyrna. He had a written source, the works of Papias, who was *"a hearer of John and companion of Polycarp"* (*AH* 5.33.4 and *HE* 3.39.1-2). Irenaeus also refers to those who had been disciples of John and the other apostles or disciples of Jesus who had settled in the area (*AH* 5.30.1). So, these four sources (the church in Ephesus, those who saw John, Polycarp and Papias) converge on Irenaeus (*Eye* p471), but they go back through John, the apostles and ultimately to Jesus himself.

The Anti-Marcionite Prologues (*CJohn* p27) inform us that the Gospel of John was published while John was still alive, and was written down by Papias, a man from Hierapolis and one of John's close disciples. However, although the rest may be true, the writing by Papias is unsupported from other sources (*FFBR* p45).

Clement of Alexandria (*HE* 6.14.7) and Origen (*HE* 6.25.6) both clearly attribute the Fourth Gospel to John the disciple.

Eusebius resumes things well:

"The beloved disciple of Jesus, John the apostle and evangelist, still surviving, governed the churches in Asia after his return from exile on the island and the death of Domitian. But that he was still living at this time, it may suffice to prove by the testimony of two witnesses...Irenaeus and Clement of Alexandria...John continued with them until the times of Trajan." (*HE* 3.23.1-4) (See also *AH* 2.22.5 and 3.3.4).

He also gives some indication of why John felt he could make a contribution, by completing the account of the beginning of Jesus' ministry (*HE* 3.24.7-17).

3. John Timeline

We will try to narrow down the possible dates of writing of John's Gospel by piecing together John's later life. Although we have already seen that Eusebius himself was an exception, the early church generally accepted (see for example Origen *HE* 6.25 and Irenaeus *AH* 4.20.11) that John the apostle wrote both the Gospel and Revelation.

Eusebius states that John died at Ephesus (*HE* 3.3.1; 3.31.4), while Jerome (in the fourth century) (*CJohn* p83) puts John's death in the sixty-eighth year after our Lord's passion, that is in AD 98, just into the reign of Trajan (AD 98-117) (*HE* 3.23.4; *AH* 2.22.5 and 3.3.4). Hence, the Gospel was published no later than AD 98.

Now the Roman Emperors during this period were Domitian (AD 81-96), Nerva (AD 96-98) and Trajan (AD 98-117) (see the John Timeline Chart 8.1[47]).

Domitian was cruel and brutal. Suetonius (*Caesars:* Domitian 10) tells us that his cruelty reached extreme heights after the rebellion of Antonius in AD 86 (*Caesars:* Domitian 6). So, the persecution and exiling of target Christians would date from AD 86 and John would probably find himself on Patmos (*HE* 3.18.2). In addition (*HSC* p4), Revelation 6:6 seems to refer to events which happened, according to Suetonius (*Caesars:* Domitian 7.2 and 14.2) and an inscription, in AD 92 and 93. From Irenaeus, we know that John wrote Revelation towards the end of Domitian's reign (*HE* 3.18.3) (say between AD 93 and 96) and narrowed down to the 15th year of Domitian's reign (*HE* 3.18.4), that is AD 95-96. This is also Hemer's (*HSC* p5) conclusion.

Nerva became Emperor in September AD 96 and reversed the exiles policy. Clement of Alexandria says that John came from Patmos to Ephesus on the death of Domitian and the accession of Nerva (*HE* 3.23.6). Tertullian (*HE* 3.20.8-9) puts it like this:

"But after Domitian had reigned fifteen years, and Nerva succeeded to the government, the Roman Senate decreed, that the honours of Domitian should be revoked, and that those who had been unjustly expelled, should return to their homes, and have their goods restored. This is the statement of the historians of the day. It was then also that the apostle John returned from his banishment on Patmos, and took up his abode in Ephesus, according to an ancient tradition of the church."

---

[47] J A T Robinson, *Redating the New Testament*, SCM Press, London, 1976, has argued that Revelation concerned the persecution by Nero, but this seems to fly in the face of the evidence.

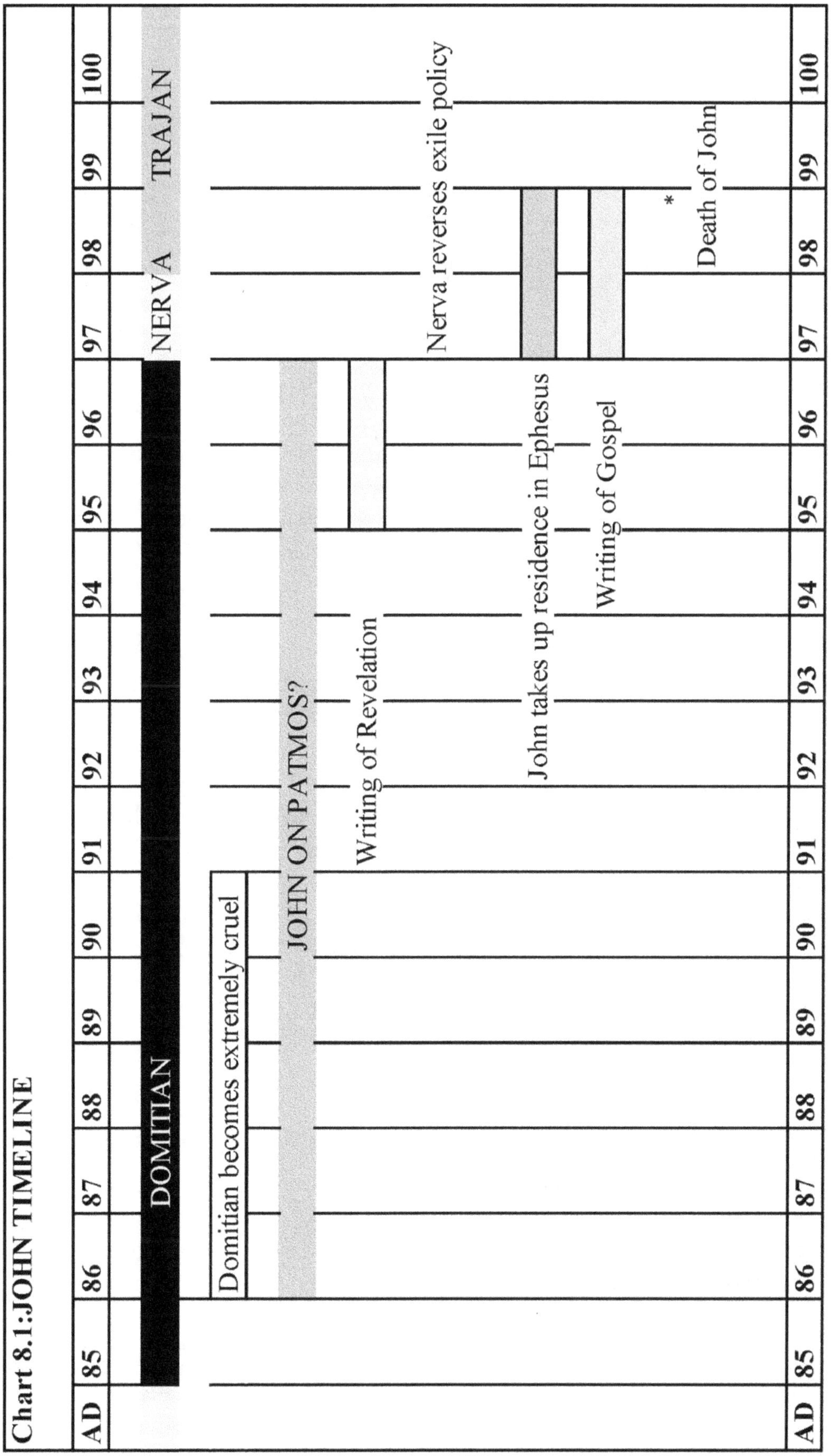

Chart 8.1: JOHN TIMELINE

AD	85	86	87	88	89	90	91	92	93	94	95	96	97	98	99	100

DOMITIAN (85–96) | **NERVA** (96–98) | **TRAJAN** (98–100)

Domitian becomes extremely cruel

JOHN ON PATMOS?

Writing of Revelation

Nerva reverses exile policy

John takes up residence in Ephesus

Writing of Gospel

* Death of John

Thus (see the John Timeline Chart 8.1 and Ramsay (*SC* p90)), John takes up his abode in Ephesus in AD 96, apparently for the first time, on his return from Patmos in AD 96, and dies there, having published his Gospel, in AD 98.

We thus arrive at the straightforward conclusion that John's Gospel dates from AD 96-98 and Revelation from AD 95-96[48].

An earlier date for the Gospel would imply that John had previously resided at Ephesus, before his exile on Patmos, between say AD 81 and 86 (which would correspond with the dating in *CJohn* p20), but we have no firm indication of this.

4. Conclusion

From the internal evidence, it is clear that the Gospel was written by "*the disciple whom Jesus loved*". Both the internal and external evidence strongly suggest that "*the disciple whom Jesus loved*" should be identified with John, the son of Zebedee, a member of the Twelve, a Jewish fisherman from Bethsaida (1:44) on the shores of the Sea of Galilee. He was a young man during the time of Jesus' ministry and therefore represented no threat to the élites in Jerusalem, although he knew them (18:16). He could thus also live to a good old age after Jesus' ascension (21:23).

He used his own eyewitness testimony and that of Peter to write his Gospel, which had an evangelistic purpose (20:31). John probably also wished to complete the account of Jesus' earlier ministry.

John died in Ephesus in AD 98, just living into the reign of Trajan (AD 98-117). We have good reason to believe that the Gospel was written down while John was still alive, perhaps by Papias himself. Papias certainly had knowledge of the written Gospel. A detailed analysis of the external evidence confirms the place of writing as Ephesus and puts the date of writing between AD 96 and AD 98.

Although this has not been underlined in the above investigation, John's Gospel covers a different time span than the Synoptic Gospels. The latter cover a period of approximately eighteen months, and much of the material concerns Jesus' ministry in Galilee. However, John's Gospel covers a three-year period, with more journeys to Jerusalem and back, and more on Jesus' earlier ministry. We will deal with this point when we consider the coherence of the four Gospels.

Thus, John, although he presumably had all three Synoptic Gospels at his disposal when he wrote, did not try to copy them. Instead, he interacted with them to produce a Gospel to complement them or fill in the gaps.

5. OVERALL CONCLUSION TO THE ORIGINS OF THE GOSPELS

We have seen in Table 7.1 and in the previous section that the Gospel writers had very different professions and profiles. In terms of profession, to a Gentile physician (Luke), a young Jewish clerk from Jerusalem (Mark) and an older Jewish border customs officer from the Galilean countryside (Matthew), we now add a young Jewish fisherman from the Tetrarchy of

---

[48] Any differences in style between the two books could then be explained, on the one hand, by the difference in *genre* and, on the other, by the idea that John employed different scribes on Patmos and at Ephesus.

Philip (John). This wide range of backgrounds and professions means that each Gospel writer is likely to contribute his own hues and colours, because their ways of looking at things are so varied.

As regards profiles, we have an inseparable companion of the apostle Paul (Luke), a young man who was like a son to the apostle Peter as he grew older (Mark) and a young man who was very close to Jesus and to Peter in his early days (John). We have two members of the original twelve disciples (Matthew and John) and one member of the inner three (John) who went nearly everywhere with Jesus. These are very solid credentials.

Then, as we consider the eyewitnesses, whose testimony these writers called upon, we also end up with a wide spectrum, as in the Table 8.1 (on the next page).

Matthew's Gospel is based on the evidence of his own eyes, as one of the original twelve disciples. John bases his Gospel on his own eyewitness testimony, as one of the inner group of three disciples (Peter, James and John) who were closest to Jesus, and on that of Peter. Mark's Gospel is based on the eyewitness testimony of the apostle Peter, as expressed in *chreiai*, the short narratives of his preaching. Luke presents the widest range of eyewitnesses, beginning with the apostle Peter. But he also includes the testimony of Mary Magdalene and Joanna, the wife of Chuza, the manager of Herod Antipas's household. These two women must have represented the extremes of the social classes of the time! Nor can we ignore the possibility that Luke used the testimony of Mary, the mother of Jesus (2:19, 51). Finally, it is possible that Luke used the evidence of Susanna (8:3), Mary the mother of James (24:10), Philip the Evangelist and Mnason (Acts 21).

These eyewitnesses were all well-placed to hear and see the life of Jesus in all its fullness. First of all, there were the two members of the inner circle of three around Jesus (Peter and John) and then Matthew, a member of the original band of twelve disciples. Luke also uses the eyewitness testimony of the women around Jesus, such as Mary Magdalene and Joanna who, among others supported him materially and financially (8:2-3). All these eyewitnesses have extremely good credentials, even if it was unusual at the time to place much value on evidence from women. If, in addition, Mary the mother of Jesus, was one of Luke's eyewitnesses, she was clearly an excellent source of information. It is therefore not surprising that, in the following chapters, we will discover that all their eyewitness testimony is of the highest quality.

In Part IV we will examine the correspondence of the Gospels with reality.

Table 8.1: THE GOSPEL WRITERS AND THEIR EYEWITNESSES

Author	Matthew	John Mark	Luke	John
Origin	Jew	Jew	Gentile	Jew
From	Capernaum, Galilee	Jerusalem	Antioch, Syria	Bethsaida
Profession	Border customs officer	Clerk?	Doctor	Fisherman
Profile	Member of 12	Companion of Paul; Filial interpreter of Peter	Inseparable companion of Paul	Member of Jesus' inner circle of three (Peter, James, John)
Eyewitnesses used	Himself	Peter, as expressed in his preaching	Peter, Mary Magdalene, Joanna, wife of Chuza	Himself and Peter
Other possible eyewitnesses used			Mary, mother of Jesus (Luke 2:19, 51)	

PART IV: THE CORRESPONDENCE OF THE GOSPELS

Chapter 9

THE BIRTH NARRATIVES

In this section we will show that the Gospels frequently talk of people and events which can be verified from other sources. In other words, they correspond with reality. We begin, in this chapter, with the Star of Bethlehem, the Magi and the shepherds. Then we move on to deal with Quirinius and the censuses and end with Lysanias.

THE STAR OF BETHLEHEM

David Hughes, Professor of Astronomy at Sheffield University, UK, has produced what is probably the most thorough recent work on this subject. He followed up two papers in the scientific journal *Nature* with his book *"The Star of Bethlehem Mystery" (Star)* in 1979. His research came to the fore once again in 2010/2011 when the BBC launched its television series *"The Nativity,"* written by Tony Jordan, scriptwriter of *"Eastenders."* This suggested that the star was, in fact, an unusually bright planetary conjunction.

The star only appears in Matthew's Gospel:

"After Jesus was born in Bethlehem in Judea, during the time of King Herod, Magi from the east came to Jerusalem and asked "Where is the one who has been born King of the Jews? We saw his star in the east and have come to worship him."" (Matthew 2:1-2)

There is already quite a lot of information here (*Star* p1):

1. Jesus was born in Bethlehem in Judea, about 6 miles south of Jerusalem

2. Jesus was born before the death of Herod the Great, that is before 11th April 4 BC

3. The Magi were more than one in number and came from the east

4. They did not know where Jesus had been born, so they went to the Palestine capital, Jerusalem, and asked Herod for information

5. The words *"his star"* indicate that the wise men thought one star was important and this was associated with *the* King of the Jews or the Messiah, whom the Jewish people were awaiting

6. In view of both the religious and astronomical tendencies of the Magi, this association must have been astrological.

The Magi considered the message important enough to travel about 750 miles to find and worship the king. There is no indication that they followed the star to Jerusalem. The implication is that they had seen the rising of the star in their homeland and simply came to Jerusalem to seek more information (*Star* p2).

The term *"in the east"* or *"en te Anatole"* almost certainly describes an *acronychal rising*. Here the star or planet rises in the east as the Sun sets in the west. The star or planet can then be seen throughout the night as it moves across the sky in an arc from east to west. It was also one of the five principal astrological positions that Babylonian astronomers studied. They calculated the positions of Mars, Jupiter and Saturn for many decades in advance. When a planet was in its acronychal rising position, it was regarded as having its maximum influence on world events.

Matthew's account continues, presumably in Herod's palace in Jerusalem:

"When Herod heard this he was disturbed, and all Jerusalem with him. When he had called together all the people's chief priests and teachers of the law, he asked them where the Christ was to be born. "In Bethlehem in Judea," *they replied,* "For this is what the prophet has written:

"But you Bethlehem, in the land of Judah, are by no means least among the rulers of Judah; for out of you will come a ruler who will be the shepherd of my people Israel." (Micah 5:2)

Then Herod called the Magi secretly and found out from them the exact time the star had appeared. He sent them to Bethlehem and said, "Go and make a careful search for the child. As soon as you find him, report to me, so that I too may go and worship him."

After they had heard the king, they went on their way, and the star they had seen in the east went ahead of them until it stopped over the place where the child was. When they saw the star, they were overjoyed. On coming to the house, they saw the child with his mother Mary, and they bowed down and worshipped him. Then they opened their treasures and presented him with gifts of gold and of incense and of myrrh. And having been warned in a dream not to go back to Herod, they returned to their own country by another route." (Matthew 2:3-12)

Clearly, Herod the local war lord, promoted puppet king by the Romans, felt insecure because of the new King of the Jews. So, he called in the Magi secretly and asked the time of the star's *heliacal rising,* the earliest rising of the star at dawn (*Star* p4). The heliacal rising, in the popular astrology of the day, was thought to coincide with the birth date of a person. Thus, Herod was asking when the child was born. This obviously has a link with the Massacre of the Innocents in Matthew 2:16-18.

A second significant star phenomenon occurred (2:9) as the Magi left Herod's palace, which made them overjoyed. Then the star *"went ahead of them"* and came to its zenith where the child was. This presents some astronomical problems because, of course, a star is so far away that it will inevitably stand over every object in the neighbourhood (*Star* p7).

Nevertheless, we can see that Matthew 2 records two significant star phenomena: one in the east (the acronychal rising) possibly before the wise men set out and then another, which must have lasted for at least one and a half hours, as they journeyed from Jerusalem to Bethlehem (*Star* p8). Thus, we can resume the main facts concerning the star (*Star* p16):

1. The star was first seen by the wise men when they were in the east

2. They observed its acronychal rising

3. At this time it had a distinct astrological meaning

4. Herod and all Jerusalem had overlooked its significance

5. A second significant star phenomenon occurred again when they were in Jerusalem and then went before them and *"stood over"* Bethlehem.

The Magi

It is difficult to pin down exactly who the Magi were. Most commentators agree (*ME* p52 and *FMatt2* p75) that their gifts of gold, frankincense and myrrh originated in Arabia, but it does not follow that the Magi came from there. For the prophet Daniel (2:2) they would have been Babylonian magicians and astrologers, and this remains the most probable identification. For Herodotus (*Star* p32), they were a priestly caste of Medes or Zoroastrian priests. So, they could have come from Media, Assyria or Babylonia. If they did indeed come from Babylonia (Is 47:13), then they would have travelled through the Fertile Crescent, following the Euphrates Valley at first, then going through Syria, via Mari, Tadmor and Damascus to Jerusalem – a distance of 750 miles. T E Lawrence, writing on the Arab Revolt in *The Seven Pillars of Wisdom*, states that a fully laden camel, under an experienced rider could cover 80-100 miles per day and that 50 miles per day was really a holiday. Thus, the journey would have taken 10-15 days. Even if two weeks' preparation were necessary to secure supplies and so on, then an overall period of one month would be sufficient (*BAH* p336 says 6 weeks; *Star* p42 says 3 to 4 months). This means that the star must have appeared in the east, carried on in the night sky and made a second significant appearance in Jerusalem after a 1–2-month interval. However, the Babylonians were capable of predicting certain planetary movements by calculation, so they could have left their home country before the acronychal rising of the "star."

What Luke's Gospel tells us

In order to consult the Chinese and Babylonian astronomical records of the time we need to zero in on the date of Christ's birth. We already know that it was not in 0 BC at all[49], but before 11th April 4 BC. We now need to look for the earliest possible date of Jesus' birth. In Luke's gospel we read:

"In those days Caesar Augustus issued a decree that a census should be taken of the entire Roman world. (This was the first census that took place while Quirinius was governor of Syria.) And everyone went to his own town to register.

So Joseph also went up from the town of Nazareth in Galilee to Judea, to Bethlehem the town of David, because he belonged to the house and the line of David. He went here to register with Mary, who was pledged to be married to him and was expecting a child. While they were there, the time came for the baby to be born, and she gave birth to her firstborn, a son...

And there were shepherds living out in the fields near by, keeping watch over their flocks by night...

---

[49] In 533 AD, Dionysius Exiguus was given the task of changing calendars from the Roman one to one based on Jesus' birth. Unfortunately, he made some errors in his calculations, omitting the four years when the Roman Emperor Augustus ruled under his own name of Octavian, for example (*BAH* p338).

On the eighth day when it was time to circumcise him, he was named Jesus, the name the angel had given him before he had been conceived.

When the time of their purification according to the Law of Moses had been completed, Joseph and Mary took him to Jerusalem to present him to the Lord." (Luke 2:1-8; 21-22)

In this way, the accounts of Matthew and Luke can be put together to obtain the Birth Narratives Timeline Chart 9.1. The holy family would have stayed in Bethlehem, at least until 40 days after the birth of Jesus, in order to be close to Jerusalem for the purification of Mary.

Now Augustus Caesar reigned from 31 BC to AD 14. He organized the Roman Empire, first of all enrolling the people in a census and then, say two years later, taxing people according to the number in the household (Poll Tax) and the land that they owned. Tacitus (*Annals* 1.11, 31 and 33) talks of censuses under Augustus and Tiberius.

QUIRINIUS AND THE CENSUS

In the late 19th century, the holding of a census when Herod the Great was still alive and Quirinius was Governor of Syria, was called into doubt. This was mainly because both Josephus and Acts 5:37 recount a census in AD 6, when Quirinius was Governor of Syria, which led to the revolt of Judas the Galilean, the founder of the Zealots. It seems best to read the Greek text of Luke 2:2 as *"This census was before* (one) *when Quirinius was governor"* (*HRNT* p60; *DBLuke* p909).

The first census, then, would have been carried out under Jewish rules, because Herod the Great was still alive and Judea was not yet under the direct rule of a Roman Prefect. Each person in the census was required to return to where his family originated. The second census, in AD 6, when Quirinius was Governor, was carried out under direct Roman rule, against Jewish custom, imposed the Roman Poll Tax, and thus sparked the revolt (*Star* p50).

So, if indeed there was a census, while Herod the Great was still alive, when did it occur? From Egypt (*BAH* p329; *Star* p52), there is evidence that such censuses were carried out every 14 years. This would place the first census 14 years before AD 6, that is in 8 BC, with a margin of error of +/- 2 years (see also *HRNT* p104).

Chart 9.1: BIRTH NARRATIVES TIMELINE

	D **Birth of Jesus**	D + 7 days	D + 40 days (see *IHML* p116)	D + about 2 months	D + about 2 years 2 months
LUKE	2:4-20 Bethlehem	chapter 2 verse 21 Jerusalem Circumcision of Jesus (see Exodus 22:30 & Leviticus 12:2-8)	2:22-38 Jerusalem Purification of Mary (see Leviticus 12:2-8)		
MATTHEW				2:1-2 Magi arrive in Jerusalem 2:9-12 Then Magi arrive in Bethlehem to worship Jesus 2:13-19 Flight to Egypt	**Death of Herod** Matthew 2:21-23 Luke 2:39
LOCATION OF HOLY FAMILY	Bethlehem			Egypt	Nazareth

87

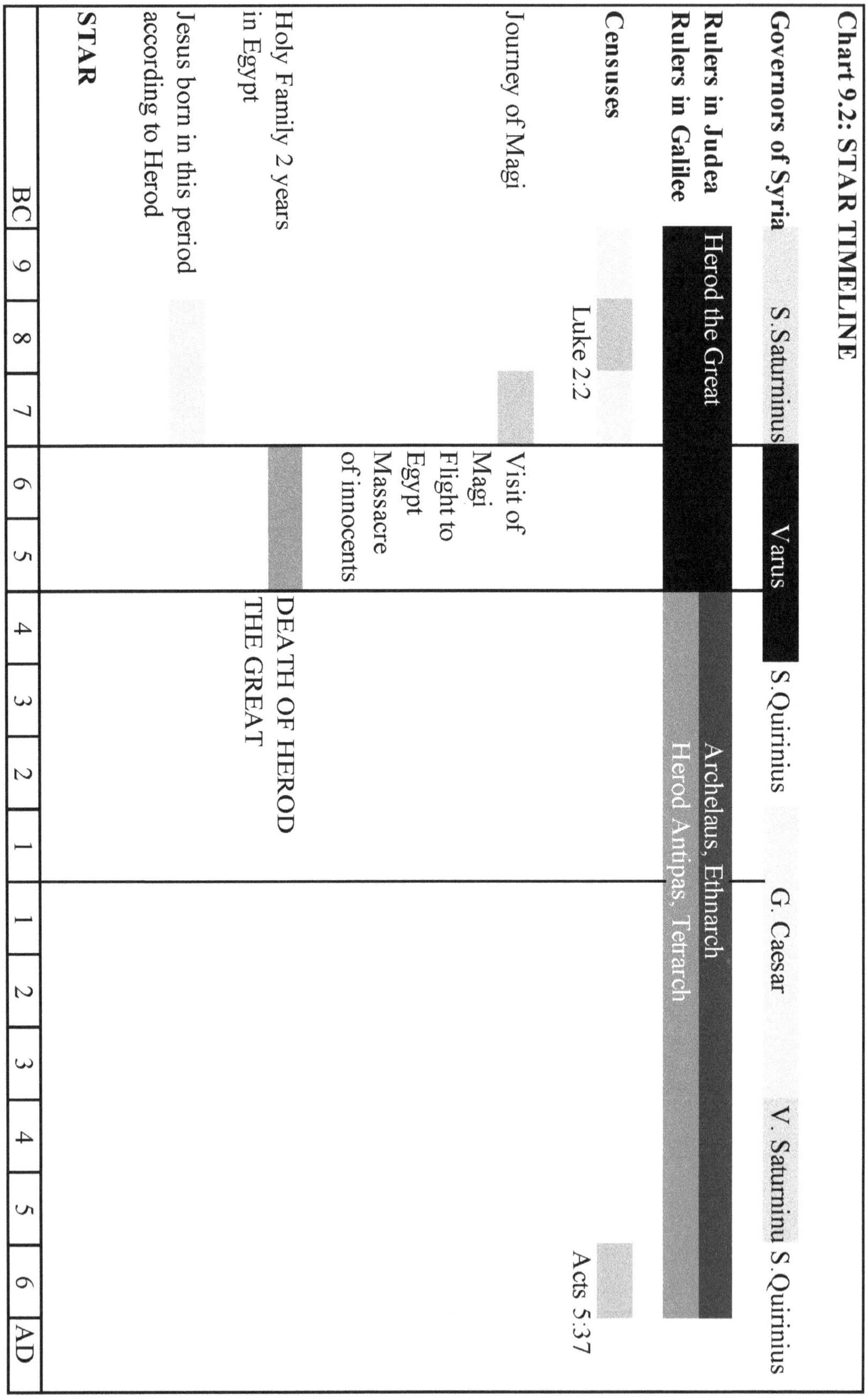

Chart 9.2: STAR TIMELINE

	BC									AD						
	9	8	7	6	5	4	3	2	1	1	2	3	4	5	6	AD
Governors of Syria	S. Saturninus			Varus			S. Quirinius			G. Caesar				V. Saturninus		S. Quirinius
Rulers in Judea	Herod the Great									Archelaus, Ethnarch						
Rulers in Galilee	Herod the Great									Herod Antipas, Tetrarch						
Censuses	Luke 2:2															Acts 5:37
Journey of Magi																
Holy Family 2 years in Egypt				Visit of Magi / Flight to Egypt / Massacre of innocents		DEATH OF HEROD THE GREAT										
Jesus born in this period according to Herod																
STAR																

The Birth of Jesus

All this means that Jesus was born somewhere between 8 BC and 11th April 4 BC, although we will follow Hughes (*Star* p 58) who suggests that between 8 BC and 6th December 5 BC is more likely. Two further points need to be taken into account. Firstly, Origen[50] and Eusebius[51] both state that Joseph and Mary stayed in Egypt for two years before the death of Herod. Secondly, Herod massacred the infant boys of two years or under (Matthew 2:16). This gives the Star Timeline Chart 9.2. Taking into account the date of the census, the length of the journey of the Magi, the death of Herod, the time in Egypt, the Massacre of the Innocents etc, we can see from the chart that Jesus was born between January 8 BC and December 7 BC, with 7 BC being the most likely date.

We also know from the Talmud (*BAH* pp338-339) that sheep flocks were put out to grass in March and brought back in at the beginning of November. This was because, firstly, the temperatures at night were below freezing between December and February and, secondly, because the rainfall was heavy in December and January.

The Nature of the "Star"

Remembering that the "Star" of Bethlehem has to fulfil the five conditions laid out previously, Hughes examines the various events which were recorded by Chinese and Babylonian astronomers: comets, novae, supernovae, planets and celestial phenomena (*Star* pp 140-176).

Novae are previously unknown stars which flare up in brightness by a factor of 10-13, before declining rapidly to their pre-nova magnitude. Supernovae are like novae but the energy emission is about 1000 times that of a nova. Such events occur about every 50 to 100 years.

However, the Babylonian astrologers did not consider comets, novae or supernovae or other unforeseen celestial phenomena as worthy of primary astrological consideration. This was reserved for planetary positions which could be predicted well in advance by detailed calculations.

The suggestion that the star was a triple conjunction of Saturn and Jupiter turns out to be much more promising. The great astronomer Johannes Kepler first proposed this in 1603/4 (*BAH* p334; *Star* p100). These two planets sometimes come together in the sky[52]. It is a slow process: they approach each other, usually stay together for a time (the conjunction), and then separate. On rare occasions, about every 139 years, Jupiter and Saturn come together three times, in about a year, to make a "triple conjunction" (*Star* p94). Triple conjunctions of Jupiter and Saturn in Pisces are even rarer, occurring about every 900 years (*Star* p110). One of these occurred between May and December 7 BC, which is exactly the time when we think Jesus was born. The Babylonians would have interpreted Saturn as meaning Yahweh or the Jews, Jupiter as the King of the Jews or the Messiah, and Pisces as the land of Palestine (*Star* p190). Jewish astrologers, and some may well have stayed behind in Babylon after the exile of their people, would have

---

[50] Origen, *Commentary on Matthew*, Frag 23.
[51] Eusebius, *Questiones ad Stephanum* XVI, 2.
[52] More precisely, the planets Earth, Jupiter and Saturn are in line in the heavens.

interpreted a conjunction of Jupiter and Saturn in Pisces as announcing the appearance of the Messiah (*BAH* p334).

The Triple Conjunction of Jupiter and Saturn in Pisces in 7 BC

During the 7 BC triple conjunction of Jupiter and Saturn in Pisces, for most of the time the two planets moved from right to left (in the forward direction) across the sky. But for about 100 days the motion was in the opposite (retrograde) direction and sometimes the two planets seemed to stop in their tracks and then recommence their normal motion from right to left. These stationary points were of particular interest to, and could be predicted by, Babylonian astronomers. Indeed (*Star* p122), these data have been preserved in Babylonian calendar tablets, the archives of the Babylonians. Moreover, during the 7 BC triple conjunction in Pisces, Jupiter would have been 500 times brighter than the brightest stars in Pisces and Saturn 38 times brighter.

All this, together with the astrological significance described above, makes the 7 BC triple conjunction of Jupiter and Saturn in the constellation Pisces, a very strong candidate for the Star of Bethlehem. It fulfils the five conditions we laid down earlier.

The Events of 7 BC

Before we try to piece together the events of 7 BC, we recall that the Babylonian astronomers could predict by calculation the heliacal and acronychal risings of Jupiter and Saturn and their stationary points. They would also have associated the heliacal rising with births, while the acronychal rising was regarded as having a maximum influence on world events. However, they could not accurately predict the planetary conjunctions (*Star* p122 Table 6.4).

In Table 9.1, we combine together Hughes' data from his Figures 17 and 18 and above all Table 10.1 (*Star* p190) for the triple conjunction of Jupiter and Saturn in Pisces in 7 BC. We note that there are a number of extraordinary events: the two planets are very close at the first conjunction, about two months after the heliacal rising. Then the two planets are very close and in retrograde motion between the acronychal rising on 14-15 September and the second conjunction on 6 October 7 BC. They then stay very close together for the two second stationary points and the third conjunction. Only in 6 BC do the planets begin to separate and leave Pisces. Two very bright objects, very close together, would certainly have attracted the attention of our Babylonian astronomers[53].

---

[53] This was impressively demonstrated in a BBC TV programme at 4.50 pm on Christmas Eve 2018: "Chris and Michaela under the Christmas Sky," presented by Chris Packham and Michaela Strachan. First, they showed a live Mars/Jupiter conjunction and then a simulation by a Jordanian astronomer of the 7 BC Jupiter/Saturn triple conjunction.

Table 9.1: The Principal Dates of Triple Conjunction of Jupiter and Saturn in Pisces in 7 BC				
Phenomenon	Date(s)	Planetary Movements		Planetary Separation (Degrees)
		Jupiter	Saturn	
Heliacal rising	11 March	F	F	7.7
First conjunction	27 May	F	F	0.98
First stationary point Saturn	6 July			2.5
First stationary point Jupiter	17 July			2.8
Mid conjunction	3 September	R	R	2.0
Acronychal rising	14-15 September	R	R	1.34
Second conjunction	6 October	R	R	0.98
Mid point of second and third conjunction	31 October	R	R	1.42
Second stationary point Jupiter	11 November			1.44
Second stationary point Saturn	19 November			1.46
Third conjunction	1 December	F	F	1.05
Jupiter, Saturn, Mars massing	mid February 6 BC			6.4
Heliacal setting	about 13 March 6 BC			8.5

NOTES: Planetary movements: F= Forward from right to left in the sky
R= Retrograde from left to right in the sky
Planetary separation: 1 degree is approximately the distance of the diametre of two full moons.

Clearly, the exact timing of events depends on when the Magi left Babylonia and how long they took to travel the 750 odd miles to Jerusalem. Werner Keller (*BAH* pp335-337) gives one scenario and David Hughes and d'Occhippo (*Star* p190) another. My own simpler version draws on these two scenarios.

I consider that the events were as follows. The Magi had already been alerted by the numerous signs (the heliacal rising, the first conjunction and the first stationary points of Saturn and Jupiter in July 7 BC). However, it was really the remarkable acronychal rising of Jupiter and Saturn which galvanized these experts, because the two planets were very close together and were both in retrograde motion. They rose together, extremely bright, separated by the diameter of two full moons, in the sky of the same evening of Tuesday September 15th 7 BC, which the Magi took to be the day of Jesus' birth. Throughout the night, the two planets stayed together, moving across the sky in an arc from east to west. The Magi would have been amazed at the potential significance of these astral events. At that time of year, the shepherds would still have been in the fields with their flocks (Luke 2:8). The Magi planned their journey and got supplies in. Then, on the day of the second conjunction (October 6th), once again with the two planets in retrograde motion, which they could not have predicted, just after the Jewish Day of Atonement on October 3rd, the Magi departed. In this way, they avoided the worst heat of the Iraqi desert from June to September. About one month later they arrived in Jerusalem on November 11th. We can thus resume the events as in Table 9.2 (0n the next page).

Once again, it seems that it was the observation of the two second stationary points of Jupiter and Saturn, which the Magi would have predicted, that made them rejoice after their interview with Herod the Great (Matthew 2:9-10). Therefore, the Magi's journey from Jerusalem to Bethlehem took place between November 11th and 19th 7 BC, and the stationary points correspond to the *stopping* or the *standing still* of the star. Did the wise men stay to see the third conjunction, which they could not have predicted accurately? Probably not; by now they had been warned in a dream not to return to Herod (Matthew 2:12). They were almost certainly on their way back to their homeland and the holy family was on its way to Egypt. Then, at the turn of the year, the two planets separated and left Pisces, signalling that the momentous event was at an end.

This scenario seems to make the most sense: it takes into account the heat of the summer, the duration of the Magi's journey, the shepherds in the fields and the astronomical phenomena of the triple conjunction of 7 BC. One consequence of this version of events is that the time of Mary's purification and the arrival of the Magi in Jerusalem are very close together. This is important, firstly because the holy family must still be in Bethlehem in order to receive the Magi and, secondly, because at the time of Mary's purification the prophetess Anna began talking about Jesus to the people she met (Luke 2:38). Therefore, for Herod the Great not to be in the know, there must not be too long a delay between the two events.

Table 9.2: THE EVENTS AROUND JESUS' BIRTH IN 7 BC

Date	Astronomical Event	Magi/Shepherds	Holy Family
Sept 15th	Achronychal rising of Jupiter and Saturn	Shepherds in fields Magi plan trip	Birth of Jesus (Bethlehem)
Sept 22nd			Circumcision of Jesus (Jerusalem)
Oct 6th	Second conjunction	Magi leave Babylonia	
Oct 25th			Purification of Mary (Jerusalem)
Nov 11th	Second stationary point of Jupiter	Magi meet Herod and begin journey to Bethlehem	
Nov 19th	Second stationary point of Saturn	Magi warned in dream	Latest date for Magi to worship the infant Jesus
Dec 1st	Third conjunction	Magi going home	Holy family to Egypt

THE SHEPHERDS AND THE MANGER

The birth narratives have been dogged by some unfortunate translations, notably the *"no room in the inn"* of Luke 2:7. Kenneth Bailey (*ME* pp25-37) points out that the word *katalyma*, translated as *"inn"* in Luke 2:7, is not the Greek word for a commercial inn. The word for a commercial inn is found in Luke 10:34 and is *pandocheion*. *Katalyma* is simply a space to stay in. Furthermore:

1. Joseph was returning to his home town and had time to make prior arrangements

2. He was from the royal line of David

3. His wife to be was pregnant.

Given this background, in a Middle-Eastern culture, the population of Bethlehem would have done everything possible to welcome Joseph and Mary.

In Figure 9.1 (see image on the next page) we see a typical Palestinian home of the period (*ME* p33). The mangers were located, not in a separate building, but on the edge of the raised family living room, where the animals, who were brought into the lower section of the house at night, could conveniently reach them. Steps led from the family living area down to the "stables"[54] and there were outside steps leading to the sturdy roof[55], made of wooden beams or branches, thatched with rushes and daubed with mud (*FMark* p123, *DBLuke* p480)[56]. The rooms were no more than five metres across because they were limited by the length of the tree trunks used for the beams. Not all houses would have had a guest room. The point of the mangers is therefore that Jesus' birth took place in a normal house, but that in that particular house the guest room (or *katalyma*,) was already occupied, probably by other visitors for the census. The baby was then placed in the most comfortable remaining area, a manger in the living room floor.

The shepherds, on the other hand (*ME* p35) were poor and, according to Rabbinic tradition, unclean. So, the shepherds were probably afraid at the sight of the angels (Luke 2:8-14), but were then invited to *visit* the child. Being considered unclean, they expected to be rejected if they did. However, the angels told them that they would find the baby *wrapped* – which was exactly what the shepherds did to their new-born children – and that he was lying in a *manger*. In other words, the shepherds would find the baby Jesus in an ordinary peasant home such as theirs. Thus reassured, they were the first to visit the Christ child. The outcasts became honoured guests (see also the translation by Tom Wright of Luke 2:7 in *TWNT* and *TWLuke* p21-22).

THE MASSACRE OF THE INNOCENTS (MATTHEW 2:16-18)

Herod the Great was, especially in his later years, an extremely violent paranoiac megalomaniac. Therefore, his decision to order the slaughter of all the children in Bethlehem who were two years old or younger was quite in character (*FMatt2* p85).

---

[54] In Judea, where the soil is limestone, there are caves which can be used to accommodate animals. Around the Sea of Galilee, where the rock is basalt, there are fewer caves.

[55] The apostle Peter would have made his way down these outside stairs after his rooftop vision in Acts 10:9-21.

[56] Hence the need of the four to *"dig out"* the roof in Mark 2:4 so that their paralyzed friend could be healed by Jesus.

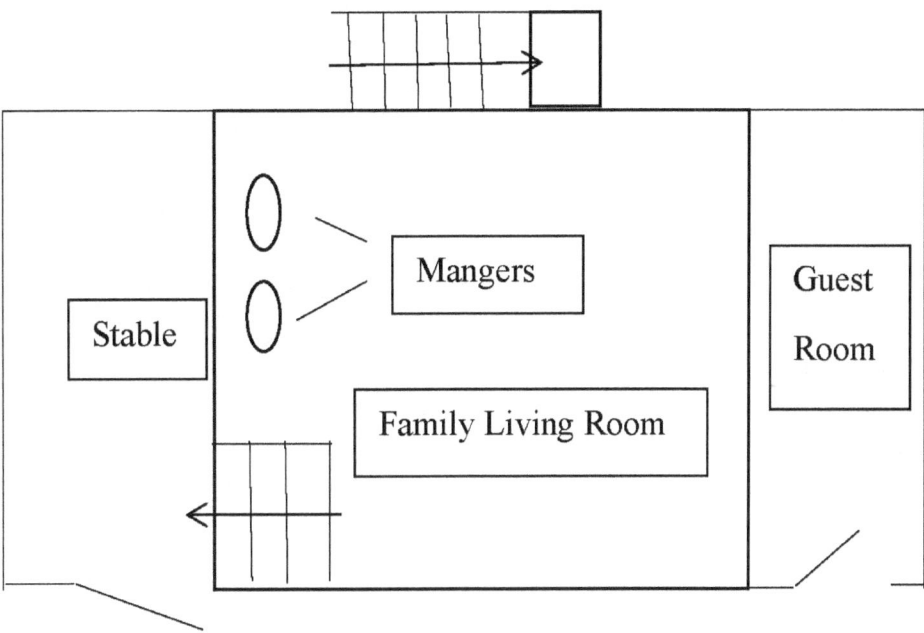

Figure 9.1: Typical Village Home in Palestine with Attached Guest Room.

Some have wondered why Josephus did not recount these events in his *Antiquities*. Firstly, this is an argument from silence and therefore unreliable (*HRNT* p105). Secondly, at the time, the population of Bethlehem was approximately one thousand, which means that the number of male children under two was probably no more than twenty or so. Therefore, although the crime was horrendous, it was small beer compared with Herod's or the Romans' other atrocities and so Josephus described more spectacular killings (*FMatt2* p85).

LYSANIAS

It is sometimes supposed that Luke made an error concerning Lysanias, who is said to have been Tetrarch of Abilene (west Damascus) in the fifteenth year of Tiberius (AD 27-28) (see Luke 3:1). The only Lysanias known from ancient history was thought to have borne the title of king and to have been executed by Mark Anthony in 34 BC. However, there is now evidence (*FFBR* pp72-73) from an inscription recording the dedication of a temple *"for the salvation of the Lords Imperial and their whole household, by Nymphaeus, a freedman of Lysanias the tetrarch."* The reference to *"Lords Imperial"* means the Emperor Tiberius and his mother Livia, the widow of Augustus, and fixes the date of the inscription between AD 14 (the year of Tiberius' accession to the throne) and AD 29 (the date of Livia's death). Josephus (*Ant* 19.5.1§275 and 20.7.1§138) seems to confirm the veracity of these inscriptions. So, once again, the external evidence shows that Luke's reference to Lysanias is entirely accurate (*DBLuke* p283).

CONCLUSION

Thus, Matthew's account of the star and Luke's account of the census are both amazingly and wonderfully true. As Professor Hughes remarks (*Star* p198), Matthew's record has the ring of truth. Modern astronomical observations and calculations confirm the Babylonian calendar tablets and the New Testament documents.

A remarkable series of astronomical events in 7 BC, with world-shattering astrological implications, led Babylonian Magi from their homeland to Palestine in order to worship the infant Messiah, Jesus. They observed precursor signs in the heavens: the first conjunction and the first stationary points of Jupiter and Saturn in the constellation Pisces. By their observation of the acronychal rising of the two planets they understood that the momentous birth of the Messiah or King (Jupiter) of Yahweh or the Jews (Saturn) in Palestine (Pisces) had taken place. By this time the two planets were extremely bright and close together in the sky and in retrograde motion. They planned their trip and set out after the second conjunction on October 6th. They arrived about one month later in Jerusalem and asked Herod the Great where the King of the Jews had been born. As they left for Bethlehem, they rejoiced because the star (Jupiter or Saturn) *stopped* or *stood still* (Matthew 2:9-10), just as they had predicted.

The Magi, wise men from Babylonia, observed and calculated the movement of the planets and interpreted their significance. They were the only people capable of this at the time. They understood that momentous events were under way; that is why they left their home country and came to Palestine. All the dates tie up: the census, the fact that Herod the Great was still alive, the shepherds in the fields, the circumcision of Jesus, the purification of Mary and the star standing still in the heavens. It is simply amazing.

Chapter 10

SOME IMPORTANT PERSONALITIES IN THE GOSPELS

In this chapter, we investigate some of the important personalities in the Gospels and whether other historical sources confirm what the Gospels say about them. We shall be looking at Pontius Pilate, John the Baptist and Herod Antipas, Caiaphas, Barabbas and Nicodemus.

Pontius Pilate

After eleven years in Judea, Gratus returned to Rome and Pontius Pilate became Prefect of Judea from AD 26-36, which means that the first years of his rule correspond with Jesus' public ministry. From Josephus, in particular, we learn that he was provocative and took every opportunity to snub the Jews. After all, his job was to collect the taxes and keep the lid on Judea, so that grain could flow freely from Egypt to feed Rome.

An inscription in Latin, dating from the reign of Pilate, was found in 1961 during an Italian archaeological excavation, led by Dr Antonio Fova, of the Herodian theatre at Caesarea Maritime. It reads:

S TIBERIEUM

TIUS PILATUS

ECTUS IUD..E

And there are indications that there was a fourth line on the original limestone block. Dr Fova believes the stone to be a dedication plaque and that the original complete text was probably:

CAESARIEN (SIBIU)S TIBERIEUM

(PON)TIUS PILATUS

(PRAEF)ECTUS IUD(AE)E

DEDIT or DEDICAVIT

Translated into English, this becomes "Pontius Pilate, Prefect of Judea dedicates (or has dedicated) this to Tiberius Caesar." The 82cm by 65cm dedication stone is now located in the Israel Museum at Jerusalem[57].

Tacitus, when recounting how the great fire of Rome broke out in AD 64 (*Annals* 15.44) has this to say about Pilate:

> "...*Nero fabricated scapegoats – and punished with every refinement the notoriously depraved Christians (as they were popularly called). Their originator, Christ, had been executed in Tiberius' reign by the governor of Judea, Pontius Pilatus. But in spite of this*

---

[57] See, for example, "Unearthing the New Testament," Premier Christianity, March 2017 p51.

temporary setback the deadly superstition had broken out afresh, not only in Judea (where the mischief had started) but even in Rome."

Whereas previous Roman Prefects had been careful to remove Caesar's effigies from their military ensigns *(signa)*, on entering Jerusalem, Pilate provoked the Jews. He moved the ensigns, with Caesar's effigies, into the city by night. The Jews protested as one man and Pilate was obliged to take the ensigns back to Caesarea (*BJ* 2.169-177; *Ant* 18.55-59).

He also took sacred money, from the Temple treasury, to finance the building of an aqueduct to bring water to Jerusalem. This time, Jewish protests were met with slaughter by Pilate's troops (*BJ* 2.177-180; *Ant* 18.60-62). Flavius Josephus continues:

"Now there was about this time Jesus, a wise man, if it be lawful to call him a man, for he was a doer of wonderful works – a teacher of such men as receive the truth with pleasure. He drew over to him both many of the Jews, and many of the Gentiles. He was (the) Christ; and when Pilate, at the suggestion of the principal men amongst us, had condemned him to the cross, those that loved him at the first did not forsake him, for he appeared to them alive again the third day, as the divine prophets had foretold these and ten thousand other wonderful things concerning him; and the tribe of Christians, so named after him, are not extinct at this day." (*Ant* 18.63-64)

Luke 13:1 describes another provocative act of Pontius Pilate:

"Now there were some present at that time who told Jesus about the Galileans whose blood Pilate had mixed with their sacrifices."

Pilate also slaughtered Samaritans, for which he was called to account before Tiberius. Marcellus took over the affairs of Judea but, by the time Pilate arrived in Rome, Tiberius was dead (*Ant* 18.85-87). Thus, we have information about Pontius Pilate from an inscription, from Tacitus and from Josephus. In addition, the Jewish historian Philo described him as *"naturally inflexible; a blend of self-will and relentlessness"* (*FMark* pp625-6). All these sources describe a person whose actions in Luke 13:1 and the rest of the Gospels are entirely in character. Archaeology and the Jewish and Roman historians present a coherent picture which corresponds with what we find in the Gospels.

John the Baptist and Herod Antipas

John the Baptist is an important figure in the Gospels because he precedes Jesus and continually points to him as, for example, *"The Lamb of God who takes away the sins of the world"* (John 1:29).

Josephus (*Ant* 18.117) describes John's mission as one of a baptism of repentance or remission of sins, in much the same terms as Matthew 3:1-6; Mark 1:3-8 or Luke 3:2-17. The Gospels and Josephus therefore agree that John's baptism was not the routine bathing of the Essenes (*BJ* 2.129-130). Nor was it the "proselyte baptism" of a Gentile in his initiation into Judaism, because John baptized *Jews* and because it seems unlikely that this rite existed as early as the time of John (*FMatt2* pp108-9). John baptized at Bethany, opposite Jericho on the east bank of the Jordan, in Perea, which was also ruled over by Herod Antipas, the Tetrarch (John 1:28).

Matthew 4:1-12 describes an incident which is also recorded in Mark 6:17-29, Luke 3:19 and by Flavius Josephus:

"At that time Herod the Tetrarch heard the reports about Jesus, and he said to his attendants, "This is John the Baptist; he has risen from the dead! That is why miraculous powers are at work in him."

Now Herod had arrested John and bound him and put him in prison because of Herodias, his brother Philip's wife, for John had been saying to him: "It is not lawful for you to have her." Herod wanted to kill John, but he was afraid of the people, because they considered him a prophet.

On Herod's birthday the daughter of Herodias danced for them and pleased Herod so much that he promised with an oath to give her what he asked. Prompted by her mother, she said, "Give me here on a platter the head of John the Baptist." The king was distressed but, because of his oaths and his dinner guests, he ordered that her request be granted and had John beheaded in the prison. His head was brought in on a platter and given to the girl, who carried it to her mother. John's disciples came and took his body and buried it. Then they came and told Jesus." (Matthew 4:1-12)

Herod Antipas had married Herodias, the wife of his half-brother Philip, and so drew the criticism of John the Baptist, whom he decapitated on the insistence of Salome (2), the seductive daughter of Herodias by her first marriage. Jesus called Herod Antipas a "fox" (Luke 13:32); he connived at the humiliation and crucifixion of Jesus (Luke 23:6-12).

We notice that Matthew has got the rank of Herod (Antipas) correct: Tetrarch, although he later more loosely calls him "king", which was not the case. Herod Antipas was Tetrarch of Galilee and Perea from 4 BC to 39 AD and thus the ruler of Galilee during Jesus' adult life.

Josephus (*Ant* 18.116-9) tells us that popular opinion attributed Herod Antipas' troubles with Aretas, the Nabatean king of Petra, to his earlier execution of John the Baptist, which had occurred in Herod's palace at Machaerus in Perea. The more specific issue mentioned above in Matthew 4:1-12 would be consistent with this, since Josephus also speaks of the political implications of Herod Antipas' marriage to Herodias, and the divorce of his previous wife which cleared the way for it (*Ant* 18.110-115; *Trust?* p96). As France (*FMatt2* p554) remarks, it was this *"brazenly irregular action which subsequently provoked the ruinous war with his former father-in-law, Aretas."*

In this way, we can see that Josephus and the Synoptic Gospels give complementary, but not contradictory, accounts of the mission, imprisonment and execution of John the Baptist.

Joseph Caiaphas

The older Annas, according to Josephus (*Ant* 20.197-200), had been High Priest from AD 6 to 15. He had five sons and all became high priests, in addition to his son-in-law Joseph Caiaphas and grandson. *Ant* 20.244-251 suggests also that the high priests, former and otherwise, acted together as a college and, in *Life* 5, Josephus describes his time living amongst the high priests and the chief of the Pharisees. We further learn from Acts 5:17 that Caiaphas, and therefore all of the Annas/Ananus family were Sadducees.

In any case, Annas as a retired high priest kept his title and must have exerted considerable power behind the scenes. Hence, when Caiaphas was High Priest, power was really a two-man affair, shared between Annas and Caiaphas (*DBLuke* p384). This is brought out in both Luke's Gospel (3:2) and John's Gospel (18:12-27).

Caiaphas, whose name was Joseph (*Ant* 18.35, 95), was installed as High Priest by the Prefect Gratus in AD 18 and continued in office until AD 37 (*IHML* p134) – a longer period than any other high priest in New Testament times, which means he must have got on well with the Romans. His existence has been confirmed by the discovery of his ornate ossuary (*Eye* pp82-3 and note 54; *HRNT* p143) as late as 1990, where he is known as Joseph bar Caiaphas.

Barabbas (Luke 23: 18-25; Mark 15 :7)

Josephus informs us that the Zealot party was "officially" founded by Judas the Galilean who led a revolt against Rome in AD 6 (*Ant* 18.1.23; Acts 5:1). These men were called Zealots because they manifested zeal for the Law of God as had Phineas and the Maccabees. They violently opposed the payment of tribute by Israel to a pagan emperor, on the grounds that it was treason to God, Israel's true king. Two of Judas's sons were crucified by the Procurator Tiberius Alexander in AD 46.

Then the name Zealot was reappropriated during the Jewish Revolt of AD 66-74; the Zealots were a major faction in the occupation of the Temple and the atrocities committed there (*BJ* 5.1-564).

However, the reality is that the spirit of violent rebellion against Rome, which the Zealots represented, was present throughout the period from AD 6 and especially from AD 40 onwards. Josephus repeatedly talks of brigands or bandits (see for example *BJ* 2.223-243). Thus, Judas the Galilean lit a Zealot flame which turned into a bush fire from AD 40 and then into full-scale revolt in AD 66-70.

On balance therefore, the apostle called Simon the Zealot (Luke 6:15; Acts 1:13) was unlikely to have been a member of the Zealot party, which was relatively quiescent in AD 27-30. His nickname came more likely from his zeal for the Jewish law (*FMatt2* p378; *Eye* p104). On the other hand, Barabbas who had *"been thrown into prison for insurrection and murder"* (Luke 23:18-25; Mark 15:7) was clearly in the Zealot party mould.

Nicodemus (John 3 :1-15)

According to John's Gospel, Nicodemus was a member of the Sanhedrin (3:1) and a Pharisee (7:47-51), who helped Joseph of Arimathea to bury Jesus (19:39). Can this be backed up from sources outside the New Testament?

Richard Bauckham (*Test* pp137-172) has carried out detailed research on Nicodemus. The name was extremely rare among Jews – even in the diaspora only two instances were known (p 171). It turns out that Nicodemus was a member of the fabulously rich Gurion family. They were one of three families who paid for essential supplies for the population of Jerusalem during the AD 70 siege of the city (p140) (see also *FFBJ* p81 and *CJohn* p186) by the Romans. One of the family was remembered not only for his immense wealth but also for his corresponding generous charity (p148).

Using information from Josephus and rabbinic sources, Richard Bauckham has managed to piece together the Gurion family tree (pp150-151).

As several have remarked (*CJohn* p186, *FFBJ* p81), the Nicodemus of John 3 cannot be identified with the Nicodemus (of *b.Git.* 56a) who supplied Jerusalem during the AD 70 siege – he would have been too young in AD 28 to occupy the prestigious functions attributed to him in John's Gospel. It is therefore more likely that he was the brother of the famous Gurion/Guria, at whose house in Jericho the Pharisees met (*Test* p167).

The Gurion family were Pharisees. John, in his Gospel, refers to the ruling group in Jerusalem as *"the chief priests and Pharisees"* (7:32, 45; 11:47, 57; 18:3), ignoring other members of the lay nobility. Josephus, when he takes the trouble to distinguish the Pharisees from other lay citizens (p163), refers to *"the powerful"* meeting with the chief priests and *"the distinguished men of the Pharisees"* (*BJ* 2.411; *Ant* 20.201-2). But on one occasion (*Life* 5), Josephus uses exactly the same terms as John's Gospel, referring to the ruling élite as *"the chief priests and the leading men of the Pharisees."* Gamaliel the Elder (Acts 5:34) and his son Simeon (*BJ* 4.159) belonged to this group of leading Pharisees. The Gurion family is probably the only other known family which can confidently be assigned to it.

Therefore, in conclusion, it appears that the name Nicodemus was extremely rare. The Nicodemus of John's Gospel was from the immensely wealthy Pharisaic Gurion family, who were not just members of the Sanhedrin, but part of the ruling inner circle in Jerusalem. That he was a teacher of the law is consistent with that. Similarly, the fact that he could supply a huge quantity of spices (34 kg or 65 lbs) (19:39), fit for a king (*DBLuke* p1875), for Jesus' burial showed that he was personally very rich, consistent with him being a member of the fabulously wealthy Gurion family.

The person of Nicodemus is fascinating. It shows how Josephus and rabbinic sources confirm the Gospels in their finest detail and gives us a greater insight into the nature of the inner ruling circle in Jerusalem.

CONCLUSION

We have shown that archaeological findings (such as inscriptions and ossuaries), rabbinic sources, Tacitus and Josephus all back up what we know from the Gospels about the important personalities of Pontius Pilate, John the Baptist, Herod Antipas, Caiaphas, Barabbas and Nicodemus.

Chapter 11

JESUS' EARLY AND GALILEAN MINISTRIES

NAMES IN JEWISH PALESTINE

The occurrence of names in the Gospels and Acts, and their occurrence in the general population of the time, present one of the most fascinating areas of correspondence.

In this section, we shall follow the investigation by Richard Bauckham (*Eye* pp67-113), who has used the database prepared by the Israeli scholar Tal Ilan of Jewish names in Palestine over the period between 330 BC and 200 AD[58]. Tal Ilan used sources such as Josephus, the New Testament, texts from the Judean desert and Masada, ossuary inscriptions from Jerusalem, papyri and legal documents and the earliest rabbinic sources. She counted people; Richard Bauckham revisited her database in order to count names (*Eye* pp67-69). His calculations resulted in 2953 occurrences of 521 names, comprising 2625 occurrences of 447 male names and 328 occurrences of 74 female names (p71) as in his Tables 6 and 7 (pp85-91).

The first thing to notice is that, among the Jews of that period, there were a small number of very popular names and a large number of rare ones. If we assemble his data from Tables 6 and 7, we find the ranking of the most popular names as shown in Table 11.1.

Bauckham then demonstrates that the overall popularity ranking of the names remains essentially the same in each of the four principal sources, namely Josephus, the Gospels and Acts, ossuaries and the Judean desert texts. For example, Simon and Joseph are the most popular male names in all four sources and Simon comes before Joseph in 3 out of 4. For female names, Mary and Salome are the most popular names in all four sources and Mary comes before Salome in all four. In fact, for both male and female names, the relative proportions of the first nine names in all four sources are strikingly close to the relative proportions for the overall figures for those names (p71).

We can further bring together Richard Bauckham's data in the Table 11.2, where we consider the following categories:

- % of men bearing the 2 most popular names, Simon and Joseph
- % of women bearing the 2 most popular names, Mary and Salome
- % of men having one of the nine most popular names
- % of women having one of the nine most popular names
- % of men bearing a name which is only attested once in the sources

---

[58] Tal Ilan, "Lexicon of Jewish names in Late Antiquity: Part I: Palestine 330 BCE – 200 CE," published in TSAJ 91; Tübingen: Mohr, 2002.

- % of women bearing a name which is only attested once in the sources

In Table 11.2, we compare in these three categories (for men and for women) the percentage of names occurring in the overall population and those occurring in the Gospels and Acts.

Table 11.1: The Nine Most Popular Names Amongst Palestinian Jews (330 BC - 200 AD)					
RANK	MALE	NUMBER		FEMALE	NUMBER
1	Simon/Simeon	243		Mary	70
2	Joseph/Joses	218		Salome	58
3	Lazarus	166		Shelamzion (1)	24
4	Judas	164		Martha	20
5	John	122	5=	Joanna	12
			5=	Sapphira	12
6	Jesus	99			
7	Ananias	82		Berenice	8
8	Jonathan	71	8=	Imma	7
			8=	Mara (2)	7
9	Matthew/Matthias	62			

NOTES (1) A longer form of Salome
(2) Probably a shortened form of Martha

Table 11.2: % of Men's and Women's Names Occurring in the Gospels and Acts Compared with those in Overall Population

	MEN		WOMEN	
	Overall Population	Gospels & Acts	Overall Population	Gospels & Acts
One of 2 most popular names	15.6	18.2	28.6	38.9
One of 9 most popular names	41.5	40.3	49.7	61.1
Bearing a name only attested once in the sources	7.9	3.9	9.6	2.5

The percentages for men in the New Testament thus correlate remarkably closely with those for the population in general. It is not surprising that the percentages for women do not match those for the overall population so closely. This is because the statistical base for women's names is considerably smaller than that for men, both in the New Testament and in the sources in general (p72).

So, even if the Gospels and Acts were written in three different regions of the Roman Empire (Palestine/Syria, Rome and Asia Minor (Ephesus), the frequency of the names used corresponds with their usage in Palestine at the time of Jesus. The usage of Jewish names during this period in Egypt, for example, was very different (*Trust?* p66). This is further evidence that, in the Gospels and Acts, we are dealing with eyewitness testimony of high quality.

Richard Bauckham also gives reasons for why certain male names were so popular at the time.

Why were some Jewish Names so Popular?

Although strictly we do not need to treat this subject, it is indeed very interesting and gives an insight into how people were thinking at the time of Jesus. It is striking that (*Eye* p74) six of the nine most popular names were those of the Hasmonean family (see Appendix 1: The Inter-Testamental Period), Mattathias and his five sons (John, Simon, Judas, Eleazar and Jonathan). Similarly, the three most popular female names (Mary (Mariam), Salome and Shelamzion (the longer form of Salome)) were also names of the Hasmonean family, who had won independence for the Jewish nation. These chosen names represented a patriotic harking back to the last period of independent Jewish statehood before the Roman occupation.

Other names were also slightly modified to include the beginning of the divine names YHWH (p76).

Thus, the most frequently used male and female names were popular because of their association with nationalistic religious expectations of national deliverance (p77).

How to distinguish Simon from Simon

Since about half the population of Jewish Palestine was called by only about a dozen personal names, a second name was often added in order to distinguish between two individuals. Tal Ilan's sources show 11 ways in which this could be achieved. These are listed below, together with examples from the Gospels and Acts which correspond to a given method:

1) Variant forms of a name. For example, Jesus' brother Joseph (Matthew 13:55) was called Joses (Mark 6:3) in order to distinguish him within the family from his father Joseph (*Eye* p78).

2) Patronymic added. A reference to the father's name (patronymic) is added. Thus, the personal name X becomes X son of (Aramaic *bar* or Hebrew *ben*) Y. There are many examples in the New Testament, among them (p79):

Levi son of Alphaeus (Mark 2:14)

Jesus son of Joseph (John 1:45).

3) Patronymic substituted. An example is Bartimaeus (=son of Timaeus) (Mark 10:46).

4) Names of husbands or sons added. Married or widowed women could be identified by reference to their husband or children. For example:

   Mary of Clopas (John 19:25)

   Mary of James (Luke 24:10)

5) Nickname added. For example: James the little (Mark 15:40), Simon the leper (Matthew 26:6; Mark 14:3). (Presumably Simon had since been healed, because otherwise he could not have taken part in any social activity, but the nickname had stayed).

6) Nickname substituted. For example, Simon Peter was often called simply Cephas or Peter, the Aramaic and Greek versions of the nickname Jesus gave him.

7) Place of origin or dwelling added. For example: Nathanael of Cana (John 21:2).

8) Place of origin or dwelling substituted. The popular prophet who led his followers out into the desert (Acts 21:38; *Ant* 20.171-2) was simply known as "the Egyptian."

9) Family name. Here the best example is the high priest known as Caiaphas, whose name was really Joseph bar Caiaphas (see *Ant* 18.35 and his ossuary).

10) Two names in two languages. For example, Silas, as he was known in the Jerusalem church (Acts 15:22), and Silvanus as he was known in Paul's letters.

11) Occupation added. For example, Simon the tanner (Acts 9:43; 10:6).

An Example from the Gospel of Matthew

Peter Williams (*Trust?* p68) gives an interesting example of where second names or qualifiers were needed to distinguish between people, namely that of the list of the twelve disciples in Matthew 10:2-4. We can summarise the situation as in Table 11.3:

Table 11.3: The Names of the Twelve Disciples in Matthew 10:2-4		
Name of Disciple	**Ranking**	**Qualifier**
Simon	1	who is called Peter
Andrew	>99	NQ
James	11	son of Zebedee
John	5	son of Zebedee
Philip	61=	NQ
Bartholomew	50=	NQ
Thomas	>99	NQ
Matthew	9	the tax collector
James	11	son of Alphaeus
Thaddaeus	39=	NQ
Simon	1	the Zealot
Judas	4	Iscariot, who betrayed him
NOTE: NQ signifies no qualifier		

We observe that, for the disciples with the most popular names (such as Simon, Judas, John, Matthew and James), Matthew adds a qualifier. However, he adds no qualifier for those disciples with less popular names (such as Andrew, Philip etc), simply because it was not necessary. Moreover, these qualifiers or disambiguation patterns would have been *necessary in Palestine, but not elsewhere* (*Trust?* p68).

CONCLUSION

The study of Jewish names in Palestine, based on Tal Ilan's database and revisited by Richard Bauckham, shows how well usage in the Gospels and Acts corresponds with that in the general population of the period. This correspondence applies for the few names in popular usage and for the multitude of rare names. Because so many people were called by so few names, there had to be a way of distinguishing between people, by adding a second name or a qualifier. Once again, this usage is found in the Gospels and in Acts and corresponds with that in the overall population at the time. The use of Jewish names in other countries, such as Egypt, was not the same. This means that, in the Gospels, we are dealing with eyewitness testimony of the highest quality.

JESUS' EARLY MINISTRY

Cana (John 2:1-11)

In John 2:1-11, we read of Jesus' first public miracle, turning a huge quantity[59] of water into wine at a wedding feast. Since the disciple Nathanael (John 1:45-51) came from Cana (John 21:2), it is likely that he was the source of the invitation. So where was Cana?

Greek Orthodox and Roman Catholic churches commemorating the water-into-wine miracle have been built at Kefr Kenna, about 7 km (4.3 miles) northeast of Nazareth.

However, the more likely location is Khirbet Qana, a ruined village some 8.5 miles (13 km) north of Nazareth (*FFBJ* p68). This is supported by Josephus' information that Cana, where he had his headquarters when he took up his military command in Galilee, lay in the Plain of Asochis (*Life* 86.207), which includes Khirbet Qana but not Kefr Kenna (*CJohn* p168). A guidebook written by a certain Theodosius between 517 and 527 AD *"The Layout of the Holy Land"* also identified Khirbet Qana as the Cana of John's Gospel.

In fact, the village of Khirbet Qana was regarded very early on as the site of the Cana of the Gospels. This is the site that most biblical atlases opt for (see for example *RDBA* p179; *SBA* map 14; *Corazin*; *NIVA* map 10).

The Pool of Bethesda (John 5:1-9)

In John 5:1-9 we read of a miracle performed by Jesus at the Pool of Bethesda (other readings say Bethzatha or much less likely Bethsaida):

"Some time later, Jesus went up to Jerusalem for a feast of the Jews. Now there is in Jerusalem near the Sheep Gate a pool, which in Aramaic is called Bethesda and which is covered by five covered colonnades. Here a great number of disabled people used to lie - the blind, the lame, the paralysed. One who was there had been an invalid for thirty-eight

---

[59] The equivalent of somewhere between 100 and 150 standard bottles of 75 cl.

years. When Jesus saw him lying there and learned that he had been in this condition for a long time, he asked him, "Do you want to get well?"

"Sir," the invalid replied, "I have no-one to help me into the pool when the water is stirred. While I am trying to get in, someone else goes down ahead of me."

Then Jesus said to him, "Get up! Pick up your mat and walk." At once the man was cured; he picked up his mat and walked."

Some less reliable manuscripts give an explanation behind the man's statement: that periodically an angel supposedly stirred the waters, and then the first one in would be cured.

The visitor to modern-day Jerusalem may find the excavations of this pool near the Church of St Anne, in the north-east quarter of the Old City (see Photo 11.1), near Nehemiah's Sheep Gate (Nehemiah 3:1, 32; 12:39).

The Copper Scroll from Qumran (published in 1960) indicates that it was *"the place of two outpourings."* Similarly, the pilgrim from Bordeaux, who visited the city in AD 313, recorded that *"inside the city is a pair of pools with five arcades, which pools are called Bethsaida."* (*FFBJ* p122; *CJohn* p242).

This is confirmed by the excavations that have been carried out on the site intermittently since 1856. It is clear that there were two adjacent pools, a northern and a southern, and that the trapezoidal area they spread over was surrounded by four covered colonnades, one on each side, with a fifth on the ridge of rock separating the two pools[60]. It was in the shelter of these colonnades that the afflicted people waited in the hope of healing. Thus, this account of the healing from John 5 is confirmed by the archaeology which can still be visited today (see Photo 11.1):

- There was a (double) pool near the Sheep Gate (verse 2)
- With five colonnades (verse 2)
- Where disabled people used to lie hoping for healing (verse 3)

It is also backed up by ancient authorities such as Origen (c. AD 241)[61] and Cyril, bishop of Jerusalem (c. AD 348)[62], who adds that the sick people lay in the middle colonnade.

---

[60] J.Jeremias, "The Rediscovery of Bethesda," Louisville, Kentucky, 1966;
"Excavations in Jerusalem-Review and Evaluation" ed. Y. Yadin, London, 1976, pp21-24.
[61] Origen, "Commentary on John," Catena fragment 61 on John 5 :2.
[62] Cyril of Jerusalem, "Homily on the Cripple at the Pool 2."

Photo 11.1 The Pool of Bethesda

JESUS' GALILEAN MINISTRY

Clearly, Jesus spent a lot of his public ministry period on or around the Sea of Galilee. This was where he performed many of his major miracles, such as the stilling of the storm or the feeding of the five thousand. However, he avoided the main centres of population, Sephoris and Tiberias, respectively built and rebuilt by Herod Antipas. Instead, he spent much time in the open air, on the shore and in the hills around the lake, which means it is difficult to trace his movements through the science of archaeology, which is based on excavating settlements and artefacts.

Various churches have been built on what were supposedly the traditional sites of Jesus' ministry, such as the:

- Sermon on the Mount, between Tabgha and Capernaum
- Feeding of the Five Thousand at Tabgha

- The Transfiguration on Mt Tabor[63]
- The reinstatement of Peter (John 21) at Tabgha

These are all plausible locations but, since these events occurred in the open air, there is little hard evidence to back them up.

Many of the other events occurred in places which still exist in modern Israel:

Nain (Luke 7:11-17): is identified with the village of Nen or Nein, about 6 miles south of Nazareth (*IHML* p384; *NBD* p799; *DBLuke* p649). (See atlases: *RBDA* p179; *SBA* map 14; *Corazin*; *NIVA* map 10).

Nazareth (Matthew (13:54-58), Mark (6:1-6) and Luke (4:16-30): essentially the modern town occupies the same site as at the time of Jesus.

Capernaum: Jesus spent much of his time in Capernaum; it was his ministry base. He seems to have set up home in the house of Simon Peter (Mark 1:29-31).

Capernaum has remains of a church from the fifth century AD which is octagonal in shape. In 1968, archaeologists discovered the remains of an earlier church underneath it (see Appendix 2). This had been built around what was originally a private house, which was apparently used by Christians as a meeting place during the second half of the first century[64]. Today, a modern church exists, suspended above the site, with the excavation visible through a glass floor; the original site is thus protected from the elements. Given that the tradition goes back to the first century, it is very likely that this is where Jesus stayed – at the home of his chief apostle, Peter (*FMark* p107).

Capernaum was an important Jewish settlement on the north-western shore of the Sea of Galilee, with the presence of a Roman centurion (Matthew 8:5) and a customs post (Matthew 9:9). Josephus (*BJ* 3.519) talks of Capernaum's economy based on agriculture and fishing. It was on the key *Via Maris* trade route and, at the time, its population was approximately 10,000. Now it is unoccupied and its ruins lie inland, due to the fall in the water level of the Sea of Galilee (see the atlases: *RDBA* p179; *Corazin*; *SBA* map 14; *NIVA* map 10).

Bethsaida: according to John 1:43-44 Phillip, Peter and Andrew and perhaps James and John, the sons of Zebedee, as well, came from Bethsaida. Bethsaida means *"house of the fisherman"* or *"Fishertown."* It lay a short distance to the east of the point where the River Jordan enters the Sea of Galilee, probably where et-Tell is located today. Sometime before 2 BC, Philip the Tetrarch had refounded it as his capital and renamed it Julias, after Augustus' daughter Julia (*FFBJ* p59).

American archaeologists have found a large house at et-Tell, dating from the time of Jesus, for a winemaker or fisherman. Unfortunately, the excavations have not been protected from the elements.

Today then Bethsaida is unoccupied. It lies approximately 500 m inland, whereas at the time of Jesus, and even in 1000 AD, the village was on the shore of the lake. The first reason is

---

[63] Another possibility is Mt Hermon, but this is unlikely (*FMatt 2* p646).
[64] Premier Christianity, March 2017, p51.

Israel's use of Jordan River water for irrigation. The second is the accumulation of alluvial deposits from the Jordan, which has pushed Bethsaida even further inland.

Corazin or Chorazin: is clearly identified with Kerazeh (*NBD* p184); now uninhabited, it is a rocky eminence about 865 ft above the Sea of Galilee (*DBLuke* p1003). See the atlases: *RBDA* p179; *SBA* map 14; *Corazin; NIVA* map 10).

Dalmanutha/Magdala: is the region mentioned in Mark 8:10, when Jesus and his disciples come back to the western shore of the lake after the feeding of the four thousand. The parallel passage in Matthew 15:29-39 has the boat landing in the region of Magdan or Magdala (= modern Migdal where the Galilean boat was found, see next section).

Bible commentaries on Mark tend to say that the whereabouts of Dalmanutha is unkown (*FMark* p309; *LMark* p275) and say that it must have been in the Magdala area (*FMatt 2* p603). The second proposition is correct; the first is inexact, because the visitor to Galilee can see a signpost to Dalmanutha. It is on the western side of the Sea of Galilee, north of Tiberias and south of Capernaum. (See atlases: *RBDA* p179; *SBA* map 14; *Corazin; NIVA* map 10).

Peter J Williams (*Trust?* p54) states that all four Gospel writers display knowledge of a range of localities, from well known, through lesser known, to obscure. In addition, no Gospel writer gains all his knowledge from the other Gospels, since each contains unique information. And all writers show a variety of types of geographical information.

In all these ways, the Gospel writers pass what Peter J Williams (*Trust?* p52) calls the Test of Geography. In particular (*Trust?* p62), the information the writers had is consistent with what we would expect if the Gospels were written by their traditional authors.

The Galilean Boat

In 1986, a typical Galilean fishing boat from the first century AD was discovered at Migdal, the Magdala of the New Testament, when the water level in the Sea of Galilee dropped very low during a drought. The boat is now conserved in the Yigal Alon Center at Ginosar in Israel. It turns out to be a typical fishing boat from the time of Jesus – exactly what Peter and his friends would have used to earn their living – and is very well preserved (see Photo 11.2).

The boat almost certainly sank during the naval battle at Migdal, between the Jews and the Romans, commanded by the future emperor Vespasian and his son Titus, during the Jewish Revolt in AD 67. Since Flavius Josephus had been appointed Governor of Galilee in AD 66, by the Jewish authorities in Jerusalem, he was probably leading the rebels. He describes the battle in *BJ* 3.462-542.

The boat, as discovered, was 8.2m (27ft) long, with a maximum breadth of 2.3m (7.5ft) and a preserved height of 1.2m (4ft). It had one sail, hanging from a central mast, four oars for rowing and two for steering. Figure 11.1 shows the author's sketch of the boat based on the brochure from the Yigal Alon Center. The boat was shallow and would have had trouble in the frequent storms on the lake.

There are several mentions of such Galilean fishing boats in the Gospels. If we set aside the references to fishing expeditions (Luke 5:1-21; John 21:1-14) or to when Jesus was simply sitting in a boat to teach (Matt 13:2; Mark 4:1-12), the other occasions talk of the twelve disciples in the boat with Jesus (Matt 14:22-36; 15:35; Mark 6:45-51; 8:9; John 6:15-22) and even of Jesus asleep in the boat along with the twelve (Matt 8:23-27; Mark 4:36-41; Luke 8:22-25). Hence the maximum capacity that Jesus expected of such boats was 12 people plus one lying down asleep.

The author's sketch in Figure 11.1, based on the Yigal Alon Center data, shows that this was indeed possible. Six disciples would have had to be close to the oars (4 for power, 2 for steering) and the four power rowers would have been disposed around the mast. There was then room for four more disciples between the front pair of rowers and the men who steered, and for two plus Jesus lying asleep behind the rear pair of rowers and the stern of the ship. The sketch shows that there was enough space in the boat for twelve disciples plus Jesus asleep, but that taking in another two or four people would have been more difficult. (*FMatt 2* p336 comes to the same conclusion).

In other words, what we read in the Gospels corresponds exactly with what we know of Galilean fishing boats of the time.

CONCLUSION

It is clear that in the Gospels we are faced with eyewitness testimony and that the places really existed and that the events described really happened. This is true, for example, of the male and female names encountered, whose usage corresponds exactly with what we know from Tal Ilan's study of the use of Jewish names in Palestine from 330 BC to 200 AD.

The important places in Jesus' early ministry can be located; in particular the account of John 5 corresponds exactly with what excavations of the Pool of Bethesda have revealed.

Similarly, the essential settlements described in Jesus' Galilean ministry can all be pin-pointed. Excavations at Capernaum suggest that the house of Peter, where Jesus lived, has been located. Then in 1986 a boat of local origin was found, dating from between AD 66 and 69. This was exactly the type of boat Peter and his friends would have used to go fishing.

In all these ways, what the Gospels describe corresponds with the reality on the ground. In the words of Peter J Williams, *"The Gospel writers knew their stuff"* (*Trust?* pp51-86). In particular, the information the Gospel writers had is consistent with what we would expect if the Gospels were written by their traditional authors. In the Gospels, we are dealing with eyewitness testimony of the highest quality.

Photo 11.2 The Galilean Boat

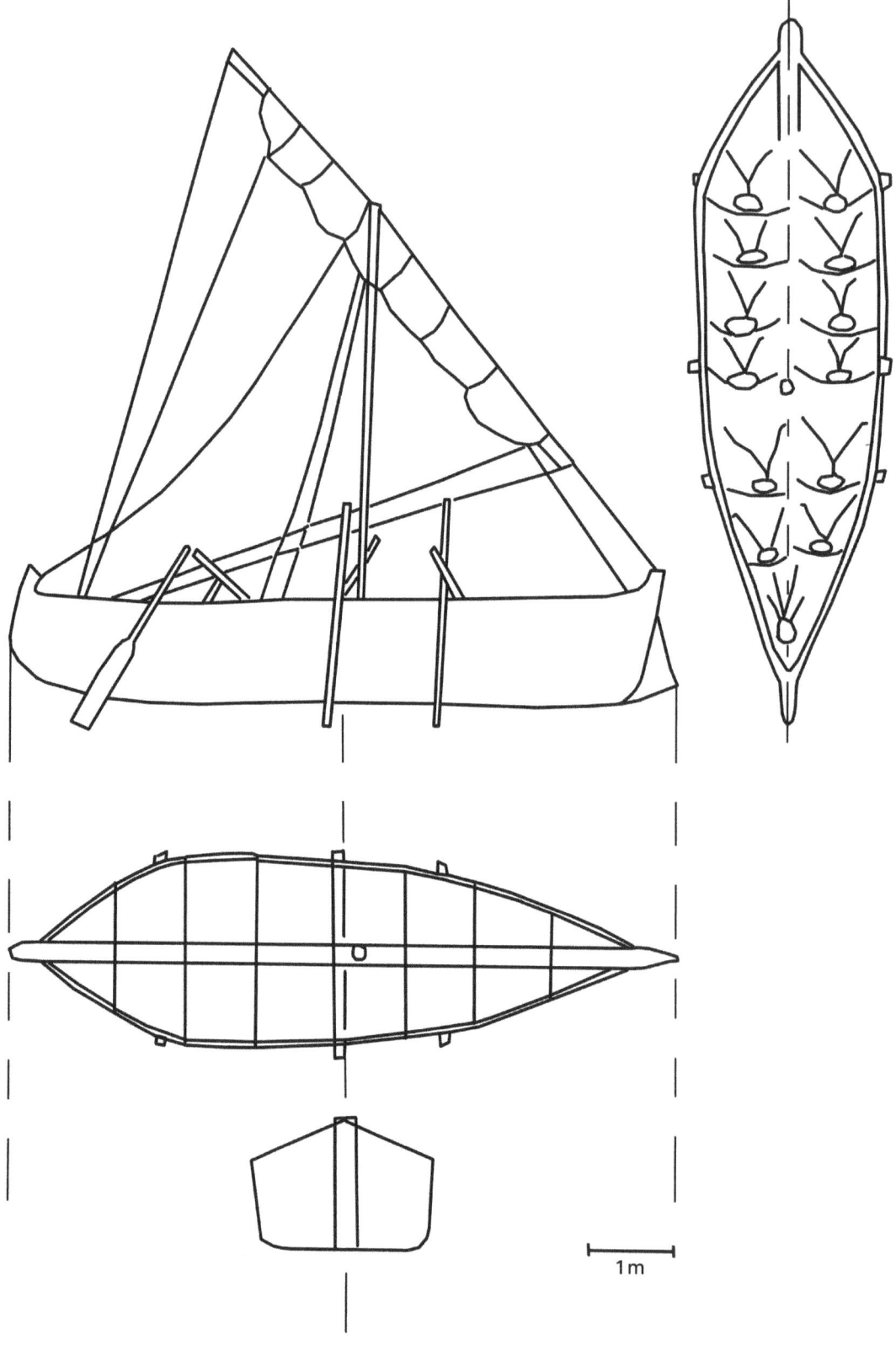

Figure 11.1: The Galilean Boat

Chapter 12

JESUS' LATER VISITS TO JERUSALEM

JESUS' DISCREET VISIT TO JERUSALEM (John 7:10-10:40; Luke 9:51-14:1)

The Pool of Siloam

The Pool of Siloam is mentioned in John 9: 7 and 11: Jesus sends a man who was blind from birth to wash his eyes there in order to be healed.

The Pool of Siloam goes back to the Old Testament. When Hezekiah, king of Judah, saw that Sennacharib, king of Assyria, was likely to attack Jerusalem, he sought to safeguard the city's water supply. He rebuilt the existing city walls and then diverted water from the Gihon Spring through a new tunnel to what Isaiah referred to as the Upper Pool (Is 7:3; 36:2). Then he built a new city wall, a section of which can be seen in present-day Jerusalem, so that the new Upper Pool reservoir fell within the new city fortifications (2 Kings 20:20; 2 Chronicles 32:2-5, 30). In this way, Hezekiah thought he would be prepared for Sennacharib's attack, which did indeed come in 701 BC (Is 22:11). This Upper Pool has now been found and is held to be the Pool of Siloam of John 9, after reconstruction no earlier than the reign of the Hasmonean Alexander Jannaeus (103-76 BC).

The pool was rediscovered in the autumn of 2004, during excavations for a sewer. First of all, stone steps were uncovered[65] and these were found to lead down to the pool. The pool is 225 ft (about 68m) long and steps existed on at least three sides – a portion of the pool remains unexcavated because the land above it is owned by a nearby Greek Orthodox Church. Coins from the reign of Alexander Jannaeus were found embedded in the plaster lining of the pool and indicate the earliest possible date for the pool's reconstruction. Other coins found date from just prior to AD 70, when the pool was covered over.

Hence the Pool of Siloam has been located and can be seen in modern-day Jerusalem. It was in operation during the life of Jesus and there seems little doubt that it is the Pool of Siloam to which Jesus sent the blind man to be healed in John 9[66].

THE FINAL PUSH TOWARDS JERUSALEM

Jericho

Jesus came to Jericho during his final push towards Jerusalem. There, he healed Bartimaeus (Matthew 20:29-34; Mark 10:46-52; Luke 18:35-43) and saved Zacchaeus (Luke 19:1-10).

---

[65] "The City of David: Revisiting Early Excavations," English translations of reports edited by Hershel Shanks pp 197-227.

[66] "Unearthing the New Testament," Christianity Magazine, March 2017 p44.

Even today the town is an oasis in the Judean desert. It is the lowest town in the world (at 320m (1050ft) below sea level) and the oldest town in the world – Joshua 6 describes the defeat of Jericho by the people of Israel and a shrine has been found dating from 9900-7700 BC (*NBD* p555). It is 5 miles (8km) west of the Jordan River and 18 miles (29km) north of Jerusalem (*LMark* p386), just north of the Dead Sea (*DBLuke* p1505). The Old Testament city has been the subject of much archaeological investigation, especially by Katherine Kenyon.

Herod the Great had built a palace at Jericho, where he died before being buried at Herodion. Herodian Jericho, the town of the time of Jesus, was about 1 mile (1.6km) from the site of the Old Testament city (*FMark* p422 note 52). Behind Jericho looms what is the traditional and plausible Mount of Temptations of Jesus. (See atlases: *RBDA* p178; *SBA* map 14; *Corazin; NIVA* map 10).

THE TEMPLE

The visitor to present-day Jerusalem, who looks down from the Mount of Olives over the Temple platform (see Photo 12.1), is astonished by its size. Herod the Great began building the Temple in 19 BC and levelled an area of about 450m (1475ft) from north to south and about 300m (980ft) from east to west. This is the platform which remains today, after the destruction of the Temple in AD 70 by the Romans under Titus. Since Herod built the Temple on the crown of a hill, the first step was to build retaining walls of massive limestone blocks 1m (3ft) high and up to 5m (16ft) long. The volume between the retaining walls and the hill was then filled in with rubble, and the Temple platform levelled off (*Ant* 15.399-400). The Wailing Wall, in front of which the Jews continue to pray, is therefore strictly not a wall of the Temple, but rather the western retaining wall.

Herod the Great built the Temple in an effort to ingratiate himself with his Jewish subjects; he had an Idumean father and a Nabatean mother, so he was not an ethnic Jew. The main structure of the Temple was finished within ten years (in 9 BC) (*Ant* 15.420-421) but work continued on it until 63 or 64 AD. It was impressive in its beauty (*Ant* 15.416), made from white marble (*BJ* 5.187). Adjoining the Temple at its north-west corner was the Fortress Antonia, with its garrison of Roman troops, always ready to subdue any unrest in the Temple. The High Priest's robes were stored there as a token of subjection (*Ant* 15.403-9) (see Map 12.1 Jerusalem in New Testament Times).

The Temple was situated close to the eastern extremity of ancient Jerusalem (see Map 12.1 Jerusalem in New Testament Times). Thus, entering the city from the Kidron Valley by the Golden Gate, in the eastern wall of the city, led almost immediately into the Temple.

Josephus has left us two descriptions of the Temple (*BJ* 5.183-247; *Ant* 15.410-416) and these are good sources, because he knew the Temple well. The description from *BJ* is more systematic and enables us to consider the Temple from the outside and gradually move in towards the centre of worship.

There were altogether 8 gates leading into the Temple courts; so far we have described one, the Golden Gate from the eastern side. There were two "Hulda" or "mole" gates on the southern side, which penetrated the retaining wall, with ramps leading up to the level of the Temple courts. These are still visible beneath the el-Aqsa mosque. There were 4 gates from the west, including the main gate for entering from the city, named after Coponius, the first Roman Prefect of Judea. It was decorated with an eagle, as a sign that the Temple had been placed under Rome's protection. Finally, there was one gate, the Tadi gate, on the northern side, but this was apparently never used (*NBD* p1158).

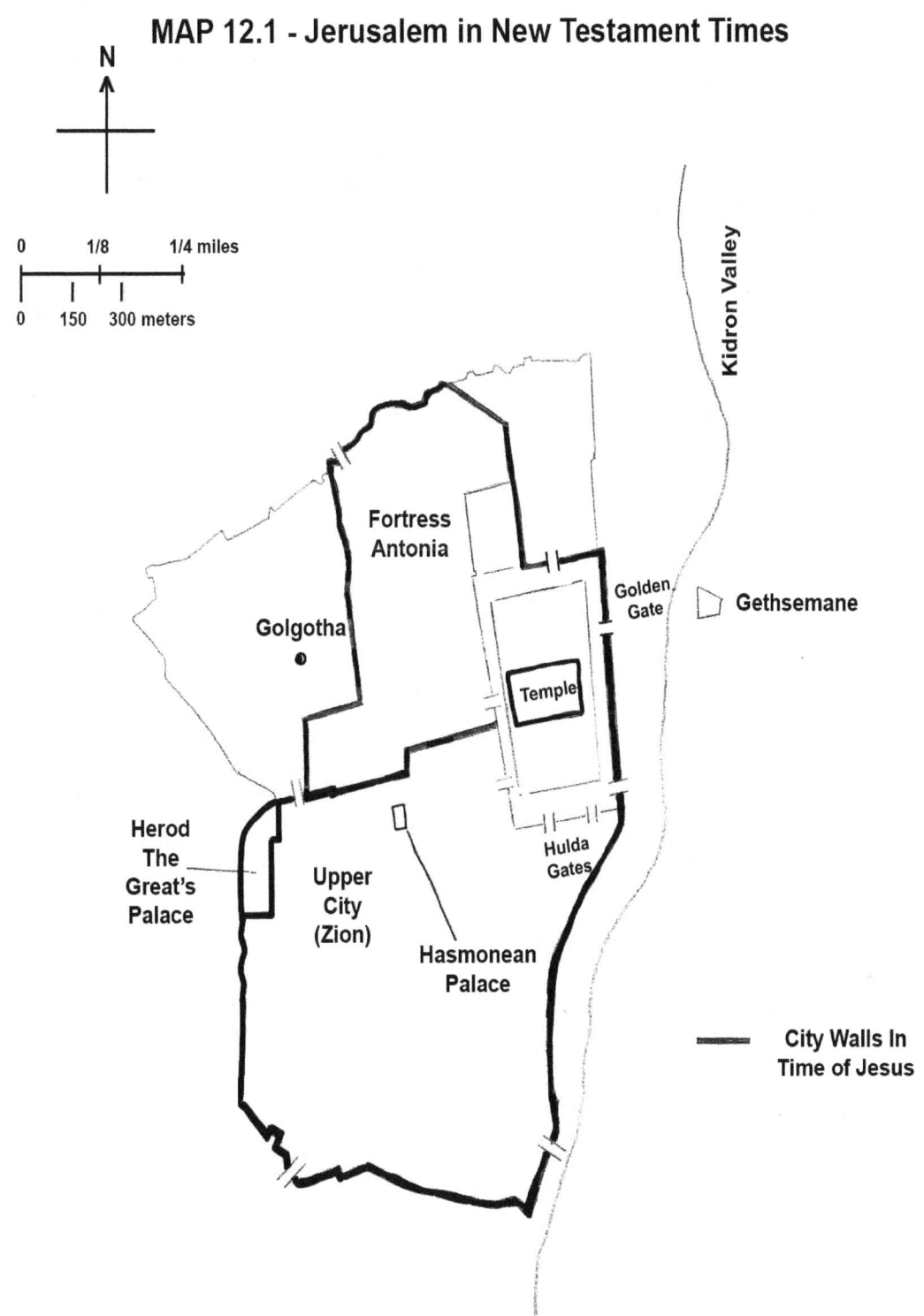

Fig 12.1 Schematic Plan of Temple

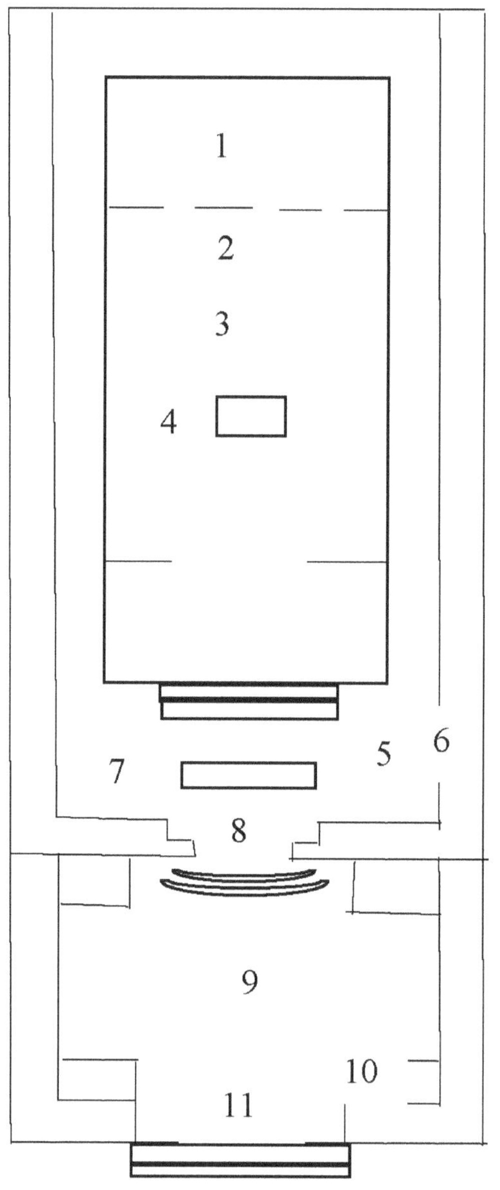

KEY

1. Holy of Holies
2. Veil (Curtain)
3. Holy Place
4. Altar of Incense
5. Court of Priests
6. Court of Israel
7. Altar of Sacrifice
8. Nicanor Gate
9. Court of Women
10. Temple Treasury
11. Gate Beautiful
12. Court of Gentiles
13. Solomon's Porch
14. Royal Porticos
15. Western Wall

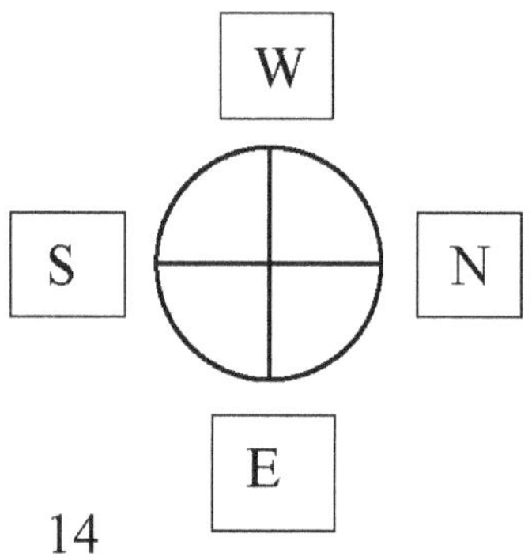

Flavius Josephus describes the Temple:

"The colonnades were all double, the supporting pillars were 37.5 feet (11.5m) high, cut from single blocks of the whitest marble, and the ceiling was panelled with cedar. The natural magnificence of it all, the perfect polish, the accurate jointing, afforded a remarkable spectacle, without any superficial ornament either painted or carved. The colonnades were 45 feet (13.7m) wide and the complete circuit of them measures ¾ mile (1.2km), Antonia being enclosed within them. The whole area open to the sky was paved with stones of every kind of colour." (*BJ* 5.187)

Here, Josephus is talking about the porticoes, with their colonnades, which surrounded the outer court, the **Court of the Gentiles** (see Figure 12.1 Schematic Plan of Temple). Solomon's Portico went down the eastern side, and here the scribes held their schools and debates, and the merchants and money changers had their stalls. The trade arose from the fact that money for the Temple, including the obligatory temple tax (see Appendix 2 for details) had to be paid in Tyrian shekel coins, with its high level of silver purity, and not in standard Roman coins. A surcharge was made, which gave rise to all sorts of irregularities (*NBD* p782).

The **inner area** was at a level a little higher than the Court of the Gentiles and was surrounded by a balustrade, with notices in Greek and Latin, warning that no responsibility could be taken for the probable death of any Gentile who ventured further (*BJ* 5.188). Four gates gave access to the inner area from the north and the south, and Josephus comments particularly on beauty of the gate from the east, made of Corinthian bronze (*BJ* 5.200), which may have been the Beautiful Gate of Acts 3:2.

Through the Gate Beautiful (11), the pilgrim arrived in the Court of Women (9) (*BJ* 5.199), which contained the Treasury chests (10) for gifts towards the expenses of the services. Penetrating further, men were allowed into the Court of Israel (6) and, at the Feast of Tabernacles, could enter the Court of the Priests (5) to go around the altar (7).

The Sanctuary was in two parts (*BJ* 5.211). A door led into the first part, the Holy Place (3); in it was a lampstand, a table and the altar of incense (4) (*BJ* 5.217). Finally, a curtain (2) separated off the Holy of Holies (1). As Josephus records it was *"unapproachable, inviolable and invisible to all"* (*BJ* 5.218).

Animals for the daily sacrifices were killed to the north of the Court of Israel. The priest would then sacrifice it on the altar (7). From the Court of Israel, people could see the priest burn incense on the altar of incense (4), once the door into the Holy Place was opened (*VQJ* p23-26). But they could not see into the Holy of Holies, and even the High Priest could only enter once a year, on the Day of Atonement (Leviticus 16:1-34; *BJ* 5.237).

In the Table 12.1 that follows, we resume the different sectors of the Temple, their reference on the Temple diagram, the paragraph of Josephus's description in *BJ* and the New Testament references to these sectors. The Table 12.1 shows that Jesus spent most of his time teaching in the Court of the Gentiles between Solomon's Colonnades. Overall, the Gospels and Acts refer to all of the different areas of the Temple, save the Holy of Holies. This is reserved for Hebrews 10:24-28.

Table 12.1: HEROD'S TEMPLE -		CORRESPONDENCE OF NEW TESTAMENT WITH JOSEPHUS	
Figure Reference	Temple Sector	*BJ* Reference	New Testament References
12	Court of Gentiles	5.187	Matt 21:12, 23; Mark 11:15; Luke 2:27
13/14	Solomon's Colonnades	5.187	John 10:23; Acts 3:11; 5:12 Scribal schools and debates: Luke 2:46, 19:47; Mark 11:27 Stalls of money changers: John 2:14-16; Luke 19:45-46
11	Gate Beautiful	5.200	Acts 3:2
9	Court of Women	5.199	Mark 12:41-44; Luke 21:1-4
10	Treasury	5.199	Mark 12:41-44; Luke 21:1-4
8	Nicanor (Greater) Gate	5.205	Luke 2:21-40
6	Court of Israel		Acts 21:30
7	Altar of Sacrifice		Luke 1:8-10
5	Court of Priests		Luke 1:8-10
3	Holy Place	5.211	Luke 1:8-10
4	Altar of Incense	5.217	Luke 1:8-10
2	Curtain	5.218	Matt 27:51; Mark 15:38
1	Holy of Holies	5.218, 5.237	

Notes
For Luke 2:21-40, see *IHML* p116   For Luke 1:8-10, see *IHML* p54

THE DESTRUCTION OF THE TEMPLE

Josephus and rabbinic sources agree that Herod's temple and its courts were awesome in size and magnificence:

"Viewed from without the Sanctuary had everything which could amaze the mind or eyes. Overlaid all round with stout plates of gold, in the first rays of the sun it reflected so fierce a blaze of fire that those who endeavoured to look at it were forced to turn away as if they had looked straight at the sun. To strangers as they approached it seemed in the distance like a mountain covered in snow; for any part not covered with gold was dazzlingly white." (*BJ* 5.222-3)

Or again:

"the most wonderful edifice ever seen or heard of, both for its size and construction and for the lavish perfection of detail and the glory of the holy places." (*BJ* 6.267)

And again, from rabbinic sources:

"It used to be said: 'He who has not seen the temple in its full splendour has never seen a beautiful building.'"[67]

Jesus' disciples were also amazed by the temple buildings:

"As he was leaving the temple, one of his disciples said to him, "Look, Teacher! What massive stones! What magnificent buildings!"

"Do you see all these great buildings?" *replied Jesus.* "Not one stone here will be left on another; every one will be thrown down."" (Mark 13:1-2)

The accounts of Matthew 24:1-2 and Luke 21:5-6 are very similar; in particular the phrase *"not one stone will be left on another; every one will be thrown down,"* is common to all three Synoptic Gospels.

Jesus' prophecy of the destruction of the temple was clear. The details of how it happened, how it was gutted by fire (*BJ* 6.249-66) before being deliberately levelled to the ground by the Romans (*BJ* 7.1-3) in AD 70 are the culmination of Josephus' masterpiece *The Jewish War* (*BJ*). Throwing every stone down was no mean effort: the stones were 12 m (39ft) (*Ant* 15.392) or 20 m (66ft) (*BJ* 5.224) long! Jesus also prophesied the partial destruction of the city of Jerusalem:

"The days will come upon you when your enemies will build an embankment against you and encircle you and hem you in on every side. They will dash you to the ground, you and your children within your walls. They will not leave one stone on another, because you did not recognize the time of God's coming to you." (Luke 19:43-44)

This corresponds with what we know from Josephus: in AD 70 Titus built a barricade around the city, whilst indescribable horrors were going on inside it (*BJ* 5.439-466; 5.508). Then he ordered the razing of the whole city and sanctuary to the ground (*BJ* 7.1-4; 7.375-377).

---

[67] *B.Suk.51b; b.B.Bat.4a* as quoted in *FMatt2* p887.

According to Josephus (*BJ* 6.421), 1.1 million Jews were killed and 97,000 taken prisoner during this terrible period.

Here we are faced with a special form of correspondence. We have demonstrated that all three Synoptic Gospels were written before AD 70. Jesus' words were therefore prophetic. Flavius Josephus and present-day Jerusalem both bear witness to the fact that these prophecies were fulfilled.

THE TRIAL SEQUENCE

Can we ever know the truth about the holy places in Jerusalem, since they have been built over so many times? As a visitor to Jerusalem, I found myself asking this question repeatedly.

Perhaps the least well attested location is that of the Upper Room. The putative site, close to the Church of the Dormition, was chosen by the Crusaders for its proximity to David's tomb, on the basis of Acts 2:29. However, there is little hard evidence in favour of this site.

On the other hand, we can be much surer of the traditional site of Gethsemane (meaning "oil press" Matthew 26:36; Mark 14:32). Matthew (26:36) describes it as an "estate," probably a walled plot, and its name suggests that it was an olive orchard (see Photo 12.2). This would fit John's description (18:1-2) of it as a "garden." Therefore, the traditional site at the foot of the Mount of Olives, facing the city, would be appropriate (*FMatt2* p1003).

After Jesus' arrest in Gethsemane, the trial sequence follows. When the four Gospel accounts are assembled, we finish up with a six-part sequence (*DBLuke* p 1793[68]). In Chapter 14, Table 14.2 gives the details of this sequence. For the moment, we extract the salient points:

Table 12.2: The Trial Sequence and its Locations

STEP	POSSIBLE LOCATIONS
1. Before Annas	House of Annas/Caiaphas
2. Evening before Caiaphas	House of Annas/Caiaphas
3. Morning confirmation by Sanhedrin	Temple Courts
4. Before Pilate (1)	Herod's Palace or Fortress Antonia
5. Before Herod Antipas	Hasmonean Palace
6. Before Pilate (2)	Fortress Antonia

Since Caiaphas was Annas' son-in-law, they probably both lived in the same house, where the first two steps of the trial sequence occurred. Here there are two possible locations: the first is the site of the Church of St Peter's Tears on Mount Zion, which is based on a tradition dating from the eighth century. The second is higher up Mount Zion, based on a tradition dating back to the fourth century, where Israeli excavations in 1972 showed the area to be one of wealthy homes in the time of Jesus. In both cases there would have been room for the mocking of Jesus to take place.

---

[68] Darrell Bock has carried out very thorough research into the Trial Sequence, notably his book *"Blasphemy"* concerning the charges levelled at Jesus.

Another interesting find is the existing stone pavement or stairway which leads from the lower city to the Church of St Peter's Tears and which dates from the time of Jesus. We do not really know which of the two above possible locations, for the house of Annas and Caiaphas, is the more likely. Either way, it seems likely that, after his arrest in Gethsemane, Jesus was led *manu militari* from the lower city to Mount Zion, via the aforementioned stone stairway (see Photo 12.3), to the house of Annas/Caiaphas.

Matthew's account of the morning trial before the Sanhedrin (Step 3) can be read as a simple continuation of the accusation in Annas/Caiaphas' house, without any change of location (see for example *FMatt2* p1035). But, according to Mark and Luke, it seems more likely that we are dealing with the "official" Jewish trial before the whole Sanhedrin or Council, in which case it would have been held in the Chamber of Hewn Stone on the western side of the Temple Mount (*BJ* 5.4.2).

However, (*BJ* 2.117 and John 18:31) only the Romans had the right to inflict the death penalty. Pontius Pilate (Step 4) normally resided in Caesarea Maritime, but came to Jerusalem when the maintaining of public order required it as, for example, during the Passover Festival. His temporary residence would become the *"praetorium"* for the time being. This would usually have been Herod the Great's Palace on the wall of the city (see Photo 12.4), where the Phasael Tower survives as the north east tower of the present-day citadel, south of the Jaffa Gate. Another possibility is the Fortress Antonia, connected by steps to the Temple area (see *BJ* 5.238; Acts 21:35,40 and *FFBJ* pp 348-9).

It seems likely that Pilate began the day at his usual Jerusalem residence in Herod's Palace and then, later in the day, as the crowds gathered, moved down to the Fortress Antonia to be closer to the Temple and any potential disturbances. This then makes Herod the Great's Palace the scene of Pilate's first meeting with Jesus (Step 4) and Fortress Antonia the place of their more public second confrontation (Step 6).

The situation of this second confrontation has been identified with the magnificent Roman pavement (see Photo 12.5), excavated beneath the *Ecco Homo* arch and the convent of Our Lady of Zion (*FFBJ* p364), originally measuring almost 3000 sqm (280,000 sqft) in area, and has been further identified as the courtyard of Fortress Antonia. In addition, the pavement seems to bear the scratch marks of the "king game," which could well have been part of the parodied coronation ceremony in which the Roman soldiers mocked Jesus (Matthew 27:27-31; Mark 15:16-20; *HRNT* p224). I have seen these marks and they are convincing. This then is where the *Via Dolorosa* begins its course, which ends in the Church of the Holy Sepulchre (*FFBJ* p369).

Most commentators consider that Jesus' appearance before Herod Antipas (Step 5) occurred in the Hasmonean Palace, a ten-minute walk from Pilate's residence at Herod the Great's Palace (*RDBA* p187; *DBLuke* pp1818-9; *IHML* p855).

The Via Dolorosa and Simon of Cyrene

The *Via Dolorosa* begins its course at the *Ecco Homo* arch (a reference to John 19:5), which ends in the Church of the Holy Sepulchre. The *Ecce Homo* arch itself dates from Hadrian's rebuilding of Jerusalem in AD 135, but may well cover approximately the right site, about eight feet (2.5 m) below the current street level (*FFBJ* p380 footnote 3).

We learn from Josephus (*BJ* 2.306-8; 5.449) that systematically prisoners were flogged before being crucified. This is what happened to Jesus (see Matthew 27:26; Mark 15:15). This form of scourging (Greek: *phragelloo* from the Latin: *flagello*) was a murderous form of torture: the whips with which it was carried out were reinforced with sharp pieces of metal or bone, which left the victim's body in a bloody pulp and the flesh hanging in ribbons (*BJ* 6.304). Not surprisingly this treatment was sometimes sufficient to cause death (*FMatt2* p1059; *FFBJ* p358; *FMark* p634).

According to John 19:16-17, Jesus was led out to be crucified carrying the horizontal cross beam of the cross. This was normal practice. However, it is reasonable to assume that, after the terrible flogging that he had been subjected to, Jesus was physically incapable of doing it (*FMatt2* p1064). Therefore, the Roman soldiers drafted in Simon of Cyrene, from the bystanders, to carry it for him (Matthew 27:32; Mark 15:21; Luke 23:26). This fits neatly with the traditional view that Simon relieved Jesus of his burden at the Fifth Station of the Cross on the *Via Dolorosa* (*FFBJ* p366).

The right of Roman soldiers to "dragoon you as a porter" was known as the practice of *angareia*. Josephus has it mentioned under the Hasmoneans (*Ant* 13.52), where it concerned the requisitioning of a donkey. But, in first century Palestine, it clearly referred to the right of a Roman soldier to enlist a member of the subject population for forced labour or to carry his equipment (see for example Matthew 5:41) (*FMatt2* p1064). And so, they dragooned Simon of Cyrene.

All this means that the present-day *Via Dolorosa* probably traces the route to the cross with substantial accuracy. However, the *Via Dolorosa* at the time of Jesus would have been about 2.5 m (8ft) lower, corresponding to the level of the Roman Pavement under the convent of Our Lady of Zion.

THE CHURCH OF THE HOLY SEPULCHRE

The visitor to present-day Jerusalem tends to get frustrated by the holy places in Jerusalem: everything significant seems deep down under the ground and to have been built over many times. Nowhere is this more the case than for Golgotha (or the Skull Matthew 27:33; Mark 15:22; Luke 23:33; John 19:17), where the Gospels say Jesus was crucified, or the nearby tomb of Joseph of Arimathea, where they say he was buried *"in a tomb cut out of the rock"* (Matthew 27:59; Mark 15:46; Luke 23:53; John 19:40-42).

The Church of the Holy Sepulchre has had an extremely chequered history, being repeatedly damaged and restored under the Muslim rulers between AD 614 and 1009. Then Pope Urban II launched the First Crusade in 1095 to safeguard the location of the Church of the Holy Sepulchre. So, what the visitor to Jerusalem sees today is essentially the Crusader church dating from 1149, renovated by the Franciscans in 1555 and rebuilt after fire in 1809-1810. However, this fire did not reach the interior of the *Aedicula*, a small building constructed by the Emperor Constantine to enclose the tomb and to protect it. Following an earthquake in 1927, the British authorities installed external scaffolding in 1947 to secure the cladding of red marble applied to the *Aedicula* in 1809-1810.

However, the Crusaders built on top of a Byzantine church which had been erected by the Emperor Constantine between AD 325 and its consecration in AD 335. The interesting question is how Helena Augusta (Constantine's mother) and the Bishop Macarius, who assisted her, knew where Jesus had been buried.

Both Joseph of Arimathea and Nicodemus were wealthy men. First of all, it is clear that the burial of Jesus as recounted in the Gospels, in the rock-cut tomb, corresponds with how wealthy Jews were buried at the time of Jesus (*FMatt2* pp1090-1).

Eusebius describes in his *"Life of Constantine"* (*DVC*) how Constantine ordered the removal of *"a gloomy shrine of lifeless idols to the impure spirit whom they call Venus"* (*DVC* 3.26) and how, *"contrary to all expectation, the venerable and hallowed monument of our Saviour's resurrection was discovered"* (*DVC* 3.28).

Now the Emperor Hadrian had razed Jerusalem completely to the ground in AD 135, following the revolt of Simon Bar Kokba in AD 132, and rebuilt it as a pagan city Aelia Capitolina. He demonstrated his victory over the Jews and the sect of the Christians by building shrines to Jupiter and Venus over the site of Jesus' tomb. However, in doing so, he inadvertently located Jesus' burial place for Constantine to find! A French television programme likened it to leaving SatNav coordinates for Jesus' tomb[69].

Thus, historically, we can be relatively sure of the location of the burial place of Jesus and therefore of Golgotha (because the tomb had to be nearby), due to the continuity of the evidence:

Table 12.3: Continuity of Evidence for the Church of the Holy Sepulchre

AD 135	AD 325-335	AD 1149
Hadrian erects shrines to Jupiter and Venus to mark the spot	Tomb rediscovered under Constantine, who builds church	Crusaders build church over same spot as Constantine

All this came once again to the fore in the world's press[70] because of restoration work on the *Aedicula* which began in 2016. The team was led by Professor Antonia Moropoulou of the University of Athens. First of all, they found a grey marble slab, marked with a cross, dating from the time of the Crusaders. Then, underneath, they found a second slab, sealed with mortar. After analysis, both proved to be from the time of Constantine. So, all this confirmed Eusebius's account[71].

Then, when the second slab was removed to expose the tomb itself, the scientific instruments went haywire. In the words of Antonia Moropoulou: *"Our instruments did not work anymore, it's a fact. We had to reinitialize them."*[72] In other words, something extraordinary happened for which there is no explanation.

---

[69] *"Jour du Seigneur,"* Programme of France 2 Television of February 19th 2017.
[70] See for example Kristin Romey on https://news.nationalgeographic.com/2016/10.
[71] La Vie, 21st-28th December 2017.
[72] Paris Match, March 23rd-27th 2017.

We cannot be absolutely certain that the Church of the Holy Sepulchre is the location of Golgotha and the burial place of Jesus. But the evidence is very strong: geographically it was outside the city walls at the time and the tomb corresponds with how wealthy Jews were buried at that period. Then, historically, Eusebius gives a convincing account of how Constantine found the correct location, which was then built on by the Crusaders. Finally, the most recent evidence during restoration of the tomb is most convincing. And the tomb is empty! Jesus is risen from the dead.

CONCLUSION

What we read about Jerusalem and the Temple in the Gospels and Acts dovetails in exactly with what we learn from Josephus and rabbinic sources. References to all the significant parts of the Temple, save the Holy of Holies, are mentioned in the Gospels and Acts, although Jesus spent most of his time teaching in the Court of the Gentiles under Solomon's Colonnades.

Herod the Great's Temple was beautiful and magnificent, made of the finest marble according to Josephus. The Gospels concur. Jesus' prophecy of the destruction of the Temple was fulfilled in AD 70 by the Romans under Titus. The Temple was razed to the ground, leaving the platform (the foundations) which still dominates the old part of the city of Jerusalem to this day.

We can be fairly sure of the locations, in present-day Jerusalem, of the Pool of Siloam, of Jesus' arrest in Gethsemane and his conviction before Pilate on the pavement of Fortress Antonia – the wonderful Roman pavement from the time is conserved under the convent of Our Lady of Zion. Similarly, the traditional route of the *Via Dolorosa,* including the drafting in of Simon of Cyrene, from Fortress Antonia to Golgotha (the church of the Holy Sepulchre marks the site) seems to fit the Gospel accounts.

However, we can be less sure of some other locations. We do not really know where the Upper Room was located and there are two possible locations for the house of Annas/Caiaphas, both in the upper part of the city on Mount Zion.

Photo 12.1 The Temple Platform Viewed from the Mount of Olives

Photo 12.2 Gethsemane

Photo 12.3 Stone Pavement leading to Annas'/Caiaphas' House

Photo 12.4 Herod the Great's Palace

Photo 12.5 Roman Pavement Beneath Our Lady of Zion

PART V : THE COHERENCE OF THE GOSPELS

Chapter 13

THE CHRONOLOGY AND THE GEOGRAPHY OF THE GOSPELS

We possess four Gospels and they are not identical in form. Whereas Matthew, Mark and Luke (which are together known as the Synoptic Gospels) include many narrative parables and short, pithy sayings of Jesus (*Jesus* p61), John adopted a different strategy, with longer discursive sermons and dialogues. We therefore have to ask ourselves two fundamental questions. Firstly, whether the four Gospels describe the same events in the same geographical context and in the same time frame. Secondly, whether their portrayal of the person of Jesus is essentially the same. The present chapter deals with the former question, the following chapter with the latter.

At first sight, the *Diatessaron* (c AD 150-160) by Tatian, which is a combination of the four Gospels into a single narrative, should be helpful. But, although Tatian puts the text into a sequence largely based on John's Gospel, the call of Levi/Matthew is mentioned at least three times, and not just once as we might expect in a real harmony of the Gospels. We are therefore obliged to carry out our own investigation.

We will show that the answers to our two basic questions are both a resounding YES. However, our investigation of the Gospels' chronology and geography, touching on the questions of Gospel contents and structure, will lead us into fascinating suggestions on the writing strategies of Matthew, Mark, Luke and John.

We begin with the chronology and geography of Mark's Gospel, because it is the shortest and the simplest in structure. We are not necessarily stipulating that Mark was the first Gospel to be written.

THE CHRONOLOGY AND GEOGRAPHY OF THE SYNOPTIC GOSPELS

The Chronology and Geography of Mark's Gospel

We may summarize the chronology and geography of Mark's Gospel as follows (see Table 13.4)[73]. Jesus begins his preparation for ministry by being baptized by John the Baptist at Bethany across the Jordan. After being tempted, Jesus returns to Galilee, calls his first disciples, and begins his Galilean ministry. When the tensions with the authorities begin to rise, he seeks rest in the north-westerly region of Tyre and Sidon. He goes back to Galilee and leads his

---

[73] Table 13.4 is based on a detailed analysis which, unfortunately, we do not have the space to reproduce here.

disciples to the north-easterly region of Caesarea Philippi, where Peter declares him to be the Messiah, which is a pivotal moment in all three Synoptic Gospels. In Mark 10:1, Jesus leaves Galilee and begins his final push towards Jerusalem. After his triumphal approach to Jerusalem, his time there, at the Passover, is marked by his confrontation with the authorities and then by his crucifixion and resurrection.

The Chronology and Geography of Matthew's Gospel

The chronology and geography of Matthew's Gospel are identical with those of Mark's Gospel. Matthew adds the Birth Narratives (chapters 1 and 2), the Sermon on the Mount (chapters 5-7), and places the Parable of the Sower in a collection of Parables in 11:2-13:53 (see Table 13.4). He adds further parables and teaching in 18:10-19:1 and in 25:1-26:1. This enables him to impose a structure on his material, based on milestone verses with the leitmotiv *"When Jesus had finished saying these things..."* as follows:

Jesus' Teaching about Discipleship (4:23-7:29)

"When Jesus had finished saying these things..." (7:28)

Jesus' Teaching about Mission (chapter 10)

"After Jesus had finished instructing his twelve disciples..." (11:1)

Parables on the Kingdom of Heaven (chapter 13)

"When Jesus had finished these parables..." (13:53)

Jesus' Teaching on the Relations between the Disciples (chapter 18)

"When Jesus had finished saying these things..." (19:1)

Confrontation in Jerusalem (21:12-25:46)

"When Jesus had finished saying all these things..." (26:1)

Nevertheless, the chronology and geography are identical with Mark's Gospel. This is why some might be tempted to oversimplify and suggest that Matthew is just Mark's Gospel with additional teaching and parables.

In terms of geography, Matthew and Mark recount Jesus' preparation for ministry at Bethany across the Jordan (Matthew 3:1-4:11; Mark 1:2-13; Appendix 5 Map 1[74]). Jesus' Galilean ministry starts when John the Baptist is imprisoned (Matthew 4:12; Mark 1:14; Map 3) and includes his wider ministry in the north in the region of Tyre and Sidon as well as the pivotal journey to Caesarea Philippi. Jesus then leaves Galilee (Matthew 19:1; Mark 10:1); Matthew and Mark describe Jesus' final push towards Jerusalem (Map 5), the confrontation with the authorities in Jerusalem and the Passion Narrative.

---

[74] The maps are to be found in Appendix 5. Unfortunately, we do not have the space to explain the crossing points on the River Jordan etc. Those who wish to investigate this aspect further should refer to the atlases and maps in the Bibliography. Craig Blomberg (*HRNT* p111) states that recent archaeology has pinpointed the previously uncertain site of Bethany across the Jordan, not far across the river from Jericho.

The Chronology and Geography of Luke's Gospel

The chronology and geography of Luke's Gospel are more complicated as Table 13.4 shows, but in all three Synoptic Gospels (Matthew 4:12; Mark 1:14; Luke 3:20) it is the imprisonment of John the Baptist by Herod Antipas that triggers Jesus' ministry in Galilee. Luke's Birth Narratives are not the same as those of Matthew and he does not include the Sermon on the Mount. He inserts the Sermon on the Plain, where Mark has the Parable of the Sower. He then completely omits (this is termed Luke's Great Omission) Jesus' Wider Ministry in the North in the region of Tyre and Sidon as well as the material corresponding to Matthew 14:22-15:20 and Mark 6:45-7:23. After Peter's pivotal declaration that Jesus is the Messiah, Luke has Jesus leave Galilee in 9:51, but adds a considerable amount of extra material (9:51-16:15) before coinciding with Matthew and Mark on the final push to Jerusalem. Even here, Luke adds more material (16:19-18:14 and 19:1-22). Finally, Luke adds material during the trial sequence of Jesus (22:66-23:12) and to the resurrection accounts (24:1-53).

There are thus some differences from the Mark/Matthew chronology, geography and contents, and the differences in content are largely by blocks of material. This can also be expressed in numbers, either by considering the number of passages or by considering the number of verses, although this obscures the blocks. This is shown in Table 13.1 (on the next page).

In terms of verses, *FFBR* pp28-29 puts it this way: *"of the 1068 verses in Matthew's gospel, about 500 contain material also found in Mark; of the 1149 verses of Luke, about 350 are paralleled in Mark. Altogether, there are only 31 verses in Mark which have no parallel either in Matthew or Luke. When we compare Matthew and Luke by themselves, we find that these two have about 250 verses containing common material not paralleled in Mark...We are then left with some 300 verses in Matthew containing narratives and discourses peculiar to that gospel and about 550 verses found only in Luke."*

The first three lines of data come from the author's own detailed analysis. Although 100% precision is not possible, the Table 13.1 shows that all four approaches give approximately the same results. Luke contains the highest proportion of his own material (between 42 and 48%). Between 45 and 54% of Matthew is material which is shared with Mark, while between 29 and 36% is his own. Only about 10-24% of Matthew is shared with Luke.

To sum up, Matthew and Mark recount the same events in the same places in the same time frame, with Matthew adding additional parables and teaching. All three Synoptic Gospels talk of Jesus attending just one Passover Feast as an adult, the one where he is crucified and rises from the dead. Luke adds a little more of his own material and we must establish when and where this fits in. It turns out that John's Gospel holds the key to understanding the chronology and geography of Luke. However, before leaving the chronology of Luke, he brings in an important piece of information.

Luke 3:1 states that John the Baptist's ministry, which immediately preceded that of Jesus, occurred *"in the fifteenth year of Tiberius Caesar."* Tiberius Caesar became Emperor in August AD 14 and so, according to the method of computation current in Syria, which Luke would have followed, his fifteenth year began in September or October AD 27. Since (*FFBR* p14; *HRNT* p110) John's Gospel mentions 3 Passover Festivals after this time, this means that the crucifixion of Jesus occurred at the Passover of AD 30.

Table 13.1: COMPARISON OF SYNOPTIC GOSPELS MATERIAL

	Matthew			**Mark**			**Luke**		
	Mark	Matthew	Luke	Mark	Matthew	Luke	Mark	Matthew	Luke
Number of passages									
TOTAL		123							132
Author's breakdown	66	44	13	78			56	16	60
%	53.7	35.8	10.6	100			42.4	12.1	45.5
DBLuke pp9-12 % breakdown				100					
FMatt pp34-35 % breakdown	45.0	35.0	20.0	100			35.0	21.0	42.5
Number of verses									
TOTAL		1068			661				1149
FFBR pp28-29 breakdown	500	318	250	661			350	250	549
% breakdown	46.8	29.8	23.4	100			30.5	21.8	47.8

We now consider the chronology and geography of John's Gospel, beginning with his account of Jewish Festivals.

THE CHRONOLOGY AND GEOGRAPHY OF JOHN'S GOSPEL

The Jewish Feasts Recorded in John's Gospel

For Matthew, Mark and Luke, the adult Jesus is present only once in Jerusalem for the Passover Feast and this is when he is arrested and crucified. John, on the other hand, mentions three Passovers, including that of his arrest and crucifixion. Listing the Jewish Festivals described in John's Gospel gives (Table 13.2):

Table 13.2: JEWISH FESTIVALS IN JOHN'S GOSPEL			
Reference in John's Gospel	**Jewish Festival**	**Jewish Calendar**	**Our Calendar**
John 2:13	Passover	14/15 Nisan	April AD 28
John 5:1	A *"Feast of the Jews"*		
John 6:4	Passover	14/15 Nisan	April AD 29
John 7:1, 14	Tabernacles	15-21 Tishri	Sept/Oct AD 29
John 10:22	Dedication	25 Chislev	Dec AD 29
John 12:1	Passover	14/15 Nisan	April AD 30

The Passover was strictly celebrated on the night of 14/15 Nisan, but the festivities probably began on 12 Nisan. The Feast of Dedication was more precisely Hannukah, the Feast of Rededication of the Temple for the worship of YHWH in 165 or 164 BC, after its profanation two or three years earlier by Antiochus IV Epiphanes (*Test* p257; *HRNT* p211). The feast of John 5:1 could have been either the Passover or Tabernacles (*CJohn* p240). We follow *Test* pp255-269, *HRNT* pp110 and 204 and *FFBR* p47 in supposing that it was Tabernacles[75]. This then gives us the base of our timeline in our Gospels Timeframe Chart 13.1, with approximately six months between Passover and Tabernacles.

---

[75] If the festival of John 5:1 were Passover, which seems unlikely, it would not alter the line of reasoning which follows. It would just mean that Jesus' earthly ministry lasted three and a half, rather than two and a half, years.

Chart 13.1   GOSPELS TIMEFRAME

JOHN CHAPTER/VERSE	2|13	5|1	6|4	7|14	10|22	12|12
FESTIVAL	Passover AD 28	Tabernacles	Passover AD 29	Tabernacles	Hannukah	Passover AD 30
JEWISH CALENDAR	14/15 Nisan	15-21 Tishri	14/15 Nisan	15-21 Tishri	25 Chislev	14/15 Nisan
MONTH/YEAR	April AD 28	Sept/Oct AD 28	April AD 29	Sept/Oct AD 29	Dec AD 29	April AD 30

Chart 13.2 JOHN'S GOSPEL TIMEFRAME

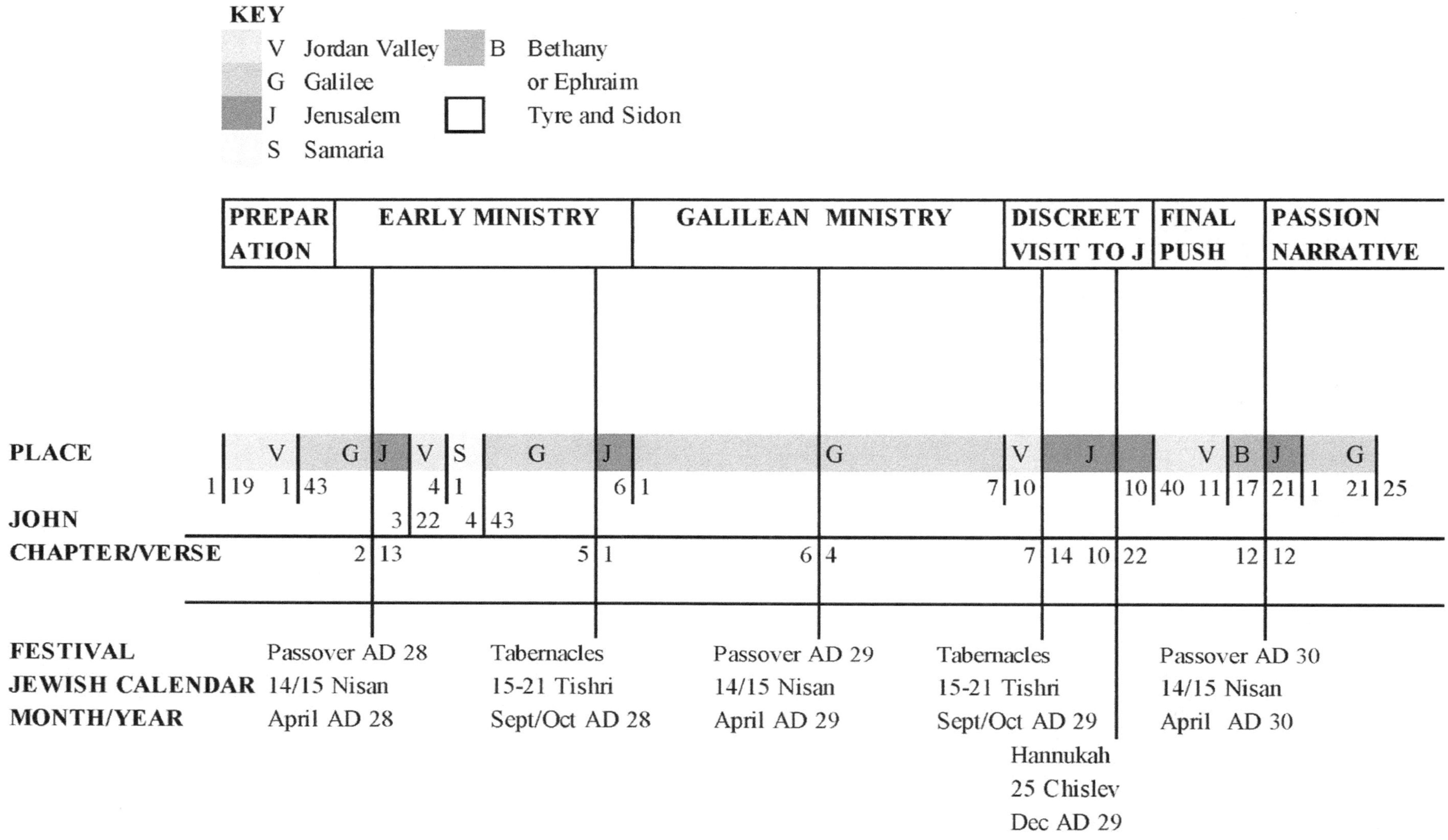

KEY
- V Jordan Valley
- G Galilee
- J Jerusalem
- S Samaria
- B Bethany or Ephraim
- ☐ Tyre and Sidon

	PREPARATION	EARLY MINISTRY		GALILEAN MINISTRY		DISCREET VISIT TO J	FINAL PUSH	PASSION NARRATIVE
PLACE	V | G | 1|19 1|43	J | V | S 3|22 4|1 4|43	G	J 6|1	G	V | J 7|10	V | B | J 10|40 11|17 21|1	G 21|25
JOHN CHAPTER/VERSE		2|13	5|1	6|4	7|14 10|22	12|12	
FESTIVAL	Passover AD 28			Passover AD 29	Tabernacles		Passover AD 30
JEWISH CALENDAR	14/15 Nisan	Tabernacles 15-21 Tishri		14/15 Nisan	15-21 Tishri		14/15 Nisan
MONTH/YEAR	April AD 28	Sept/Oct AD 28		April AD 29	Sept/Oct AD 29 Hannukah 25 Chislev Dec AD 29		April AD 30

Tracing John's Basic Timeline

The second step is to trace John's many place markers onto this basic timeline to give us the John's Gospel Timeframe Chart 13.2. We note two important points. Firstly, the bulk of the Galilean ministry of Jesus must have occurred between Tabernacles AD 28 and Tabernacles AD 29, that is between John 6:1 and 7:10. Secondly, Jesus went up to Jerusalem for Tabernacles AD 29 and stayed there until the Feast of Hannukah (John 10:22), but then retired to the Jordan Valley for several months (John 10:40), because *"the right time had not yet come"* (John 7:6), before making the final push to Jerusalem for the Passover of AD 30 (*FFBR* p47). Thus, in the John's Gospel Timeframe Chart 13.2, the adult Jesus makes four separate visits to Jerusalem, and we have essentially six stages in Jesus' ministry: his preparation for ministry (Map 1), his early ministry including his first and second visits to Jerusalem (Map 2)[76], his Galilean ministry (Map 3), his discreet visit to Jerusalem (Map 4), the final push towards Jerusalem (Map 5) and the Passion Narrative.

---

[76] No map is necessary for the second visit to Jerusalem, because Jesus would have followed the same route as the first, apart from the bifurcation into the Judean desert on the way back.

Chart 13.3A GOSPELS CHRONOLOGY: PASSAGES FROM JOHN AND THEIR CORRESPONDING PASSAGES IN THE SYNOPTIC GOSPELS

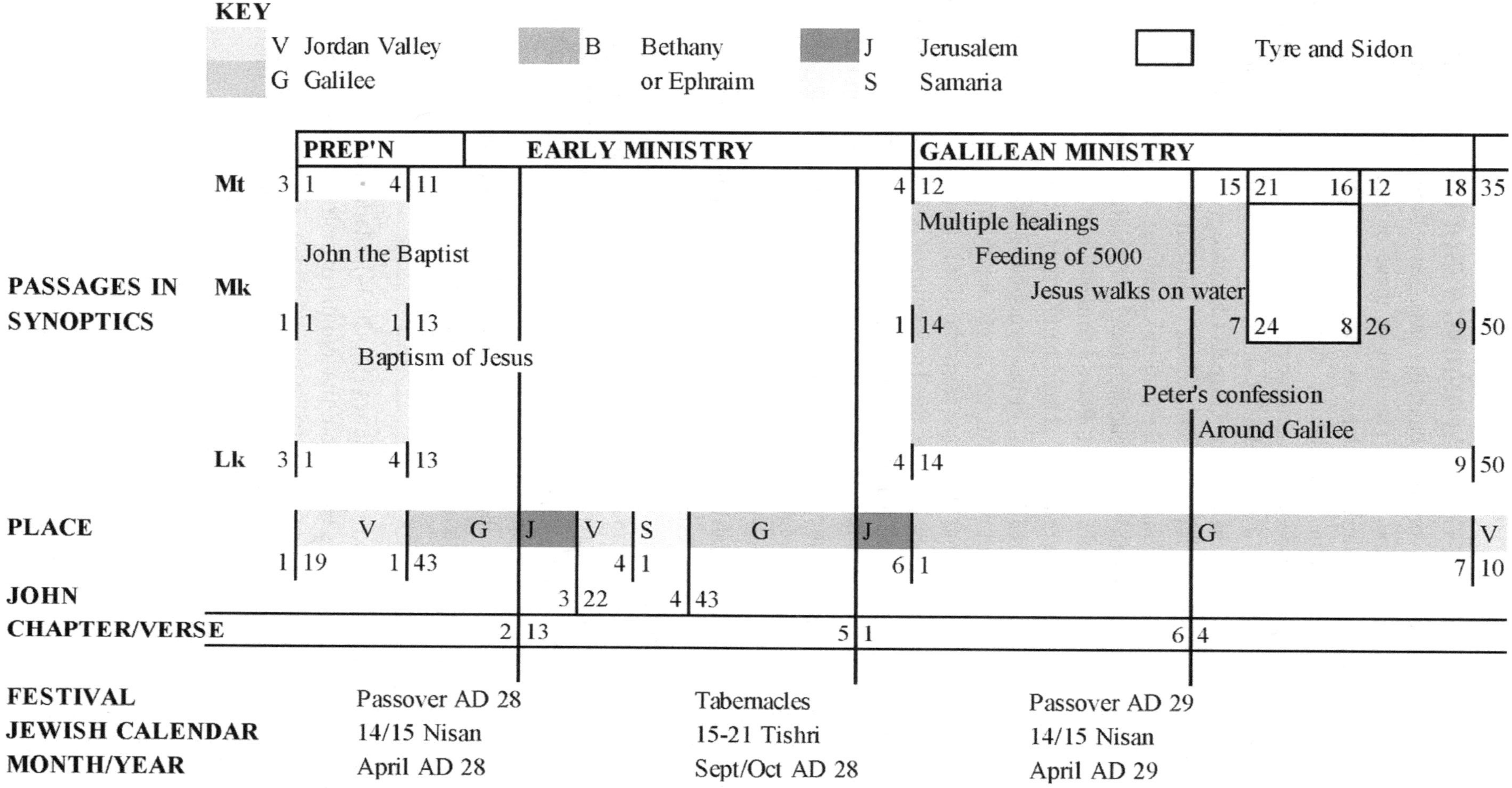

KEY

- V Jordan Valley
- G Galilee
- B Bethany
- J Jerusalem
- S Samaria
- [ ] or Ephraim
- Tyre and Sidon

	PREP'N	EARLY MINISTRY	GALILEAN MINISTRY
PASSAGES IN SYNOPTICS Mt	3|1 — 4|11 John the Baptist		4|12 — 15|21 16|12 18|35
Mk	1|1 — 1|13 Baptism of Jesus		1|14 — 7|24 8|26 9|50
Lk	3|1 — 4|13		4|14 — 9|50
			Multiple healings / Feeding of 5000 / Jesus walks on water / Peter's confession / Around Galilee
PLACE	V	J V S G	J G
JOHN CHAPTER/VERSE	1|19 — 2|13	3|22 4|1 4|43 5|1	6|1 6|4 — 7|10
FESTIVAL	Passover AD 28	Tabernacles	Passover AD 29
JEWISH CALENDAR	14/15 Nisan	15-21 Tishri	14/15 Nisan
MONTH/YEAR	April AD 28	Sept/Oct AD 28	April AD 29

INCORPORATING THE CORRESPONDING SYNOPTIC PASSAGES

The third step is to place on our time chart the passages of John which clearly correspond with those from Matthew, Mark and Luke. The first of these blocks (see the Gospels Chronology Chart 13.3A) concerns the ministry of John the Baptist, and the baptism of Jesus, beginning in the Valley of the Jordan (John 1:19), before moving to Galilee in John 1:43. The equivalent passages in the Synoptic Gospels are found after the birth narratives of Matthew and Luke, in Matthew 3:1-4:11, Mark 1:1-13 and Luke 3:1-4:13; they are often known as Jesus' Preparation for Ministry[77]. We duly place these on the Gospels Chronology Chart 13.3A.

The second block of material represents Jesus' Galilean Ministry, which we find between John 6:1 and John 7:9. Here, John describes multiple healings, the feeding of the 5,000 and Jesus walking on the lake. In Mark 6:39, we read that the 5,000 could sit on green grass, which fits the time of the Passover as in John's account. Peter's confession of John 6:68 *"Lord to whom can we go? You have the words of eternal life"* should be taken as the equivalent of his confession that Jesus is the Messiah at Caesarea Philippi in the Synoptic Gospels. In all four Gospels, it can be regarded as the pivotal moment which triggers Jesus' determination to go to Jerusalem, where he knows he will be crucified and then rise from the dead. Finally, John states that Jesus went around Galilee, which probably includes the Transfiguration. The Wider Ministry in the North, in the region of Tyre and Sidon, which is described in Matthew 15:21-16:12 and Mark 7:24-8:26 (see the Gospels Chronology Chart 13.3A on the next page), is absent from Luke.

Hence, Jesus' Galilean Ministry is recounted in Matthew 4:12-18:35; Mark 1:14-9:50 and Luke 4:14-9:50 and matches John 6:1-7:9.

The third block of material in John's Gospel which clearly matches that of the Synoptic Gospels is the Passion Narrative, beginning with Jesus' triumphal entry to Jerusalem and continuing through his trial, crucifixion, resurrection and resurrection appearances. Matthew, Mark, Luke and John are manifestly describing the same climactic events in Jerusalem. John 12:12-21:25 thus corresponds to Matthew 21:1-28:20; Mark 11:1-16:8 and Luke 19:28-24:53 in the Gospels Chronology Chart 13.3B, although the confrontation with the Jewish authorities is only found in the Synoptic Gospels (Matthew 21:12-25:46; Mark 11:12-13:37; Luke 19:45-21:38).

We can in this way identify these three blocks of material or events, which are common to the four Gospels, and place them in an overall coherent time frame.

The Final Push to Jerusalem

This block of material found in Matthew (19:1-20:34), Mark (10:1-52) and Luke (14:1-19:27) does not really figure in John's Gospel but fits into the overall timeframe, between Jesus leaving the Jordan Valley and his Triumphal Entry to Jerusalem (see Gospels Chronology Chart 13.3B). This is where John introduces the raising of Lazarus as the curtain raiser to the Passion Narrative.

---

[77] The call of the first disciples seems to have occurred in two stages, the first recounted in John: 1:35-51, the second in Matthew 4:18-22, Mark1:14-20 and Luke 5:1-11.

Chart 13.3B: GOSPELS CHRONOLOGY
PASSAGES FROM JOHN AND THEIR CORRESPONDING PASSAGES IN THE SYNOPTIC GOSPELS

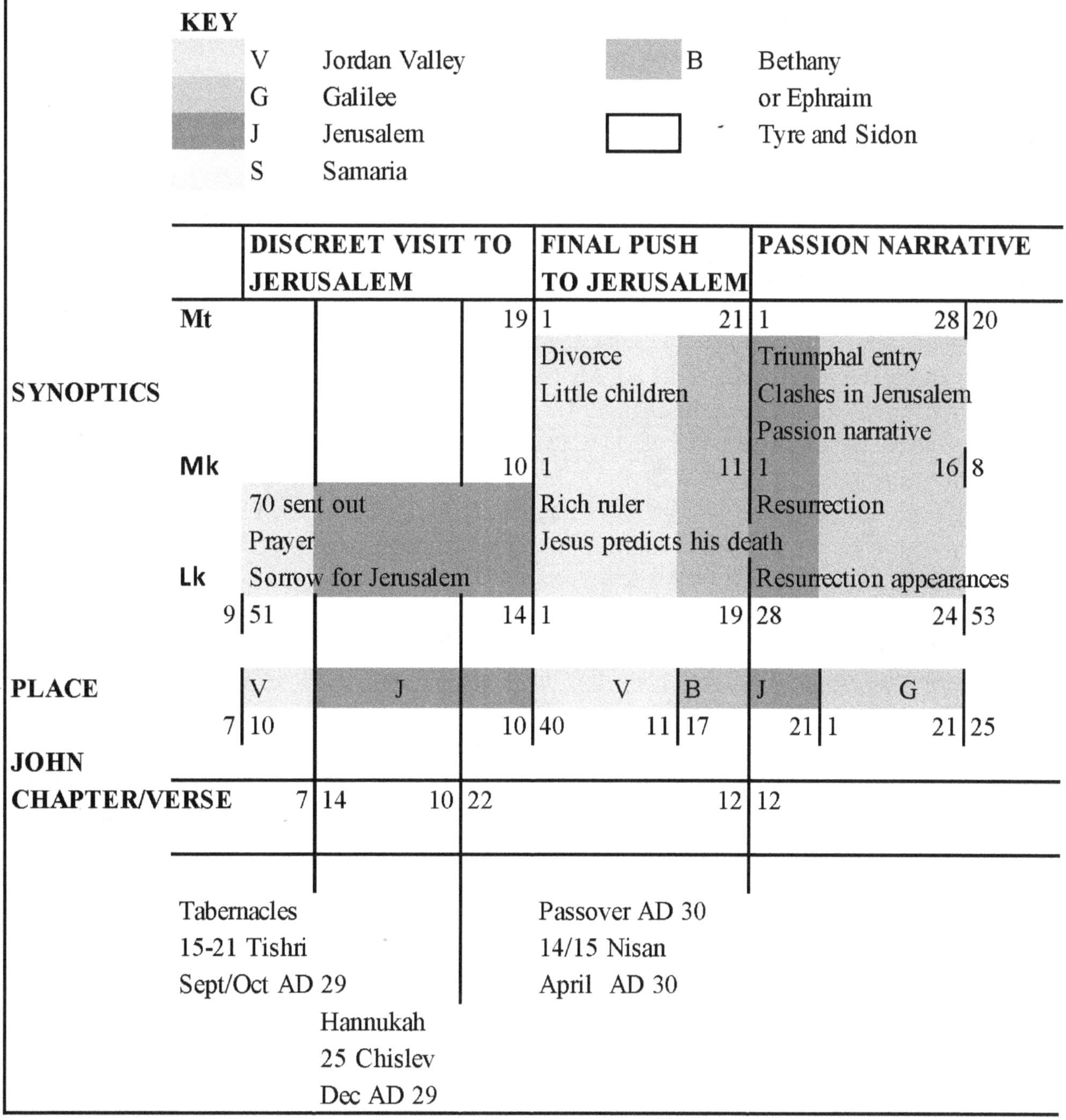

KEY

	V	Jordan Valley		B	Bethany
	G	Galilee			or Ephraim
	J	Jerusalem		-	Tyre and Sidon
	S	Samaria			

		DISCREET VISIT TO JERUSALEM		FINAL PUSH TO JERUSALEM		PASSION NARRATIVE	
SYNOPTICS	Mt			19|1 Divorce Little children	21|1	Triumphal entry Clashes in Jerusalem Passion narrative	28|20
	Mk			10|1 Rich ruler Jesus predicts his death	11|1	Resurrection Resurrection appearances	16|8
	Lk	70 sent out Prayer Sorrow for Jerusalem					
		9|51		14|1	19|28		24|53
PLACE		V	J	V	B	J	G
JOHN CHAPTER/VERSE		7|10 7 14	10|22	10|40 11|17 12		12|21 12|1	21|25

Tabernacles
15-21 Tishri
Sept/Oct AD 29

Passover AD 30
14/15 Nisan
April AD 30

Hannukah
25 Chislev
Dec AD 29

Jesus' Discreet Visit to Jerusalem

It is clear that Luke joins John in recounting Jesus' discreet visit to Jerusalem because, long before the final push towards Jerusalem, Luke places Jesus at Martha and Mary's house (10:38) and then expressing his sorrow over Jerusalem (13:34) (see also *Trust?* p60). Unfortunately, we do not have the space to give a more detailed analysis of all the geographical pointers in this section of Luke's Gospel. Suffice it to say that this block of material in Luke (9:51-14:1) can be located on the Gospels Chronology Chart 13.3B in the same period as John 7:10 - 10:40.

SUMMARY OF GOSPELS CHRONOLOGY AND GEOGRAPHY

We have been able to construct a coherent Gospels Chronology in Charts 13.3A and B, which faithfully situates the material of the four Gospels, and maps which describe Jesus' journeys in detail. The basic timeline and place markers come from John's Gospel, because Jesus' ministry spans a longer period in this Gospel than in the three Synoptic Gospels.

All four Gospels treat Jesus' Preparation for Ministry. John continues (2:13-6:1) by recounting Jesus' early ministry in Galilee, Jerusalem, Samaria, and then again in Galilee and Jerusalem. Then all four Gospels describe Jesus' Galilean ministry of about one year, including the feeding of the 5,000 and Peter's confession of faith, between the Feasts of Tabernacles of AD 28 and 29, in varying degrees of detail. Matthew and Mark include in this Galilean ministry a wider ministry in the north, in the region of Tyre and Sidon. John's account of Jesus' Galilean ministry concentrates on certain milestone events which enable us to make the link with the Synoptic Gospels.

Only John and Luke then describe a discreet visit to Jerusalem for the Feast of Tabernacles in AD 29. John recounts how Jesus stayed on in Jerusalem for Hannukah, before retiring to the Jordan Valley (Perea) to wait for his time to come. The final push to Jerusalem is present in all four Gospels, but John's account is different because he introduces the raising of Lazarus as a curtain raiser to the Passion Narrative. Once again, all four Gospels recount Jesus' arrest, trial, crucifixion and resurrection, before ending his time on earth back in Galilee. Whereas the Synoptic writers describe the confrontation with the Jewish authorities in the lead-up to Jesus' arrest, John does not, presumably because he has already explained these tensions in earlier chapters. Similarly, in the account of the Upper Room, John does not deal with the installation of the Eucharist, which he has already prefigured in chapter 6, leaving us instead an important discourse on the Holy Spirit.

Nevertheless, the four Gospels present a coherent whole in terms of chronology and geography: the same events occur in the same places in the same time frame. In fact, the four Gospel writers have, by leaving us four complementary biographies of Jesus, combined together to give us a very rich portrait of Jesus, his person and his life. This allows us some reflections on the different strategies of the four Gospel authors.

THE INTERLOCKING GOSPELS OF LUKE AND JOHN

It is interesting to return to our conclusions on the origins of the four Gospels. Here, we resume some of the main points in Table 13.3:

Table 13.3: MAIN POINTS ON GOSPEL ORIGINS

Author	Matthew	John Mark	Luke	John
Inclusio evidence on eyewitnesses	None	Peter	Peter plus women	Peter plus John
Language	Hebrew/Aramaic, then Greek	Greek	Greek	Greek
Place of writing	Palestine or Syria	Rome	Caesarea, then Rome	Ephesus, Asia Minor
Date of writing	Syriac AD 55-57	AD 59-60	Feb AD 60 - Feb AD 62	AD 96-98

From the dates of writing, we see that John was written much later than the other three Gospels, and that Luke was written just after Matthew and Mark[78]. So, John would have had copies of Matthew, Mark and Luke in front of him as he wrote, and the fact that he was able to disclose the identity of witnesses that the other three had protected (see the section on Protective Anonymity) confirms this. Similarly, Luke would have had copies of Matthew and Mark to work with. Luke himself confirms this in 1:1, where he states that others (plural) had already written accounts of the life of Jesus. We note that none of the following argument is dependent on Mark being the first Gospel to be written, or for that matter Matthew: it is, however, dependent on them both being written, in some form, before Luke.

CJohn pp49-57 says that, in this way, the Gospel of John *interlocks* (see also *HRNT* p165) with the Synoptic Gospels, in the sense that John reacts to them and completes them. However, in reality we see that there are two interlocking Gospels: Luke interlocks with Matthew and Mark, while John interlocks with Matthew, Mark and Luke. This is shown in Table 13.4: Gospel Interactions.

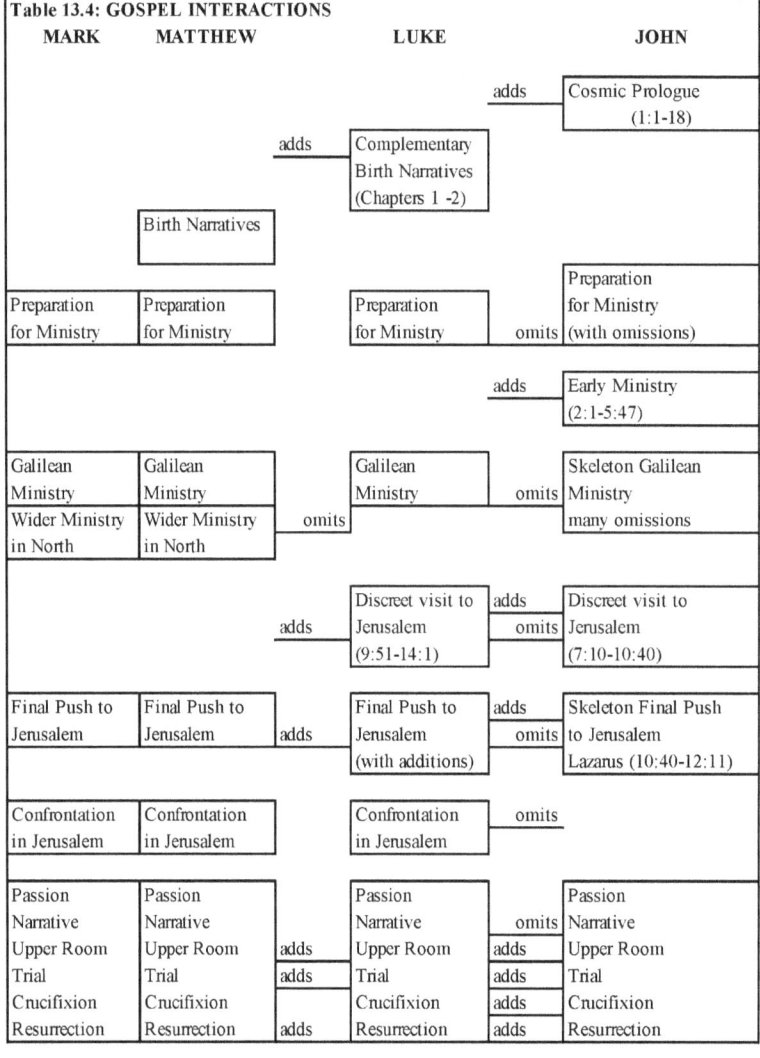

---

[78] This is especially the case if we suppose that Luke possessed the Syriac version of Matthew when he was in Caesarea between AD 57 and AD 59.

We see that Luke interacts with Matthew and Mark by adding and omitting. He omits Jesus' wider ministry in the north and subsequent material, presumably because he considered that Matthew and Mark had already covered these points in sufficient detail. On the other hand, Luke complements Matthew and Mark by adding additional birth stories, the discreet visit to Jerusalem, more important parables during the final push towards Jerusalem and extra detail in the Passion Narrative.

John's strategy was different again. He interacted with Luke and with Matthew and Mark. Considering that the birth narratives had already been fully dealt with by Matthew and Luke, he placed Jesus as the cosmic Lord of creation in his prologue (1:1-18). In Jesus' preparation for ministry, John ignores Jesus' testing by Satan, already treated by Matthew and Luke. However, John adds a huge chunk of material concerning Jesus' early ministry (2:1-5:47), before giving us a skeletal account of the Galilean ministry, already recounted in great detail by the three Synoptic writers. However, even in this skeletal account, he gives us milestones, so that we can discern the correspondence with the Synoptic Gospels. For Jesus' discreet visit to Jerusalem, he omits most of Luke's material, instead giving us a series of discourses and confrontations with the Pharisees in Jerusalem. Similarly, John omits the Synoptic material in the final push towards Jerusalem and the confrontation with the Jewish authorities, instead introducing the raising of Lazarus as the curtain raiser to the Passion Narrative. While omitting the installation of the Eucharist, John brings a considerable amount of extra detail to the Passion Narrative.

Thus, we can see that, partly because Luke was written after Matthew and Mark, and John after Luke, the strategies of the four Gospel writers were different. John interacted or interlocked with Luke, Matthew and Mark; Luke had already interlocked or interacted with Matthew and Mark. They were thus able, by complementary accounts to build up a rich picture of Jesus' actions and life. In the next chapter, we will consider whether the four Gospels portray Jesus' person in the same way and two particular cases of chronology.

Chapter 14

THE PERSON OF JESUS

We have previously shown that the Gospel writers had impeccable credentials, but contrasting professions and profiles. They also based their Gospels on different eyewitness testimonies, albeit testimony of the highest quality. Therefore, in this chapter we will ask the question: do the four Gospel writers present us with essentially the same portrait of Jesus as a person? Then we will deal with two particular difficulties which are sometimes brought up concerning the coherence of the Gospels: the genealogies in Matthew and Luke and the chronology of the Passion Narratives.

THE PERSON OF JESUS

Although each of the four Gospel writers casts a different light on the person of Jesus, they all view him as, on the one hand, the Messiah (*Christos* in Greek; literally *the anointed one*) and the Son of God and, on the other hand, as fully human. There is therefore no essential difference in the portrayal of the person of Jesus on the four Gospels, but there are variations of shade and colour.

Messiah and Son of God

The four Gospel writers make it clear from the outset that Jesus is the Messiah and Son of God, in their prologues, birth narratives and when Jesus was baptized:

"The beginning of the gospel about Jesus Christ, the Son of God." (Mark 1:1)

"A record of the genealogy of Jesus Christ the son of David." (Matthew 1:1)

"And a voice from heaven said, 'This is my Son, whom I love; with him I am well pleased.'" (Matthew 3:17)

"So the holy one born to you will be called the Son of God." (Luke 1:35b)

"Today in the town of David has been born to you; he is Christ the Lord." (Luke 2:11)

"For the law was given through Moses; grace and truth came through Jesus Christ." (John 1:17)

"I have seen and I testify that this is the Son of God." (John 1:34)

Jesus is also named as the Son of God and Messiah towards the end of all four Gospels, particularly in the trial and crucifixion scenes:

"The high priest said to him, 'I charge you under oath by the living God: Tell us if you are the Christ, the Son of God.' 'Yes, it is as you say,' Jesus replied." (Matthew 26:63-64a)

"Again, the high priest asked him, 'Are you the Christ, the Son of the Blessed One?' 'I am,' said Jesus." (Mark 14:61-62a)

"'If you are the Christ,' they said, 'Tell us.' Jesus answered, 'If I tell you, you will not believe me.' They all asked, 'Are you the Son of God?' He replied, 'You are right in saying I am.'" (Luke 22:67-70)

"The Jews insisted, 'We have a law, and according to that law he must die, because he claimed to be the Son of God.'" (John 19:7)

"When the centurion and those with him who were guarding Jesus saw the earthquake and all that had happened, they were terrified, and exclaimed, 'Surely, he was the Son of God!'" (Matthew 27:54)

"And when the centurion, who stood there in front of Jesus, heard his cry and saw how he died, he said, 'Surely this man was the Son of God.'" (Mark 15:39).

Nevertheless, to avoid getting killed straightaway at the beginning of his ministry, Jesus tried to avoid saying outright that he was the Messiah or Son of God. When, for example, Peter and the disciples finally figured it out, in the following verse(s) we read that immediately Jesus warned them not to tell anyone (see Matthew 16:16, 20; Mark 8:29, 30; Luke 9:20, 21). Even so, Jesus' announcement at Nazareth that he was the Messiah was barely veiled (Luke 4:18-21).

Therefore, Jesus used codes to get his message across but still stay alive, at least for a time.

Codes

Jesus used many codes which are found in all four Gospels. These often took the form of direct quotations from, allusions to, or echoes of, the Old Testament (*Echoes* p10). At other times the Gospel writers conjured up images inspired by the Old Testament. We do not have the space to do justice to this subject; the reader who wishes to investigate it further is encouraged to study *Echoes* by Richard B Hays. We will restrict ourselves to two codes which Jesus used about himself: My Father, Our Father and Son of Man.

Code 1: My Father, Our Father

The first code was hardly one at all: he talked of God as *"My Father"* or to his disciples as *"Our Father,"* the latter especially in the Lord's Prayer. Jesus is recorded as using the term *"My Father"* above all in John's Gospel, where numerous examples are to be found in chapters 5, 8, 10, 14 and 16, culminating in *"I and the Father are one"* (John 10:30). However, Matthew also has Jesus using the same term, especially in the Sermon on the Mount (chapters 6 and 7), in chapter 11 and in the Upper Room (chapter 26). Luke has the term *"Father"* in chapter 11 and in the Upper Room (chapter 22) and all three Synoptic Gospels describe Jesus using it in Gethsemane (Matthew 26:39; Mark 14:36 and Luke 22:42).

Code 2: Son of Man

The second code was the one Jesus used most often (*Trust?* p103) for himself: *"Son of Man."* There are many examples in all four Gospels. This was more subtle because it could be understood in two ways. Read as *"a son of man"* it would have meant just a man. But Jesus referred to himself as *"The Son of Man or man"* and charged the name with all the contents of

Daniel 7:13-15. This term was not in current use in Judaism as a messianic title at the time of Jesus, even though the messianic significance of Daniel 7 was recognized and developed in later Jewish literature. Thus, Jesus' use of *"Son of Man"* enabled him to evoke his messiahship without using the clear nationalistic content of terms such as *"Messiah"* or *"Son of David"* (*FMark* pp127-128). *"In Daniel 7:13-15,* 'one like a son of man' *is the true representative of God's people. He is opposed by the forces of evil; but God vindicates him and rescues him, proves him to be in the right, and gives him authority...to dispense God's judgment"* (*TWMark* p17). Jesus saw this as a pithy description of his mission on earth: he was the Messiah, the true representative of Israel; he would suffer and die on the cross, as in the Servant Songs of Isaiah 42:1-53:12 (*FFBJ* p63), but God would declare him in the right by his resurrection. Here are some of the most significant things Jesus said about himself using the code the *"Son of Man or man"*:

- He had power on earth to forgive sins, which only God could normally do (Mark 2:10)

- He was Lord of the Sabbath, which was God's prerogative (Mark 2:28)

- He will dispense definitive judgment on men, which is God's job (Matthew 13:41)

- He *"came to serve and to give his life as a ransom for many."* (Mark 10:45)

- He *"came to seek and to save what was lost."* (Luke 19:10)

- He was *"going to be betrayed into the hands of men. They will kill him, and on the third day he will be raised to life."* (Matthew 17:22-23a)

- *"Just as Moses lifted up the snake in the desert, so the Son of Man must be lifted up, that everyone who believes in him may have eternal life."* (John 3:14-15)

Thus, in spite of using coded terms for himself, such as *"My Father"* and *"Son of Man,"* Jesus was able to underline that he was indeed the Messiah (Christ) and the Son of God. All four Gospels attest to this.

Fully Man

However, the Gospels also maintain that Jesus was fully man. He suffered hunger and was tempted (Matthew 4:1-11; Luke 4:1-13), was extremely sensitive to the distress of others (Luke 7:11-17) and wept when his friend Lazarus died (John 11:35).

Certainly, his ministry was not that of an ordinary man: according to all four Gospels he was a miracle worker, healer and raised the dead. The Synoptic Gospels are full of Jesus' healings and exorcisms and all four Gospels include the miraculous feeding of the 5,000. John's Gospel also includes major healing miracles (4:43-54; 5:1-15; 9:1-41) and the turning of water into wine (2:1-11). Finally, Jesus raises the dead in all four Gospels: Jairus' daughter (Matthew 9:18-26; Mark 5:21-43; Luke 8:40-56), the widow of Nain's son (Luke 7:11-17) and, of course, Lazarus (John 11:1-44).

Alongside Jesus' miracle-working and healing ministry, Jesus was also a prophet. In particular, he seemed to have insights into what people were thinking and what was going on deep down in their hearts (John 4:16-19). There are examples of this *"cardiognosis"* (literally knowledge of the heart) in all four Gospels, and it was an important expression of Jesus' love and compassion.

Thus, all four Gospels declare that Jesus was the Messiah or Christ, the Son of God and yet fully man. As Tom Wright says, *"Jesus can only be properly understood as the human being who embodies or incarnates the fullness of divinity"* (*TWPrison* p167). There is no essential difference between the Gospels in what they tell us of the person of Jesus. Rather, they combine together, like complementary colours, to give us a wonderful and complete portrait of Jesus.

Did Jesus Speak Greek?

There is a long history of viewing Jesus as speaking only in Aramaic, and indeed Mark records Jesus as speaking Aramaic to a little girl (5:41) and to a deaf and mute person (7:34). However, as Peter J Williams points out (*Trust?* pp107-110), Greek language and influence had spread throughout the areas Alexander the Great (356-323 BC) had conquered, including Palestine. Sepphoris, the capital of Galilee in Jesus' early years, was substantially Jewish but possessed a Roman amphitheatre. As both Jesus and his father Joseph are described by the term *tekton*, meaning carpenter or builder, they would probably have been involved in construction projects in the area and would have had to conduct business transactions in Greek.

As Peter J Williams explains, some of Jesus' sayings actually reflect Greek word play. For example, four Beatitudes (Matthew 5:3-11) begin with alliteration of the Greek letter *pi* ("p" in English). Similarly, the four woes of Luke 6:24-26 have alliteration with *pi*. In addition, of course, two of Jesus' disciples – Andrew and Philip - had Greek names and (in John 12:20-22) acted as intermediaries for Greeks who wanted to see Jesus.

Thus, it is likely that Jesus spoke Greek, along with Aramaic, and that, in the Greek text of the Gospels, we have the words that Jesus really said.

We will now consider two apparent difficulties which concern the coherence of the Gospels: the genealogies in Matthew and Luke and the chronology of the Passion Narratives.

TWO APPARENT DIFFICULTIES

The Genealogies of Jesus in Matthew and Luke

The genealogies recorded in the Gospels of Matthew and Luke are not identical, even though both go down Joseph's side of the family. Both tell essentially the same story and the differences have never really been an obstacle to considering the New Testament documents as absolutely reliable.

Matthew (1:1-17) starts at Abraham and goes down through his descendants to David, through the Kings of Judah, and the line after the return from exile to Joseph. Luke (3:23-38), on the other hand, reverses the order, starting with Joseph and going back through David's line to Adam. Matthew stops occasionally to explain the significance of an entry; Luke does not. Matthew lists some women (e.g. Rahab and Ruth) but Luke does not – a curious difference given Luke's usual attention to women (*DBLuke* pp918-923). Although the two genealogies differ in detail, they agree completely between Abraham and David (following 1 Chronicles 2:1-15 and Ruth 4:18-22), and both go through the same important figures of Jewish history as shown in Table 14.1:

Table 14.1: KEY FIGURES OF JEWISH HISTORY IN MATTHEW'S AND LUKE'S GENEALOGIES OF JESUS

	Adam	Abraham	David	Shealtiel, Zerubbabel	Joseph	Jesus
Verse from Matthew 1		2	6	12	16	16
Verse from Luke 3	38	34	31	27	23	23
	First human	Father of the nations	King after God's own heart	Leaders of Judah after the exile		

Matthew's is probably an "official" genealogy of the Jewish nation (*FMatt* p72), whereas Luke presents a more judicial or physical point of view, placing Jesus in the line of all humanity. They are thus both recounting essentially the same story: Jesus comes from Abraham, the father of the nations, and from the royal line of David[79]. Thus, the reliability of the Gospels is not affected.

The Chronologies of the Passion Narratives

In the Passion Narratives, all four Gospels give their versions of basically the same events. Mark and Matthew cover essentially the same material, whereas Luke and John introduce other details. In the Synoptic Gospels, the Jewish authorities have come to the point where they believe they must get rid of Jesus at all costs. In John's Gospel, the raising of Lazarus adds to the pressure on them.

Although each of the four Gospel accounts is self-consistent, it is frequently asserted that the chronologies of the Passion Narratives in the Synoptic Gospels and John's Gospel are difficult to reconcile.

However, this position ignores the fundamental fact that all four Gospels say that Jesus died on the day of Preparation for the Passover (see Matthew 27:62; Mark 15:42; Luke 23:54 and John 19:31). Hence all four Gospels and the early church historians (see for example *HE* 5.24.2-7) were clear that Jesus died as the Passover Lamb, i.e., that he was crucified on Nisan 14 at the same time as the Passover lambs were being slain, on the eve of the Passover (Nisan 15) itself. Astronomical calculations back this up: Nisan 15 did not fall on a Friday between AD 27 and 34 (*FMatt* p 365).

The matter could really be left there, but the question seems to have arisen from a cultural misunderstanding (*FMatt2* p982): the Gospel writers adopted the Jewish time system and not the Roman, or even less our contemporary system. This means that the days were counted from sunrise to sunset and not from midnight to midnight as we do.

This means that the Last Supper was held on the evening which began Nisan 14. For this it would have to have been a "Passover meal" without a lamb (no lamb is mentioned) a day early, but Jesus was sufficiently non-conformist for that! This would have put Jesus and his disciples in the same situation as Jews who were not in Jerusalem and could therefore not slaughter lambs in the Temple: a meal of unleavened bread would have had to suffice (*FMatt 2* p984). For the rest of that evening and night, the other events unfold (see Table 14.2): Jesus is arrested, tried before Annas (John 18:12-23), probably at Caiaphas's house, then before Caiaphas, then at dawn before the Sanhedrin and between dawn and noon before Pilate (twice) and Herod Antipas. Jesus then is crucified at noon on Nisan 14 and dies at 3pm. As evening approaches, Joseph of Arimathea asks Pilate for Jesus' body (John 19:38-42). We are still Nisan 14, the Day of Preparation, but the burial must be carried out quickly, before sunset, to avoid encroaching on the Passover Sabbath (Nisan 15).

All this fits together (see Table 14.2). The only remaining glitch on a perfect landscape is that Mark 15:25 has Jesus crucified at *"the third hour"* whereas in John 19:24 Pilate finally

---

[79] The custom of levirate marriage (Deuteronomy 25 :1-10) is often proposed to explain any remaining differences, but it is not certain that it resolves everything.

sentences Jesus to death at *"about the sixth hour."* However, it might be considered a little odd if the testimony from at least four different eye-witnesses agreed on every detail. It is clear that the four Gospels are recounting the same climactic earth-shaking events in Jerusalem and that they make a coherent whole[80].

In the next chapter we will consider the miracles of Jesus.

---

[80] In fact, it is even possible to resolve the difficulty of *"the third hour"* of Mark, but this does not really add anything.

Table14.2: THE GOSPELS - THE PASSION AND RESURRECTION

Page 1

PLACE	SUBJECT	JOHN 12:20-20:18	MATTHEW 26:2-28:15	MARK 14:1-16:8	LUKE 22:1-24:12	DAY	TIME
Jerusalem	Jesus Meets Greeks	12:20-36					
	Reflections	12:37-50					
Jerusalem	The Plot (1)		26:2-5	14:1-2			
Bethany	Jesus Anointed at Bethany		26:6-13	14:3-9			
Jerusalem	The Plot (2)		26:14-16	14:10-11	22:1-6		
Upper Room	Jesus Washes Disciples' Feet	13:1-17				N S N	1
Upper Room	The Lord's Supper including Jesus' Prediction of his Betrayal	13:18-30	26:17-30	14:12-26	22:7-23	A	EVENING
Upper Room	Who is the Greatest?				22:24-30	N	
Upper Room	Jesus Predicts Peter's denial	13:31-38	26:31-35	14:27-31	22:31-38		
Upper Room	The Holy Spirit	14:1-31					
Upper Room	The Holy Spirit	15:1-16:33					
En Route	Jesus' Prayer	17:1-26					
Gethsemane	Jesus' Prayer		26:36-46	14:32-42	22:39-46	1	
Gethsemane	Jesus Arrested	18:1-11	26:47-56	14:43-52	22:47-53	4	

156

Table 14.2: THE GOSPELS - THE PASSION AND RESURRECTION

PLACE	SUBJECT	JOHN	MATTHEW	MARK	LUKE	DAY	TIME
	Trial Sequence						
House of Annas/ Caiaphas	Jesus before Annas	18:12-14				N	
	Peter's First Denial	18:15-18				I	
	Reprise Jesus before Annas	18:19-23				S	
	Jesus before Caiaphas	18:24	26:57-66	14:53-64	22:54	A	
	Mocking		26:67-68	chap14:65		N	
	Peter's (2nd & 3rd) denials	18:25-27	26:69-75	14:66-72	22:55-62		DAWN
	Mocking				22:63-64		
Temple Courts	Jesus before Sanhedrin		27 verse 1	15 verse 1a	22:66-71		
Herod's Palace	Jesus before Pilate (1)	18:28-40	27: verses 2, 11-14	15:1b-5	23:1-7		
Hasmonean Palace	Jesus before Herod				23:8-12		
Fortress Antonia	Jesus before Pilate (2) publicly	19:1-16	27:15-26	15:6-15	23:13-25		
Fortress Antonia	Flogging		27:27-31	15:16-20			
Golgotha	Crucifixion	19:17-27	27:32-44	15:21-32	23:26-43		NOON (6th hour)
							15h00 (9th hour)
	Death and Resurrection						APPROACH
Golgotha	Death of Jesus	19:28-37	27:45-56	15:33-41	23:44-49	NISAN 15 1	OF EVENING
Near Golgotha	Burial of Jesus	19:38-42	27:57-61	15:42-47	23:50-56	NISAN 4	
Near Golgotha	Guards for Tomb		27:62-66				
Near Golgotha	Resurrection	20:1-18	28:1-10	16:1-8	24:1-12	NISAN 1	DAWN
Jerusalem	Guards' Report		28:11-15			6	

Chapter 15

THE MIRACLES OF JESUS

Thomas Jefferson, the principal author of the American Declaration of Independence, once decided to make himself a Bible, from which he cut out the miracles with a pair of scissors. He ended up with a very 'holey' (!) Bible; in particular the Gospels were like Gruyere cheese (*HRNT* p664).

It is clear that the question of the veracity of the miracles of Jesus, as described in the Gospels, is absolutely pivotal. If Jesus can/could work miracles, then it must be allowed that God can intervene in his universe, that he is all-powerful, that he can modify the laws of nature and that this power was revealed in the person of Jesus of Nazareth. This is obviously extremely difficult for deists, such as Thomas Jefferson, and atheists to acknowledge (*BAV* p95).

In the end the choice is clear-cut. If we reject the supernatural character of Jesus, we will reject his miracles. But if we accept the Gospels' portrait of Jesus, then his miracles will cease to be a stumbling block (*FFBR* p53).

THE HISTORICAL VIEW

The Internal Evidence

First of all, as we have demonstrated throughout this book, the accounts of the miracles in the Gospels are a matter of historical evidence. They have been written down by eyewitnesses or by others whose testimony we have shown to be trustworthy.

We have already shown that, in writing his Gospel, Luke interacted with Matthew and Mark and that, in turn, John interacted with all three of the Synoptic Gospels. Therefore, there are not many miracles which are recounted in all four Gospels; the exception is the feeding of the five thousand. In Table 15.1, we show a breakdown of the four Gospel accounts of this miracle, with the special contributions of each author in bold type.

John states that the Jewish Passover Feast was near, which ties in with Mark's remark that the grass was green – because the Passover is celebrated in April when indeed the grass is green in Palestine[81]. Luke informs us that the miracle happened near a town called Bethsaida. Matthew and Luke tell us that Jesus healed those who were sick, before feeding the five thousand. Luke has the disciples suggesting that the crowd should be sent away in order to find food *and lodging*.

Whereas the disciples (the Twelve according to Luke) remain anonymous in the Synoptic accounts, John describes the discussion with Jesus in more detail. Peter J Williams (*Trust?* p92) points out the particular coherence of the accounts of Luke and John. Luke says that the miracle

---

[81] Peter J Williams (*Trust?* p93) even produces the rainfall figures from the town of Tiberias to back this up!

occurred near Bethsaida. John describes how Jesus first of all asked Philip *"Where shall we buy bread for these people to eat?"* And it is Andrew who finds *the boy* with five *barley* loaves and two small fish. All this is entirely logical because (John 1:44) Philip and Andrew were from Bethsaida.

When the sitting down of the crowd is related, each Gospel writer uses slightly different Greek words to describe basically the same action (*BAV* p101). Finally, while all four Gospels describe the presence of 5,000 men, only Matthew underlines the fact that this number does not include the women and children who were also present.

We notice that all four Gospel writers, who had very different profiles, describe the same events, even down to the details, without any contradictions. Nevertheless, each author brings his own specific touches to the narrative.

This is exactly what we would expect if the Gospels were all based on genuine eyewitness testimony.

Secondly, unlike the 'miracles' recounted in the so-called gnostic gospels (*TWSC* p152), the miracles in the Gospels are 'in character': they are the kind of miracles that might be expected from the Jesus portrayed in these documents. As F F Bruce states: *"Not even in the earliest Gospel strata can we find a non-supernatural Jesus"* (*FFBR* p53).

The External Evidence

Thirdly, there is external evidence from non-Christian sources. Early non-Christian writers who refer to Jesus at any length do not dispute the fact that he performed miracles. We recall that Josephus called him a miracle-worker and that he appeared to those who loved him on the third day alive again:

"Now, there was about this time Jesus, a wise man, if it be lawful to call him a man, for he was a doer of wonderful works – a teacher of such men as receive the truth with pleasure. He drew over to him both many of the Jews, and many of the Gentiles. He was (the) Christ; and when Pilate, at the suggestion of the principal men amongst us, had him condemned to the cross, those that loved him at the first did not forsake him, for he appeared to them alive the third day, as the divine prophets had foretold these and ten thousand other wonderful things concerning him; and the tribe of Christians, so named after him, are not extinct at this day." (*Ant* 18.63-64)

Jewish rabbinical writings attribute his miracles to sorcery but do not deny them (*HRNT* p686). Sorcery is also the explanation given by Celsus, the philosophic critic of Christianity in the second century (*FFBR* p57).

The Nature of the Miracles

Many of the Gospel miracles are healing miracles which demonstrate Jesus' love, power and compassion, and thereby reveal the love, power and compassion of God himself. The criterion of coherence with the core teaching of Jesus is thereby satisfied (*HRNT* p686). Modern tendencies, to treat these as healings from 'psychosomatic' diseases, are simply an attempt to put a label on things which are not understood, in order to explain them away.

Similarly, to suppose that there was no real raising from the dead of Jairus's daughter (Mark 5:21-43) or the widow of Nain's son (Luke 7:11-17), because ignorant ancient peoples did not know for certain when people were dead, is merely another form of modern arrogance. The people at the time of Jesus could tell the difference between someone who was alive and a corpse. However, not even this false idea can be applied in the case of the raising of Lazarus (John 11:1-44), because he had been four days in the tomb.

However, these were not the only types of miracle performed by Jesus. There were also what may be termed *nature miracles*. One example is, of course the feeding of the 5,000, considered above and described in all four Gospels, which occurred on Jewish soil at the time of the Jewish Passover. Matthew (15:32-39) and Mark (8:1-10) record the feeding of the 4,000 in Gentile territory. Other nature miracles in Mark's Gospel include the calming of the storm (4:35-41), walking on water (6:45-53) and the cursing of the fig tree (11:20-25) and that is just Mark's input. These miracles are very different in scope and are extremely difficult to explain away. They demonstrate Jesus' mastery over the created order.

Miracles in John's Gospel

For John all the miracles are *"signs"*, to point us to something about Jesus. For example, the healing of the man who was born blind in John 9 confirms Jesus' announcement that he is *"the light of the world"* (John 8:12 and John 9:5) and reveals the spiritual blindness and obduracy of the Pharisees. Similarly, each of the nature miracles shows us something. John includes what is one of the most interesting of the nature miracles in 2:1-11: the turning of water into wine at a wedding in Cana in Galilee. Here, the stone jars usually contained water for Jewish purification rites. Jesus turns the water into wine for the wedding celebration. The message is clear and reinforced by the clearing of the Temple which follows: the demands of the Law of Moses are being transformed out of all recognition. God has come to earth in human form and that is cause for celebration.

THE RESURRECTION OF JESUS

Nevertheless, the above is in many ways merely a preamble or a starter before the main course. If the central decisive event in human history is the death of Jesus on the cross and his rising from the dead after three days, then the miracle of the Resurrection towers in importance over all the others. It may be stated that if the Resurrection is true, then so is the reality of the Christian faith. If, on the other hand, Jesus did not rise from the dead, then the Christian faith is empty and vain, perfectly useless and untrue. This is, of course, Paul's argument in 1 Corinthians 15:14-19. A consensus exists on a hard core of historical facts (*FFBR* p55):

1. Jesus really died and was placed in a well-marked tomb
2. On the third day after this the tomb was found to be empty
3. Jesus appeared to various individuals and groups of disciples in both Judea and Galilee
4. The Jewish authorities could not disprove the disciples' claim that Jesus had risen from the dead.

When, about fifty days after the crucifixion, the disciples began their public proclamation of the Gospel, their chief argument for their claims about Jesus was the fact that he had risen from the dead. "We saw him alive" they asserted (*FFBR* p53). Paul summarises the evidence and testimony that he himself had received (1 Corinthians 15:5-7).

Table 15.1: THE FEEDING OF THE FIVE THOUSAND

*Special contributions from the various gospel authors are in **bold** type*
In Matthew, Mark and Luke, this miracle occurs after the death of John the Baptist

Matthew 14:13-21	Mark 6:30-44	Luke 9:10-17	John 6:1-13
Jesus withdrew by boat to a solitary place (13)	So they went away by themselves in a boat to a solitary place (32)	They withdrew to a town called **Bethsaida** (10)	**Jesus crossed to the far shore of the Sea of Galilee…Jesus went up on a mountainside…The Jewish Passover Feast was near** (1-4)
Jesus landed and saw a large crowd (v14)	Jesus landed and saw a large crowd (v34)	The crowds learned about it and followed him (11)	A great crowd of people followed him (2)
He had compassion on them. He **healed their sick** (14)	He had compassion them. He taught them (34)	He spoke to them about the kingdom of God, and **healed those who needed healing** (11)	
As evening approached (15)	By this time it was late in the day (v35)	Late in the afternoon (14)	
The disciples said, "Send the crowds away, so they can…buy themselves some food." (15)	The disciples said, "Send the crowds away…so they can buy themselves something to eat." (36)	The Twelve said, "Send the crowd away…to find food **and lodging**." (v14)	Jesus said to **Philip**, "Where shall we buy bread for these people to eat?" (v5)
Jesus answered, "You give them something to eat." (16)	But he answered, "You give them something to eat." (37)	He replied, "You give them something to eat." (13)	**Philip** answered him, "Two hundred denarii would not be enough." (7)
	"That would take two hundred denarii." (37)		

162

Table 15.1: THE FEEDING OF THE FIVE THOUSAND

Matthew 14:13-21	Mark 6:30-44	Luke 9:10-17	John 6:1-13
"Only five loaves of bread and two fish." (17)	"Five loaves and two fish." (38)	"Only five loaves of bread and two fish." (13)	**Andrew** spoke up. "Here is a **boy** with five small **barley** loaves and two small fish." (8-9)
He directed the people to sit down on the grass (19)	Jesus directed them to have all the people sit down in groups on the **green** grass. (39)	"Make them sit down" (14)	"Make the people sit down." (10) There was plenty of grass in that place. (10)
	In groups of **hundreds** and fifties (v.40)	"in groups of about 50 each." (14)	
Looking up into heaven, he gave thanks and broke the loaves (19)	Looking up into heaven, he gave thanks and broke the loaves (41)	Looking up into heaven, he gave thanks and broke them (the loaves) (v.16)	Jesus took the loaves, gave thanks and distributed (11)
They all ate and were satisfied (20)	They all ate and were satisfied (42)	They all ate and were satisfied (17)	When they had all had enough to eat (12)
They picked up 12 basketfuls (20)	They picked up 12 basketfuls (43)	The disciples picked up 12 basketfuls (20)	They filled 12 baskets with the pieces…left over (13)
The number of those who ate was 5000 men, **besides women and children** (21)	The number of men who had eaten was 5000 (44)	About 5000 men were there (14)	The men sat down, about 5000 of them (10)

The public proclamation of Jesus as risen from the dead, and therefore that he was the Messiah and the Son of God, obviously made an immediate impact on the inhabitants of Jerusalem. Acts informs us how the Jewish authorities tried to stop the spread of the new movement. But they were spectacularly unsuccessful.

If Jesus was still dead, then his body was available somewhere and the Roman and Jewish authorities had sufficient power and resources to find it and produce it. But they could not; the best story they could come up with was that the disciples had stolen the body. The fact that the Roman and Jewish authorities did not simply produce the body of Jesus, in order to achieve their aim of stopping the new Jesus movement, is a major argument in favour of the Resurrection.

The rising of Jesus from the dead proved that he was the Messiah and the Son of God (Romans 1:4). He was not just one of the list of bandits, false prophets and messiahs, who sought to liberate Israel from Rome's grip by military means (*HRNT* p708). This also had significance for his followers. The power that had raised Jesus from the dead became available to them in their proclamation of the Gospel and in their daily lives (*FFBR* p56).

Recent history has many accounts of how people who were once sceptical about Jesus' resurrection, but carried out thorough investigations of the subject and ended up convinced Christians[82]. For the more detailed arguments the reader should refer to these works[83]. For example, Frank Morison, thought the life of Jesus was one of the most beautiful ever lived, but when it came to the Resurrection, he assumed that someone had tacked a myth onto the story. He was persuaded that a rational inquest would disprove the Resurrection. However, when he examined the facts, he had to change his mind. Instead of refuting the Resurrection, he finally wrote the best-seller *"Who Moved the Stone?"*[84]. The title of the first chapter was *"The Book that Refused to be Written."*

We will now continue to review the other main evidence in favour of Jesus' Resurrection. Several of these arguments concern the eleven disciples remaining after the suicide of Judas Iscariot.

Firstly, they claimed to have seen the risen Lord. Would they have died for a lie? It is generally accepted that ten of these eleven men died violently for their faith at the hands of their persecutors (*MTAC* p90). The possible exception is the apostle John. He suffered for his faith in exile on the island of Patmos, through a difficult period of persecution under the Emperor Domitian, but then appears to have died peacefully in Ephesus in AD 98, after the Emperor's successor, the Emperor Nerva, rescinded the sentence. The others died as martyrs: six by crucifixion (such as Simon Peter), and two by the sword (such as James in Acts 12).

Sometimes, the argument goes, people die for a lie. So what does this prove? Well, it may be that many people have died for a lie, but they did so believing it was the truth. The case of the disciples is different. If the Resurrection had not happened then the disciples would have died for a lie, knowing it to be a lie. It's unlikely that under these circumstances their faith would have

---

[82] Two of the more recent examples being Josh McDowell (*MTAC*) and Lee Strobel, former crime reporter for the Chicago Tribune, with his book and film *"The Case for Christ."*

[83] Or to Tom Wright, writing as N T Wright, "The Resurrection and the Son of God," London, SPCK, 2003.

[84] Frank Morison, "Who Moved the Stone?" Faber & Faber, London, 1954.

held up under the persecution, suffering and threat of death if, from the outset, it had been based on a lie.

Furthermore, when Jesus died, the apostles had thought it was all over. They fled after his arrest (Mark 14:50) and did not at first believe that Jesus had risen from the dead (Luke 24:11). Only after seeing convincing evidence did they believe. Thomas was typical of them. He had not been present at Jesus' other appearances, and therefore asked for further proof (John 20:24-25). A week later he got it (John 20:26-29) and believed.

So, the eleven disciples were not gullible mystics. They were, for the most part, down-to-earth Galilean fishermen, who needed to be convinced of the truth of Jesus' Resurrection before proclaiming it until their deaths as martyrs.

Thirdly, the disciples became courageous. Before they were fearful (John 20:19). Then, after the Resurrection and Pentecost, their boldness was amazing (see for example Peter's message in Acts 2:14-41). Blaise Pascal, the great French philosopher, sums up the situation (*MTAC* p97):

"The allegation that the Apostles were impostors is quite absurd. Let us follow the charge to its logical conclusion. Let us picture those eleven men meeting after the death of Christ, and entering into a conspiracy to say that he has risen. That would have constituted an attack upon both the civil and religious authorities. The heart of man is strangely given to fickleness and change; it is swayed by promises, tempted by material things. If any one of those men had yielded to temptations so alluring, or given way to the more compelling arguments of prison, torture, they would have all been lost."

Fourthly, as Tom Wright points out (in *"Resurrection of the Son of God"* p413), the concept of the bodily resurrection of *one person* in advance of others would have been very odd within Judaism. It is therefore unlikely that the early Christians would have invented it, in an effort to continue the Jesus movement after the death of their leader.

Finally, and this is a major point, there is the argument of the phenomenal growth of the Jesus movement, the early church. Starting in AD 30, it had already made its way around the eastern Mediterranean to Rome by AD 54 and to the rest of Europe and North Africa by AD 180. As Tom Wright says[85]:

"The historian has to say, 'How do we explain the fact that this movement spread like wildfire with Jesus as the Messiah, even though Jesus had been crucified?' The answer has to be, it can only be, because he was raised from the dead."

I remember once listening to a BBC Radio programme which weighed the evidence for and against Jesus' Resurrection. They left the last word to C F D (Charlie) Moule, then Professor of Theology at the University of Cambridge. He stated that, in the final analysis, the case was straightforward. If the Resurrection of Jesus were not a historical fact, then the early church could not have grown as it did. He used a space-age metaphor: "Your rocket motor would not be powerful enough to launch my missile," he explained.

The Witness of James

From the Jewish Roman historian Flavius Josephus we know that James, the brother of Jesus, became the leader of the church in Jerusalem, with a reputation of attractive piety (*Ant* 20.200-

---

[85] Tom Wright, "Jesus: The Search Continues" on www.johnankerberg.org.

201). He goes on to explain that, when James was assassinated in Jerusalem at the order of the current High Priest in AD 62, the whole (mainly devoutly Jewish) population of the town was scandalized.

James's position as leader in the Jerusalem church is confirmed by Luke in Acts 15:13 and by Paul in Galatians 1:19 and 2:12, as well as by the other early church historians.

We have to ask ourselves how this came about, because the Gospels tell of only strained relations between Jesus and his family. In Mark 3:21 we read that they thought he was *"out of his mind."* In John 7:5 we read that *"even his own brothers did not believe in him."* So, what changed so drastically that this same brother James should later call himself *"a servant of God and of the Lord Jesus Christ"* (James 1:1)?

The answer is that the risen Jesus had appeared to James (1 Corinthians 15:4) as his Lord. This is the only fact which can explain the complete change in how James thought of his brother. Thus, the conversion of James, the brother of Jesus, is another strong argument for the Resurrection of Jesus.

Epilogue

I suppose that for most of my life I regarded the Gospels as a fairly reliable solid object, like say a wooden coffee table. After our trip to Israel and my subsequent rereading of Flavius Josephus' *"The Jewish war" (BJ)* in the high-speed train between Colmar and Paris, I began to have even more respect for it. It was more like a coffee table my dad had made – he tested his coffee tables by standing on them! Among other things, I had seen the excavations of the Pool of Bethesda (John 5), the Pool of Siloam (John 9), the Galilean Boat and the *Gabbatha* pavement where Pontius Pilate had condemned Jesus to be crucified.

Then one Sunday afternoon, around Eastertime, while walking in our village in Alsace, I suddenly realized that I possessed a systematic method, for establishing the time and place of writing of the Gospels. I dug out the translations of Suetonius and Tacitus that I had purchased when I first became a disciple of Jesus and which, to my shame, had remained largely unread for the best part of forty years. I then started burrowing into the origins of the Gospels with the help of Irenaeus (*AH*), Eusebius (*HE*) and Richard Bauckham's study of Papias (*Eye*). I was determined to carry out this investigation systematically and to avoid the usual trap of starting historically and then, half way through the argument stipulating, for example, that Mark's Gospel had to be written first. In other words, I wanted the evidence to speak for itself and to see where it led.

I believe the results of this evidence-based approach are extremely enlightening, especially when we combine them with an examination of the contents and geography of the four Gospels. We end up with two Gospels probably written independently (Matthew in a Semitic language to begin with and Mark) and then two interlocking Gospels (Luke and John). Luke could have used the Syriac or Aramaic versions of Matthew and collected eyewitness testimony when he was imprisoned with Paul in Caesarea, before interviewing Mark and Peter in Rome. Hence, Luke interlocks with Matthew and Mark and, on this basis, makes certain editorial decisions as to what to include or delete from his Gospel – notably his *"grand omission"* where he omits the material of Matthew 14:22- 16:12 and Mark 6:45-8:26. Finally, John writing much later, between 96 and 98 AD, is able to use all the other three Gospels. He gives but a skeleton account of Jesus' Galilean ministry, but gives us milestones so we know where we are in the other Gospels. It is to John that we owe the basic chronology of the four Gospels and our knowledge of Jesus' early ministry. This approach can be very helpful when studying the Gospels in small groups.

It is clear that the Gospels were *all based on eyewitness testimony and were written during the lifetimes of those eyewitnesses*. In this they resemble other Roman and Greek biographies of the time. Therefore, the four Gospels are essentially biographies of Jesus and they really hold together: they describe the same events in the same place and at the same time. They all portray the person and character of Jesus as Messiah, the Son of God and yet fully man. And they are all based on eyewitness testimony of the highest quality.

When we turn to the correspondence of the Gospels with scientific reality, we possess a very plausible explanation for the mystery of the Star of Bethlehem: modern astronomy combined with ancient archives of the Babylonian astrologers, gives us the fascinating probability that the

Star of Bethlehem was caused by a triple planetary conjunction of Jupiter and Saturn in the constellation Pisces in 7 BC (*Star*).

Then we have the icing on the cake: recent research on Jewish names shows that their frequency of use in the Gospels corresponds closely with that found in other ancient sources of the same period (*Eye*). We can even (*Test*) reconstruct the family tree of Nicodemus (John 3).

Finally, we must come back full circle. In terms of the number, quality and early dates of manuscripts, the New Testament documents are quite simply in a class of their own, dwarfing the reliability of all other ancient historical documents.

The Gospels are more solid than one of my dad's coffee tables. You can still stand on them, because in every detail the Gospels, when tested, turn out to be 100% reliable. So, they are more like a huge block of marble, solid rock, towering over time and free from erosion. As the apostle John says:

> *"Jesus did many other miraculous signs in the presence of his disciples, which are not recorded in this book. But these are written that you may believe that Jesus is the Christ, the Son of God, and that by believing you may have life in his name."* (John 20:30-31).

APPENDIX 1

THE INTER-TESTAMENTAL PERIOD

We cannot hope to understand the political and religious structures of the time of Jesus, and their representatives, without going back to the exile of Judah in Babylon and the period between the Old and New Testaments: the Inter-Testamental Period.

The Hopes of Judah after the Exile

Neither the ten tribes of Israel nor the two tribes of Judah had been faithful to God. Judah had been faithful for longer, but they were finally sent off into exile in Babylon in 587 BC. Through Jeremiah the prophet (see Jeremiah 29:10-14), God promised to bring them back to the Promised Land after 70 years, and this did indeed happen, beginning not later than 522 BC[86].

Presumably the Jews thought that God would reestablish them in the land as before. There would once again be the three-fold hierarchy, with each branch being anointed by the Holy Spirit. There would be the Davidic line of kings, from the tribe of Judah, the prophets to keep the kings in line with the will of God, and the priests to gather up the worship of the people, from the line of Aaron, from the tribe of Levi.

However, things turned out differently. The prophet Daniel, who lived in Babylon under Nebuchadnezzar and Belshazzar, and then under the Medo-Persian Empire, had some very important dreams, visions and insights. In a night vision (Daniel 7:3), he saw four great beasts come up from the sea, and received the interpretation that these represented four kingdoms which would arise in succession (Daniel 7:17). In other words, Judah would not be free of their enemies, and the kings would not be able to reign. They would be under the control of these four empires: firstly, the Babylonians, then Medo-Persia, then Greece (under Alexander the Great) and finally Rome. Daniel was particularly interested in the fourth Empire, Rome, because it was terrifying and devoured the whole earth. The third Empire was also interesting because, as Daniel intimated, on the death of Alexander, it was split into four regions, each under one of Alexander's former generals.

So, what happened to the prophets, priests and kings when, as Isaiah had predicted (Isaiah 45:1), Judah went back to Jerusalem and to the Promised Land, under Cyrus the Persian?

The Return of the Exiles

The exiles from Judah returned under the leadership of Ezra and then Nehemiah. The exact dates and chronology of these two returns are notoriously difficult to pin down[87]. Kitchen gives a

---

[86] Lion Handbook to the Bible p306, Lion Publishing, Berkhamstead, England, 1973.
[87] New Bible Commentary Revised, Ezra and Nehemiah pp395-411, Inter-Varsity Press, London, 1970.

date between 539 and 405 BC[88]. However, the fixed point would appear to be the return of Nehemiah in 445 BC. Ezra was a scribe, a teacher of the law (Nehemiah 8:1), whereas Nehemiah was a Governor, appointed by the King Artaxerxes I. Straightaway we have a picture of the new power structures: Medo-Persia pulled the strings, while the teachers of the law and the scribes increased their influence.

The prophets Haggai and Zechariah were there, essentially to encourage Zerubbabel son of Shealtiel and Jeshua son of Jehozadak, the high priest, to rebuild the temple (Haggai 1:12-15; Ezra 5:1-2). Zerubbabal was a Governor, preceding Nehemiah, and he was in the Davidic line (Matthew 1:13), but he could not be king.

After Haggai and Zechariah, the final prophet was Malachi (480-430 BC), who ministered during the time of Nehemiah. He began to talk about a Messianic messenger (Malachi 3:1), whose coming would be preceded by that of Elijah (Malachi 4:5-6), but it seemed that even this would not necessarily be good news for Judah.

The only leg of the authority tripod which still functioned, on the return from Exile, was the Aaronic priesthood, with Jeshua and then Eliashib (Nehemiah 3:1).

Thus, things were pretty grim for Judah. They were still under the Medo-Persian Empire, their royal line could not be kings and there were no prophets left to speak of. They were not free from their enemies and only the Temple and the priesthood were still operating. It was as if the period of exile was still continuing; it was just getting longer. But things were going to get worse.

Judea under the Greeks

As Daniel had predicted, from 336 BC the armies of Alexander the Great swept through the known world, and even into India. The apocryphal book 1 Maccabees and the Jewish-Roman historian Flavius Josephus (*Ant* Books 12-13) describe the events in detail. On Alexander's death in 323 BC, his four former Macedonian generals vied for power. Judea was first of all ruled from Egypt by the Ptolemies, then by the Seleucids, who were based in Turkey, but who saw themselves as the guardians of Greek culture.

Peace was shattered in 167 BC by an outbreak of religious persecution in Jerusalem (*Ant* 12.5.248-264). The new Seleucid ruler Antiochus IV looted the Temple and proscribed Judaism and its practices, such as circumcising males, observing the Sabbath, not eating pork. A cult of the Greek god Zeus replaced the worship of God in the Temple - this was the "abomination of desolation" predicted in Daniel 9:17.

However, a Jewish priest named Mattathias Hasmoneas started a revolt at Modein. The Hasidim (the "pious ones"), who were Jews dedicated to the observance of the Mosaic Law, rallied to him, but opposition came from Jews who had already accepted Greek culture (the Hellenizers) (*Ant* 12.6.265-286). Mattathias had five sons; he designated Simon to lead the rebellion and Judas (nicknamed Maccabeus, the hammer) as military commander. After much fighting, including the death of Judas, in the spring of 142 BC, Judea became politically independent and Simon High Priest.

---

[88] K A Kitchen, "On the Reliability of the Old Testament," Eerdmans, Grand Rapids, Michigan, 2006.

The Hasmonean Dynasty

Simon, the High Priest, was given hereditary rights by the people and this was approved by the Senate at Rome. However, one group of Jews called Simon or another Hasmonean "the wicked priest" and withdrew to Qumran, to become the Essenes sect and the source of the Dead Sea Scrolls.[89]

The Hasmonean Dynasty is shown in Table A1.1

Table A1.1: THE HASMONEAN DYNASTY		
Dates of Reign (BC)	**Name**	**Rank**
142-135	Simon	High Priest
135-105	John Hyrcanus I	High Priest
105-104	Aristobolus I	King and High Priest
104-78	Alexander Janneus	King and High Priest
78-69	Hyrcanus II	High Priest
69-62	Aristobolus II	King and High Priest
63-40	Hyrcanus II	High Priest
40-37	Antigonus II	King

John Hyrcanus and Alexander Janneus took more and more territory, where they enforced conversion to Judaism, including Samaria, Perea and Galilee to the north and Idumea to the south of Judea. Thus, the ancestors of Herod the Great, who were Idumeans, converted to Judaism.

But divisions began to appear towards the end of John Hyrcanus' reign, between the Sadducees, who supported him, and the Pharisees (the successors of the Hasidim), a political-religious group devoted to strict observance of the Mosaic Law. Aristobulus I took the title "King," although the Pharisees objected, saying (rightly) that only a descendant of David could be king (*RDBA* p160). These tensions gave rise to civil war under Alexander Janneus, on whose death in 76 BC, Hyrcanus II became High Priest. By now things were very complicated. In 64

---

[89]When visiting Israel, our guide explained to us that there is a theory by which Simon, or another Hasmonean, expelled the cream of the Levitical priests in order to consolidate his power. This seems plausible and would explain the large number of priests in the Qumran community. However, Flavius Josephus does not confirm this.

BC, Pompey the Great (one of the triumvirates with Crassus and Julius Caesar) took Antioch in Syria, finally ending the Seleucid Empire, and turned south towards Judea.

Jewish history cites the Hasmonean Dynasty as a high point, because they were independent again. But there were several worms in the fruit (*FMark* p329). The Hasmonean kings were not descended from David. The source of prophecy had dried up and the end of the dynasty was plunged in intrigue and murder. Even if the high priests came from the line of Aaron, they had obtained their position by violence and bloodshed. They were in it for the power, not to worship the living God. In reality the Jews were still in "exile"; it had just got worse.

Enter the Romans

Daniel's fourth empire (Daniel 7) had arrived on the scene. Rome had invariably supported the Hasmoneans against the Seleucids. Now Rome initiated a very complicated period of political and military manoeuvres in the Middle East. Pompey's troops took Jerusalem in 63 BC and he then designated four administrative regions: Judea, Samaria, Galilee and Perea. After Crassus' death in 53 BC, it was only a matter of time before Pompey and Caesar confronted each other. Antipater II, Herod the Great's father, and a local warlord, switched his allegiance to Caesar and won his (*VQJ* p8) spurs by helping to expel the Parthians and to suppress a revolt in Galilee. As a result, Caesar confirmed Hyrcanus II as hereditary High Priest and appointed Antipater as Procurator of Judea. His job was to "procure" everything Rome needed and to raise taxes and diverse revenues. He became richer than he ever dreamed and appointed his first son as Governor of Jerusalem and his second, Herod, as Governor of Galilee.

However, in 44 BC, Caesar was assassinated in Rome and a year later Antipater II was poisoned. In Judea the situation became even more complicated. Herod fled to Rome, where Mark Anthony gave him the title "King of the Jews," (*VQJ* p12) even though at that time he was a king without a kingdom. Nevertheless, in 37 BC, Herod took Jerusalem and married a second Mariamme (he had killed the first) from the Hasmonean family. He killed members of the opposing aristocracy and, after five years, calm returned. In 31 BC, Octavian defeated Mark Anthony at the battle of Actium, and became undisputed ruler over the Roman world. Herod switched allegiance to the future Emperor Augustus, who confirmed his royal status (*Hist* 5.9).

APPENDIX 2

THE GEOGRAPHICAL AND ECONOMIC BACKGROUND

MAP A2.1 Palestine During New Testament Times

Palestine was, and Israel today still is, a land of amazing contrasts. From east to west, we drop down from the Perean Mountains to the Dead Sea, at 392m (1,300ft) below sea level, the lowest point on the planet. It is, of course, well known for its high concentration of mineral salts, which means one can float in its waters with great ease. Continuing westwards, we cross the hill country of Judea at about 900m (3,000ft), before descending to sea level on the coastal plain.

The south of Palestine, the Negev desert, Judea and, above all, Jerusalem is all limestone, the colour of clotted cream. Galilee is grey or black basalt. Galilee and Samaria are fertile, whereas much of Judea is desert.

The name of the game is water. Even the deserts of the Negev and Judea are potentially fertile, as the Israelis have proved; all you need is water. Jericho, for example, is a fertile oasis in the middle of a desert.

THE GEOPOLITICAL AREAS

We know about the geographical divisions set up by the Romans from Josephus (especially *BJ* 3.30-50). Galilee and Perea were under Herod Antipas, while Trachonitis, Gaulanitis and Batanaea were ruled by Philip the Tetrarch. Judea, ruled by the Roman Prefects, included Samaria and Idumea.

Idumea

Herod the Great was from Idumea. Jesus did not venture into Idumea.

The Decapolis

Jesus did, however, go into the Decapolis, when he crossed the Sea of Galilee to free the demonized man at Gadara (Mark 5:1-20; Matthew 8: 28-34; Luke 8: 26-37). The Decapolis was a league of ten independent pagan cities, comprising Scythopolis, Pella, Dion, Gerasa, Philadelphia, Gadara, Raphana, Kanatha, Hippos and Damascus. Scythopolis was the capital of the Decapolis and the only one of the ten towns on the western bank of the Jordan. The visitor to modern Israel can visit the archeological site (the Israeli name for the town is Bet Shean) and it is thoroughly pagan, with many temples to Greek and Roman gods. People in the Decapolis would have eaten pork, which explains the pigs in the account of the deliverance of the demonized man. The prodigal son (Luke 15:11-32), when he left home, would have had the choice of the Decapolis or Caesarea Philippi if he was looking for the night life.

The Plain of Syro-Phoenicia

Jesus also went into the Province of Syria, near Tyre and Sidon, in present-day Lebanon, to seek some peace and quiet. He ended up healing the daughter of a woman of the region (Matthew 15:21-28; Mark 7:24-30).

Tetrarchy of Philip

Gaulanitis, Trachonitis, Auranitis, Bathanaea and Iturea comprised the Tetrarchy of Philip, which was inhabited (*BJ* 3.56) by a mixture of Jews and Syrians. Philip rebuilt Panias (modern Banyas) as Caesarea Philippi; he refounded Bethsaida, sometime before 2 BC, as Beth-saida Julias (*Ant* 18.28 and *BJ* 2.168), named after Augustus's daughter Julia. He was the first Jewish prince to press the heads of the Roman emperors on his coins.

Jesus' farthest journey to the north-east was to the pagan city Caesarea Philippi, inhabited by Greeks, Romans, Sidonians etc. Jews refused to live there; they regarded it as totally evil. There were a large number of pagan temples, including one to Caesar Augustus, and there were animal and child sacrifices to the god Pan (hence the name Panias). It was in this oppressive region that Peter declared that Jesus was the Messiah, the Son of the living God (Matthew 16:16).

Jesus spent a lot of time in the triangle Chorazin, Capernaum and Beth-saida Julias, this last village being in Philip's Tetrarchy, a short distance east of the point where the River Jordan enters the Sea of Galilee. According to John 1:44, Andrew, Peter and Philip all came from Bethsaida Julias. The mixture of a Hellenistic forename (Andrew) and a Semitic one (Simon) in the same family agrees with what we know of the mixed Jewish/Hellenistic culture of the region from Josephus (*BJ* 3.56).

Perea

Perea was a district on the east bank of the Jordan. At the time of Jesus, it was inhabited by Jews but, as Josephus remarks (*BJ* 3.44-46) was less productive agriculturally than Galilee or Samaria.

Since, like Galilee, it was ruled over by Herod Antipas, the Tetrarch, it tended to be regarded by the Jews as having the same status as Galilee and Judea. The name Perea is not mentioned in the Gospels, but we know from Josephus that John the Baptist was imprisoned in the palace of Machaerus in Perea and John tells us that Jesus baptized at Bethany, on the other side of the Jordan (John 1:28; 10:40). We consider that the Gospels record Jesus as spending significant periods of time in Perea, and that the *"Judea across the Jordan"* of Matthew 19:1 and Mark 10:1 in fact refers to Perea (*FMatt2* p709; *Trust?* p98).

Judea

In the time of Jesus, Judea was ruled directly by Rome, through Roman prefects, such as Pontius Pilate, whose headquarters were at Caesarea Maritime, and who would sometimes go up to the Jewish capital Jerusalem.

Judea represented the heartland of the Jewish nation; its Temple and main political and religious institutions were all located in Jerusalem. The Roman Province of Judea included the regions of Samaria and Idumea.

Samaria

Eating with Samaritans was equated with eating pork[90]. Such people were unclean and to be avoided (*DBLuke* p1031).

There seem to be three possible origins for the fact that Jews did not associate with Samaritans (John 4:9). The first is to identify the Samaritans with the people who came from other lands, to replace the ten tribes of Israel carried off into captivity in Assyria (in 722/721 BC), after their chronic unfaithfulness (2 Kings 17:6). According to 2 Kings 17:33, the people who resettled the land *"served the Lord, but they also served their own gods in accordance with the customs of the nations from which they had been brought."*

Secondly, these people could have been the same as those who opposed the rebuilding of the Temple in Jerusalem in around 445 BC (see Ezra 4).

However, it seems more likely that the contention arose during a later period when Alexander the Great ruled over the region. Ecclesiasticus 50:26, 2 Maccabees 5:22-23 and Josephus (*Ant* 11.321-347) all refer to the Samaritans as being based at Shechem. Alexander, to reduce the

---

[90] *m.Seb* 8.10; *b.Sanh.*57a.

power of the Jerusalem clergy, allowed the construction of a second temple on Mount Gerizim. Those accused of breaking the Mosaic Law in Jerusalem could then escape to the Shechemites.

Then, when Antiochus Epiphanes tried to dedicate the two temples to Zeus, the Shechemites acquiesced, whereas the Maccabees (Hasmoneans) rebelled. When Hasmonean influence extended over Samaria, John Hyrcanus I destroyed the Mount Gerizim temple in about 128 BC (*NBD* p1052).

All this is sufficient to explain the mutual resentment between the Jews and the (Shechemite) Samaritans of Jesus' day. It also exactly fits what the Samaritan woman said (John 4:20).

Galilee

Galilee is beautiful and peaceful. Ruled over by the Tetrarch Herod Antipas, Jesus spent most of his time here, in Cana, Nain, on Mount Tabor etc, and especially around the Sea of Galilee where they grow oranges and lemons. He passed a lot of his time in the Chorazin/Bethsaida/Capernaum triangle. These villages are no longer inhabited and have been the subject of archeological excavations. The Bethsaida site is largely unprotected but, at Capernaum, the probable site of Peter's house can be seen, where Jesus lived with Peter's extended family (Mark 1:21-34). This is one of the earliest examples of a house that was used as a house church. There is also the suggestion that the house of Jairus (Mark 5:22-43) and his family has been found (*HRNT* p125).

BOTANY

Peter Williams (*Trust?* p82) points out that the Gospel authors are even accurate about botany. In Luke 19:4, in Jericho, Zacchaeus the tax collector, climbs a sycamore tree in order to get a view of Jesus. Such sycamores are absent from north and central Africa, Arabia and the other countries of the Middle East and the northern Mediterranean. They are present in southern Africa and that small corner of the world around Jericho. So, Luke has got his botany right.

THE ECONOMY

Trade routes

The Nabateans (see Map A2.1 of Palestine in New Testament Times) were Arabs who had come from Yemen. They managed the **Spice Road**, which brought spices from India, through Yemen, up the west coast of Arabia by camel caravan, to Gaza. They were Bedouins who had become sedentary, and they could build towns and cities on the Spice Road, in the middle of the desert, because they had mastered the storage of water in underground cisterns. Such a city was Avdat, in the Negev. Their capital was Petra.

However, the most important trade route, from the New Testament point of view, was the **Via Maris, meaning Way of the Sea.** The route dates from the Bronze Age and its name comes from the Vulgate (the Bible translated into Latin by Saint Jerome):

*"In the past he (the Lord) humbled the land of Zebulun and Naphtali, but in the future he will honour Galilee of the Gentiles, by the **way of the sea**, along the Jordan."* (Isaiah 9:1 also cited in Matthew 4:15-16).

The starting point of the Via Maris was Heliopolis, in Egypt. It then went along the north coast of the Sinai Peninsula and the west coast of Gaza and Palestine. It then forked into two branches, one continuing up the Mediterranean coast to Akko (Ptolemais or St John of Acre) and into Phoenicia. The other went inland into Galilee via Hazor, Megiddo and Capernaum and over the Golan Heights to Damascus.

It means that Galilee was a cross roads for all sorts of economic and cultural reasons.

Money, coins

Tacitus (*Annals* 1.17) describes a group of mutineering Roman soldiers demanding pay of 4 sesterces (1 denarius) per day. Thus, the **silver denarius** was worth one day's wages, exactly as in Matthew 20:12.

Tyrian sliver shekel coins were used for the payment of Temple services and taxes. At the time of Jesus' ministry, they were worth 4 denarii (*VQJ* p98).

Taxation

The Roman Empire controlled territory stretching from the Atlantic to the Caspian Sea and from Britain to the Sahara. Administering the Empire was a complex affair, more difficult than the initial military conquest. The Province of Judea posed the questions of the co-existence of two religions (emperor worship and Judaism) and above all the issue of money – who paid taxes to whom, who profited from the Empire and who did not (*Baker* pp247-251)?

On the religious question, the Romans came to an accommodation with the Jews: the Jews would pray and sacrifice *for* the Roman Emperor, but not *to* him.

For the successful administration of provinces such as Judea, the Romans relied on the locals, first of all on client rulers such as Herod Antipas, then on groups of elders or elected councils and magistrates. In particular, the Roman Prefects or Procurators needed help in gathering taxes (a tax on the land and a poll tax), and turned to the local élites.

The Poll Tax (*phoros*) was imposed by Rome from the beginning of direct rule in Judea in AD 6, and provoked the rebellion of Judas the Galilean (*BJ* 2.118; *Ant* 18.4-10). This tax went directly to Caesar (Tiberius). It was collected by the Jewish high priests and a council of rich Jerusalem Jews; the indirect taxes (*telos*) on produce of the land were collected in toll booths by local businessmen. There was also a local sales tax (*DBLuke* p331). In practice only the wealthy could be tax gatherers (*telones*). The right to collect taxes was sold at auction and the successful bidder was obliged to pay the Prefect or Procurator a significant sum in advance, with the expectation that he would earn more money through the conscientious execution of his task. At times they could hire subordinates, becoming head tax collectors (*Baker* pp247-251). So, the successful rule of the Romans in Palestine depended not only on Roman force and power but on the passive compliance of these provincial élites.

But in the rocky and dry mountains of Judea it was hard enough to make a living, pay the rent, feed a family and pay one's dues to the Temple and tithes to the priests, without having to pay out even more for Caesar to the tax-gatherers. So, these Jewish tax-collectors were rich and unpopular (*Baker* pp247-251).

In the Gospels, we meet two tax-collectors: Matthew or Levi (Matthew 9:9-13; Mark 2:13-17) based at Capernaum, and Zacchaeus (Luke 19:1-10) at Jericho in Judea. So, Zacchaeus would have been a chief tax collector (*architelones*) working for the Romans, according to the system described above. However, Matthew (a *telones*), at Capernaum was on the important commercial route, the Via Maris. He was based in Galilee, so he would have worked for the Tetrarch Herod Antipas, collecting taxes and especially customs duties and tolls for crossing the border from Galilee into the nearby Tetrarchy of Philip and vice-versa (see Map A2.1 of Palestine in New Testament Times and *Trust?* p82).

The Jews excommunicated tax collectors (*DBLuke* p312).

The 2-drachma temple tax

In Matthew 17:24-27, Jesus is staying at Peter's house in Capernaum. Peter is asked whether Jesus pays the 2-drachma or half-shekel temple tax, which had its origins in Exodus 30:11-16. This annual tax was paid by most adult male Jews and was a matter of patriotic pride. It was also a subject of controversy, because the Sadducees disapproved of it and the Qumran Essenes paid it only once in a lifetime. So, Jesus' answer, via a miracle, maintains his independence without causing offence. He was biding his time. He would sort out the Temple later (*FMatt* p267-8).

The payment would normally have to be made in Tyrian silver shekels, at the Temple, via the money-changers, at the Passover celebrations. But it could also be paid one month before in other parts of Palestine (*Ant* 18.312-3). So, Peter has to go and fish for a coin equivalent to one shekel.

After AD 70, when the Temple was destroyed, the Romans diverted this tax to the temple of Jupiter at Rome. The fact that Matthew has recorded this incident is an indication that Matthew's Gospel should be dated before AD 70.

CONCLUSION

We have carefully examined the geographical and economic background to the Gospels. Most of the information came from Flavius Josephus and from archaeology.

The Gospels confirm what we know from Josephus and other historians concerning the geography, economy and taxation in Palestine at the time of Jesus and amplify the details in our possession. The Gospel writers even get their botany right.

Once again, the Gospels are reliable in every area tested.

APPENDIX 3

OTHER ANCIENT WORKS

THE OLD TESTAMENT CANON

The Bible consists of two parts, which Christians refer to as the Old Testament and the New Testament. The Old Testament is much longer and it came into existence over a period of more than 1000 years. It deals essentially with the relationship between God and his chosen people, the people of Israel. On the other hand, the New Testament is about a third as long and came into existence roughly between AD 40 and AD 100. It deals with the life of Jesus of Nazareth and the early church.

The Old Testament comprises 39 books in all. The first five books (Genesis, Exodus, Leviticus, Numbers and Deuteronomy) were foundational and ascribed to Moses himself. They are known as *Torah* (or Law). The next collection of books, known as *the Prophets* includes some of the historical books (1 and 2 Samuel, 1 and 2 Kings) as well as the books of the Major Prophets (Isaiah, Jeremiah, Ezekiel) and Minor Prophets, such as Hosea etc. The third division, known as *the Writings*, is headed by the Psalms and includes some material, such as the book of Daniel, which was only accepted within the last 200 years BC. Even around the time of Jesus, some were still debating whether Esther or the Song of Solomon should be included, but in the end they were.

These 39 books became the official list of the sacred books of the Jewish people. The Greek word for such an official list is *Canon*, which means "rule or measuring rod" (*TWSC* p150).

THE DEAD SEA SCROLLS

The Dead Sea Scrolls and the Old Testament

Qumran, a site situated on the shore of the Dead Sea, was occupied in the first century AD by a group from the Essenes sect. They took no part in society and led a secluded life, waiting for a Messianic figure from their own ranks called "The Teacher of Righteousness."

During the spring of 1947 a Bedouin herdsman, searching for his animals, came across several caves and, in them, large clay jars which were found to contain manuscripts on copper rolls, wrapped in cloth. Many of the manuscripts concerned the future Teacher of Righteousness and the "Rules for the (Essene) Community." However, there were also 220 copies or fragments of books of the Old Testament; in fact, all of the Old Testament books were represented apart from Esther. Although most of the materials dated from around 100 BC, they had been placed in the caves in AD 68, to hide them from the Roman armies, sent to quash the Jewish Revolt of AD 66-74.

Before the discovery of the Dead Sea Scrolls, the earliest known manuscript of the Old Testament was the Masoretic Text, dated from AD 916, 1300 years after the completion of the writing of the Old Testament. One of the Dead Sea Scrolls had a complete copy of Isaiah in the original Hebrew, dated from around 125 BC, so a thousand years were gained. In addition, comparison of the Qumran Isaiah scroll and the Masoretic text revealed no significant changes (*TTQ* p45-49).

The Dead Sea Scrolls and the New Testament

The Essene community at Qumran were ardent students of the Old Testament, especially the prophets, so it is not surprising that they possessed a large number of Old Testament manuscripts. The question of whether the Dead Sea Scrolls contain any New Testament material has led to some debate. The Jesuit palaeographer José O'Callaghan controversially proposed that fragments found in 1972 in Cave 7, previously categorised as "non-identified" were in fact fragments of Mark dating from AD 50 and fragments of Acts (dating from AD 60), Romans, 1 Timothy, 2 Peter and James, dating from AD 70 (*TTQ* p48; *LMark* p21 and footnote). However, the general view is that the fragments are too short (of the order of 20 letters per fragment) and the letters too difficult to decipher, to permit identification with any degree of certainty (*LMark* pp18-20). Furthermore, the Essenes lived as recluses, cut off from society. For this reason, and the very early dating of Mark which would be implied, it seems unlikely that the Dead Sea Scrolls will prove to be a source of New Testament material. Tom Wright puts it even more forcefully: *"The Dead Sea Scrolls say nothing whatever about Jesus or the early Christians."* (*TWSC* p82).

THE SEPTUAGINT AND THE APOCRYPHA

Over the two hundred years before the time of Jesus, all the books of the Hebrew Bible, or Old Testament, were translated into Greek, probably in Egypt, for the benefit of the increasing number of Jews for whom Greek was the primary language. The Greek Old Testament they produced was, in various different versions, the one used by most of the early Christians. It was known as the "Septuagint" (usual abbreviation: *LXX*), because it was supposed there were seventy translators.

This was also the point at which the books which came to be known as the "Apocrypha" (literally: "hidden things") first appeared. Their validity and status were argued about and this rumbled on in the early church and re-emerged at the Reformation. As a result, some Bibles include them, placed between the Old and the New Testaments, while others exclude them (*TWSC* p151). Nevertheless, even if the doctrinal value of these books remains controversial, books such as 1 and 2 Maccabees give us great insight into the history of the Jews between the Old and New Testaments – the so-called Inter-Testamental Period, roughly between 400 and 0 BC. They therefore enable us to better understand how the Jews of the time of Jesus thought and lived, in much the same way as the Dead Sea Scrolls and the works of Flavius Josephus.

In addition, there are other works which do not enter into these categories, known as *"pseudepigrapha."*

THE NAG HAMMADI GNOSTIC MATERIAL

Dan Brown, in his cleverly written thriller *The Da Vinci Code*, insists, among many other things, that Jesus married Mary Magdalene and fathered a child[91], but this is largely a figment of his imagination. Some may suppose that it comes from a twisted interpretation of a passage from the gnostic "gospel of Philip", written somewhere around the third century, but this interpretation is extremely suspect on at least six counts (*HRNT* pp567-8). He also claims that *"More than 80 gospels were considered for the New Testament, yet only a few were chosen for inclusion – Matthew, Mark, Luke and John among them."*

We have demonstrated in Chapter 4 that this is an erroneous view of how the choice was made of the books entering the New Testament Canon. But what can be said about the Nag Hammadi documents discovered in Upper Egypt in 1945?

In terms of literary *genre*, the four New Testament Gospels and the so-called gnostic gospels found at Nag Hammadi are very different kinds of work. The four Gospels all tell a continuous narrative about Jesus, beginning with the outset of his ministry or his birth, continuing through his death on a Roman cross, and ending with accounts of his resurrection from the dead. This is the kind of work that early readers would have identified as biography (*Jesus* p7).

The gnostic gospels are different on four counts. Firstly, there is very little about what Jesus did or about how he lived. Most are set after the resurrection of Jesus and are long teaching discourses. They tell of the gnostic myth of redemption, according to which this material world was made by an ill-intentioned demi-god who bungled the job. The gnostic Christ was not really human and the gnostic gospels abstract the figure of Jesus into an almost entirely mythical world (*Jesus* p8; *TWSC* pp82-83). This was the heresy which Irenaeus fought against.

Secondly, the gnostic gospels presuppose that the stories and sayings of Jesus after his resurrection are well known. The gnostic gospels were designed to *add*. They belong after the four Gospels, not only chronologically, but also logically. Thirdly, the Jewishness of Jesus, which is integral to his portrayal in the four Gospels, is absent from the gnostic gospels. Finally, the four Gospels place their narratives of Jesus firmly in a historical context that can be verified. They have every appearance of being good history. The gnostic gospels do not (*Jesus* p9; *TWSC* pp82-83). For example, they have few mentions of place names (*Trust?* p63).

One of the longest and best known of the Nag Hammadi documents is a collection of the sayings of Jesus known as the "Gospel of Thomas." However, the Syriac traditions that "Thomas" embodies can be dated reliably, not to the first century AD at all, but to the second half of the second century AD. That is over a hundred years after Jesus' own day; in other words, 70 to 100 years after the time when the canonical Gospels were in widespread use across the early church (*TWSC* p83).

Tom Wright continues (*TWSC* p83), explaining that, when "Thomas" uses the canonical Gospels as its source, they have, in many cases, been quietly doctored to express the gnostic viewpoint.

---

[91] For the arguments against see for example *Le Figaro (hors-série)* "Jésus Christ cet Inconnu," November 2019.

APPENDIX 4

WAS MARK THE FIRST GOSPEL TO BE WRITTEN?

The external evidence of the early church fathers and historians (such as Origen (*HE* 6.25.3-6) and Irenaeus (*AH* 3.1.1) indicates that Matthew was the first Gospel to be written and that the order of writing of the four canonical Gospels was Matthew - Mark - Luke - John. This view remained unchallenged until the late 18th century, when Storr[92] proposed in 1786 that Mark was the first Gospel to be written. Lachmann[93] in 1835 compared the Synoptic Gospels in pairs and inferred that Mark best preserved a relatively fixed order of events in Jesus' ministry. Wilke[94] and Weisse[95] extended Lachmann's reasoning to say that Mark was Matthew's and Luke's source. It is important to realize that all this was based on a very particular form of internal evidence: a comparison of the contents of the three Synoptic Gospels. There is no external evidence to back it up.

Arguments for the priority of Mark are usually based on attacking its main rival: the priority of Matthew. Modern arguments deal with redactional plausibility, that is whether it is more reasonable to suppose that Matthew and Luke could have written with Mark in their hands, or whether Mark could have written as he did with Matthew and Luke in his hands. However, we do not have the space to examine these aspects in greater detail.

Similarly, we do not have the space to dwell on the multitude of theories which have been derived from this supposed priority of Mark. The best known, and most widely accepted, is the "two-source theory" of Streeter[96], whereby Matthew and Luke each independently drew from Mark and another hypothetical source, known as Q.

The problem is that many scholars in the 20th century regarded the priority of Mark's Gospel no longer as a hypothesis, but rather as an established fact. But fresh challenges from W R Farmer[97] and J A T Robinson[98] have proved influential in reviving the hypothesis of the priority of Matthew's Gospel, so reducing the adhesion to Markan priority. There are also more eager moves to explore other alternatives (*FMark* pp41-45).

---

[92] Gottlob Christian Storr, "Über den Zweck der evangelischen Geschichte und der Briefe Johannis," 1786, p274ff.

[93] Karl Lachmann, "De ordine narrationem in evangelis synopticis," 1835.

[94] Christian Gottlob Wilke, "Der Urevangelist oder exegetisch kritische Untersuchung über das Verwandtschaftsverlältniss der drei ersten Evangelien," 1838.

[95] Christian Hermann Weisse, "Die evangelische Geschichte kritisch und philosphisch bearbeitet," 1838.

[96] Burnett Hillman Streeter, "The Four Gospels: a Study of Origins, Treating of the Manuscript Tradition, Sources, Authorship & Dates," 1924.

[97] W R Farmer, "The Synoptic Problem: a Critical Review of the Problem of Literary Relationships between Matthew, Mark and Luke," 1964.

[98] J A T Robinson, "Redating the New Testament," SCM Press, London, 1976, pp92-117.

Thus, the priority of Mark's Gospel is uniquely based on a particular form of internal evidence. There is no external evidence whatsoever to support it. Indeed, the early church fathers and historians never mention any Gospel writer using the material of another, and were virtually unanimous on placing Matthew as the first Gospel to be written.

The priority of Mark is more and more contested by scholars. There are probably several very different reasons why the notion has not yet disappeared from our consciousness. Firstly, there is the inevitable inertia of academic theology, where new ideas take time to trickle down into the seminaries and theological faculties and then into the training of priests, pastors and preachers. Secondly, there are those skeptical theologians who have a hidden agenda. They wish to question the resurrection of Jesus, which is dealt with at less length in the versions of Mark than in the other Gospels handed down to us. So, they favour the priority of Mark.

Finally, there are perhaps some more intuitive reasons. Mark is the shortest Gospel, so it is easy to imagine it being the first and the other Gospel writers adding to it. And Mark contains lots of detail, which the other Gospel writers could have précised down. Although these notions are intuitive, they are perhaps relatively powerful in our collective consciousness.

Nevertheless, when all is said and done, the priority of Mark is not an established fact. As a theory, it is now severely contested, as it should be, because it stands wobbling on the one foot of a particular form of internal evidence, rather than firmly on the two feet of internal and external evidence.

APPENDIX 5

MAPS

MAP 1 Jesus' Preparation For Ministry

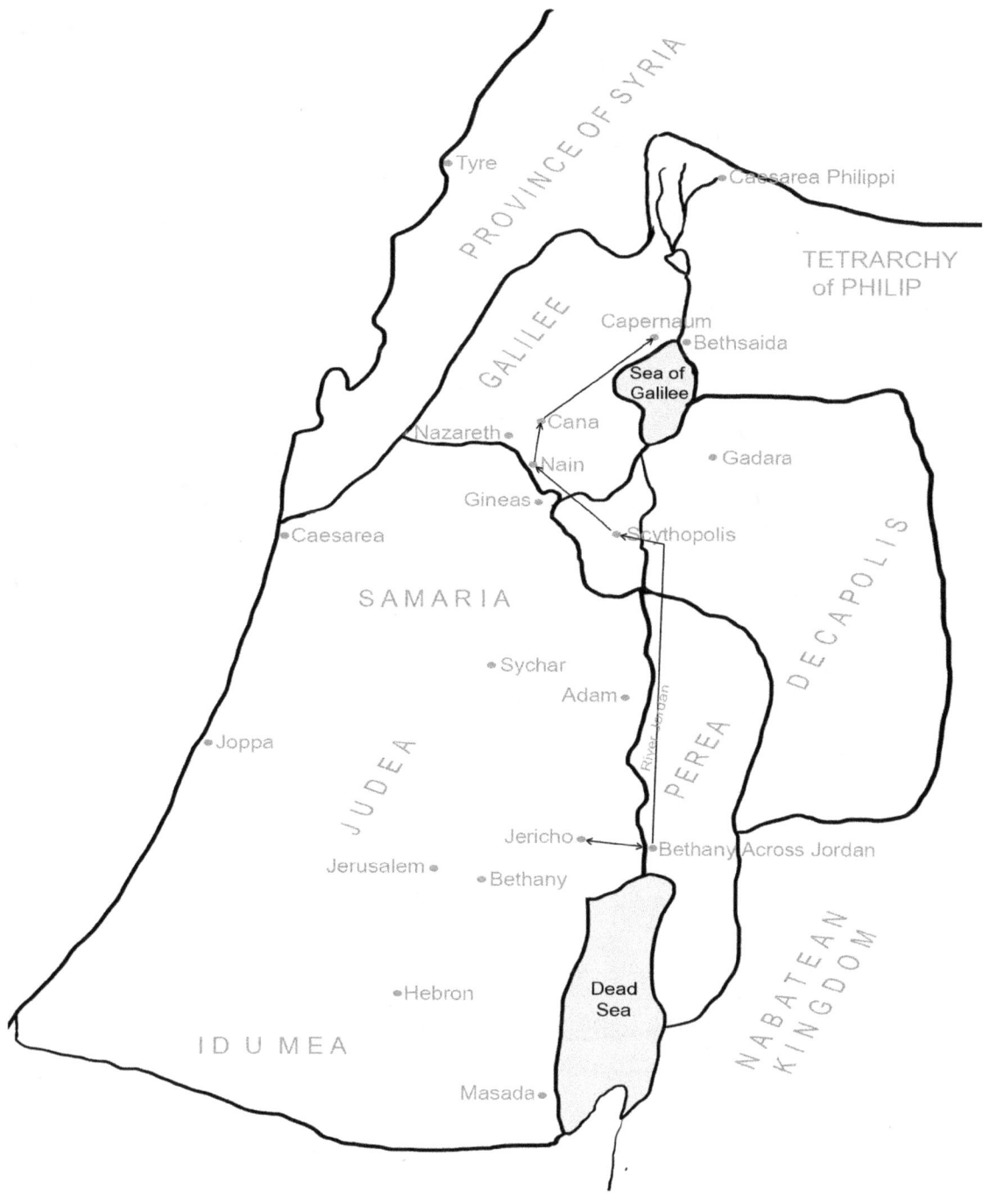

MAP 2 Jesus' Early Ministry and First Visit to Jerusalem

MAP 3 Jesus' Galilean Ministry

MAP 4 Jesus' Discreet Visit to Jerusalem

MAP 5 The Final Push to Jerusalem

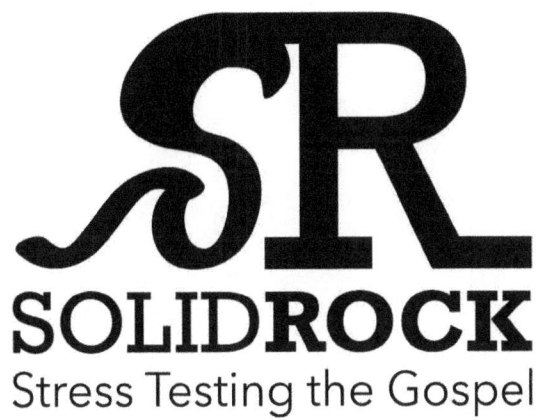

You may also follow Peter Murfitt's videos and podcasts on his YouTube channel SOLID ROCK – Stress Testing the Gospel

https://www.youtube.com/channel/UCDCbRAuZhQk7iS0dKaWBbiQ

www.ingramcontent.com/pod-product-compliance
Lightning Source LLC
Chambersburg PA
CBHW081131170426
43197CB00017B/2816